Talking about Politics

Studies in Communication, Media, and Public Opinion
A series edited by Susan Herbst and Benjamin I. Page

Talking about
POLITICS

Informal Groups and Social Identity
in American Life

Katherine Cramer Walsh

The University of Chicago Press
Chicago and London

Katherine Cramer Walsh is assistant professor of political science at the
University of Wisconsin–Madison.

The University of Chicago Press, Chicago 60637
The University of Chicago Press, Ltd., London
© 2004 by The University of Chicago
All rights reserved. Published 2004
Printed in the United States of America

13 12 11 10 09 08 07 06 05 04   5 4 3 2 1

ISBN (cloth): 0-226-87218-1
ISBN (paper): 0-226-87220-3

Library of Congress Cataloging-in-Publication Data

Walsh, Katherine Cramer.
    Talking about politics : informal groups and social identity in
  American life / Katherine Cramer Walsh.
        p.   cm.—(Studies in communication, media, and public opinion)
    ISBN 0-226-87218-1 (cloth : alk. paper)—ISBN 0-226-87220-3 (pbk. : alk. paper)
    1. Communication in politics.   2. Group identity.   3. Discussion.
  4. Political sociology.   I. Title.   II. Series.
  JA85.W35   2004
  320.973′01′4–dc21

                                                      2003009993

♾ The paper used in this publication meets the minimum requirements of the
American National Standard for Information Sciences—Permanence of Paper
for Printed Library Materials, ANSI Z39.48-1992.

Differences

My neighbor lives on the hill,
    And I in the valley dwell,
My neighbor must look down on me,
    Must I look up?—ah, well,
My neighbor lives on the hill,
    And I in the valley dwell.

My neighbor reads, and prays,
    And I—I laugh, God wot,
And sings like a bird when the grass is green
    In my small garden plot;
But ah, he reads and prays,
    And I—I laugh, God wot.

His face is a book of woe,
    And mine is a song of glee;
A slave he is to the great "They say,"
    But I—I am bold and free;
No wonder he smacks of woe,
    And I have the tang of glee.

My neighbor thinks me a fool,
    "The same to yourself," say I;
"Why take your books and take your prayers,
    Give me the open sky";
My neighbor thinks me a fool,
    "The same to yourself," say I.

Paul Laurence Dunbar

CONTENTS

Figures

Tables

APPENDIXES

Acknowledgments are a glimpse into a writer's history. Mine will reveal that I have been incredibly fortunate to cross paths with many generous and kindhearted people in the course of writing this book.

In the pages that follow, I describe the everyday act of making sense of our place in the world and the related task of making sense of politics. It is a very human process, and therefore one rife with parochialism, stereotypes, and other inherited rules of thumb. I have opened the doors to the meetings of several groups not to indict their modes of interpretation, for we are each at the center of a universe we do our best to understand. Instead, my intent is to present the following analyses as a contribution toward the ongoing conversation about the life we wish to live together, and as a step toward establishing how we might go about achieving it. Therefore my first debt is to the people I observed for this study. Thank you for letting me, and the glare of public, academic light, into your lives so that I could learn about political understanding. In the process, I learned much more. I am forever indebted to you and extend to you my sincere respect.

I also owe a special word of thanks to Bill Gamson. Bibliography pages usually convey a person's intellectual debts, but my title is an acknowledgment that Gamson's book *Talking Politics* greatly inspired me. His work provided many of the tools necessary to think about political understanding. My thanks to Wendy Rahn for introducing me to that book and for inviting me into the world of political science.

I enjoyed a vast community of scholars at the University of Michigan, where I was a graduate student when this project began. Thanks to Chris Achen, Scott Allard, Adam Berinsky, Alison Bryant, Martha Feldman, Kim Gross, Khristina Haddad, Don Herzog, Heather Hill, Margaret Howard, Vince Hutchings, Amaney Jamal, Cindy Kam, John Kingdon, Ken Kollman, Conrad Kottack, Su-Feng Kuo, Ann Lin, Yukio Maeda, Deb Meizlisch, Jennifer Mittlestadt, Anna Maria Ortiz, Madelaine Pfahler, Rosemary Quigley, Alexander Shashko, Abigail Stewart, Michael Traugott, Jennifer Widner, Elizabeth Wingrove, and Nick Winter for your conversations and feedback on this project. I also thank members of the social network study group in the School of Education and the reading group on Race, Gender, and Politics within the Institute for Research on Women and Gender for inspiring conversations. To Paula Pickering especially, thank you for your insight on this project and for years of coffee, conversation, and unwavering camaraderie.

In particular, there are five faculty members at the University of Michigan that made this book possible through their wisdom, and through their unqualified support. To Don Kinder, thank you for encouraging me, from the earliest stages of this project, to think clearly while listening to my heart. To John Jackson, thank you for teaching me to strive simultaneously for humbleness, rigor, and confidence. To Mark Mizruchi, thanks for helping me see the utility of this project beyond the bounds of political science. To Nancy Burns, you have inspired me with your unmistakable joy in working hard, arguing clearly, and making the most of every moment. Thank you for your constant support and ongoing friendship. To Kent Jennings, thank you for mentoring me from the moment I stepped into graduate school. Your generosity is a model for the ages. I am grateful to all of you for your guidance, time, and friendship.

I also had the great fortune of sharing my work on this project with scholars who were located elsewhere at the time. Thank you to Jake Bowers, Margaret Conway, Ann Crigler, Michael Delli Carpini, Rick Doner, Jamie Druckman, Rod Hart, Leonie Huddy, Sharon Jarvis, Taeku Lee, Paul Martin, Jeffery Mondak, Robert Putnam, Paul Sniderman, Laura Stoker, Randy Strahan, Cara Wong, and seminar participants at Emory, Boston College, Oberlin, the University of Texas at Austin, and Yale. I am indebted to you for your helpful and motivating feedback.

The University of Wisconsin–Madison has welcomed me and given me the opportunity to benefit from the generosity and wisdom of a talented set of colleagues. My special thanks go to Nina Eliasoph, Charles Franklin, Ken Goldstein, Dave Leheny, Paul Manna, Dick Merelman, Gina Sapiro, Dhavan Shah, participants in the Political Communication seminar, and members of the Political Behavior Research Group for their helpful comments on the manuscript and to the staff in North Hall for many laughs and a heck of a lot of help.

I also owe a debt of gratitude to the participants and organizers of the City of Madison Study Circles on Race. Thank you for moving me closer to understanding the privileges I enjoy, and all the responsibilities that entails.

Working with the University of Chicago Press has been a delight. Thanks to John Raymond and Claudia Rex for fine-tuning this manuscript, and to the anonymous reviewers for outstanding advice. To my editors, Susan Herbst and John Tryneski, thank you for your wisdom and guidance, and for celebrating along with me. Also, thank you, Susan, for your special dose of encouragement early on in this project.

I would also like to thank the National Science Foundation, the Ford Foundation, and the Institute for Social Research for generous funding through graduate research fellowships during the time of this study, and the University of Wisconsin–Madison Graduate School for assistance in the later stages of the project. Of course, any opinions, findings, conclusions, or recommendations expressed here are my own and do not necessarily reflect the views of these organizations or the many people who have provided guidance on this project.

Most of all, I thank my family, including all of the Cramers, Geissmans, and Walshes. I dedicate this book to my mom and dad, Pat and Kip Cramer. Thank you for giving me a social conscience and the resources and encouragement to pursue it. To Scott and Joan Cramer, my brother and sister (in law), thanks for making me laugh via long distance and now (with Ben, too) over Sunday dinners. And to Bailey Walsh Jr., whose path I was lucky enough to cross while riding my bike to the Old Timers' corner store, I thank you so very much. I'm glad I have a lifetime to show you just what I mean.

CHAPTER 1

Introduction: The Public's Part of Public Discussion

Bob: Ever since [Governor] Engler's been in there they haven't paved a single road [in the Upper Peninsula of Michigan]. We used to have the best roads in the country. Now they're the worst.
Skip: Yep, it's going to take billions to fix them.
Rose: Well, Election Day is coming up, you can vote him out.
Bob: I suppose . . .
Rose: But I tell you I wouldn't vote for that lawyer of [Jack] Kevorkian [Geoffrey Fieger, at the time a candidate in the Democratic primary for the Michigan gubernatorial election] . . . No way.
Bob: Oh yeah, right . . .
Rose: No way.
Bob: Well, by the time they get through campaigning, he may not be in it anymore.
Rose: Well, yeah, I don't know. No one else will be in it then either.
Skip [Turning to Kathy]: You're too young to vote [joking], but it's still good to listen to these conversations.

"These conversations" are the casual exchanges about political topics that take place among a group of elderly people who meet every morning while drinking coffee in a neighborhood corner store.[1] They arise in the midst of informal talk with the same fanfare that accompanies talk about the latest lottery winner, the summer's crop of tomatoes, or someone's recent vacation. These people are taking part in public discussion, engaging in informal political talk.

Not everyone has the opportunity to spend time chatting casually with friends and acquaintances every morning. But the experience of September 11, 2001, demonstrated that people, at least occasionally, rely on one another to make sense of public affairs. As people struggled to make sense of the terrorist attacks, they watched the news, read the papers, and,

1

more poignantly, turned to their friends and family members to express their disbelief, bewilderment, grief, and rage. Stranded in airports, shell-shocked in workplaces and around dinner tables, people wondered aloud, together.

This is the public's part of public discussion. It is a common part of everyday life, but political scientists know very little about it. It is an awkward topic for us, for two reasons. First, we generally believe that democracy hinges on deliberation, but the political talk that arises as a by-product of casual interaction does not fit prevailing definitions of this venerable act.[2] As such, it has slipped through the cracks of recognition of objects worthy of serious study (Mansbridge 1999). Second, we have evidence that the transmission of information among members of the public matters for their individual opinions (Huckfeldt and Sprague 1995), yet we have little faith that members of the public actually engage in meaningful political talk. We view "public discussion" not as discussion among members of the public but as discussion about public issues that takes place among political professionals.[3] We think that the central tendency of public opinion results from "collective deliberation," but we conceptualize this deliberation largely as a process that occurs among political professionals within the mass media, the government, and interest groups (Page and Shapiro 1992; Page 1996).

I argue that informal interaction should not be overlooked, because it is a way in which people collectively develop fundamental tools of political understanding. Political scientists have given the act of understanding politics, also referred to in this book as the act of interpreting or making sense of politics, far less attention than the act of evaluating or making political choices (Kuklinski and Hurley 1996). In analyzing processes of interpretation, the dependent variable is no longer *preferences* but *perspectives*. Preferences are attitudes about particular issues. Perspectives are the lenses through which people view issues. They are psychological knowledge structures that result from the interaction of identities, values, and interests. They are the reason two people can make sense of the same message in entirely different ways. They influence interpretations by suggesting which categories are useful for making sense of the world.

No individual has the same view of the world, but perspectives vary in systematic ways across racial, ethnic, gender, and socioeconomic lines. In this book, I argue that the systematic variation we see in interpretations of politics by members of different social groups is not innate but is, instead, created through the process of developing and clarifying one's social identity during casual interaction with other people. Social identities are the psychological attachments people make between themselves and social groups in their environment. This concept is central to the processes theorized about in this book for the following reasons. Across variations in the concept of perspective, such as worldviews, standpoints, and even culture, there is a similar emphasis on the creation of these views through social interaction.[4] I build on existing conceptions of perspective by emphasizing the centrality of social identities in the way people interpret and communicate about the world around them. Some aspects of a person's perspective or outlook on life are not necessarily tied to their social context.[5] Yet, how people look at the world is grounded in where they place themselves in relation to others. Social identities are not just one component of our worldviews. Instead, we see the world *through* ideas of where we place ourselves in relation to others.

Real People Talking in Their Own Terms on Their Own Turf

In this book you will meet several groups of people. These are groups whose conversation and interaction I began observing because existing research was insufficient to explain what goes on when people talk to each other casually in natural settings about politics. *Deliberation* has been brought to empirical light, through direct investigation of decision making in town hall meetings (Mansbridge 1983), public hearings (Mendelberg and Oleske 2000; Burke 1994), meetings of activist organizations (Mansbridge 1983), food cooperatives (Gastil 1993); the design and investigation of deliberative opinion polls (Luskin and Fishkin 1998); talk sessions sponsored by the National Endowment for the Humanities (Merelman, Streich, and Martin 1998); laboratory experiments (Sulkin and Simon 2001); and survey-based studies of the cognitive effects of participating in the National Issues Forums (Gastil and Dillard 1999). However, *casual* political talk—talk that is not organized for the sake of decision making—has received far less attention, and has almost always been investigated in settings manufactured by the researchers, such as through focus groups or in-depth interviews (Gamson 1992; Sigel 1996; Conover, Crewe, and Searing 1991, 1999; Conover, Searing, and Crewe 2002; Hibbing and Theiss-Morse 2002). The exceptions—studies that investigate informal political talk directly in natural settings—are few and have been conducted by sociologists, anthropologists, or social work scholars (e.g., LeMasters 1975; Duneier 1992; Eliasoph 1998; Lichterman 1999). When interpersonal interaction within social contexts is expected to influence vote choices or other political attitudes, only the existence—not the *content*—of this talk has been the object of study (Lazarsfeld, Berelson, and Gaudet 1944; Berelson, Lazarsfeld, and McPhee 1954; Huckfeldt and Sprague 1995).[6]

In my attempts to understand how people make sense of politics through informal talk, I gave the bulk of my attention to "the Old Timers," who are quoted at the start of this chapter.[7] They are a group of retired, white, middle-class to upper-middle-class (objectively defined) men who meet every morning over coffee in a neighborhood corner store in Ann Arbor, Michigan. I use the term "corner store" to describe this place because it is more akin to a convenience store that serves coffee than to a café as it is normally understood today. The choice of beverages includes "regular," "decaf," or "black tea," not lattes, mochas, and so forth. After the morning hours, more patrons use it to buy items to take home than use it for drinking coffee. About thirty-five men attend the "Old Timers" group on a regular basis, though the pool of occasional participants numbers approximately ninety.

I selected this group after searching for a group of people who meet regularly in a public place to hang out and occasionally talk about politics. I spent approximately three years (from the fall of 1997 through the summer of 2000, and for a short period in January of 2001) with the Old Timers and others who gather in the store, as well as with a group of retired white and African-American blue-collar workers who also meet there and a group of white middle-class men and women who gather in the store later in the morning.[8] I supplemented these observations with fieldwork with a group of elderly women who meet in a craft guild at an Ann Arbor church and, for a short time, with a group of homeless people who gathered during a breakfast program.

The Old Timers are not meant to represent all voluntary associations or informal discussion groups. And, indeed, they are unique. First, this group is very cohesive: the people involved share a great number of overlapping acquaintances and experiences (Mizruchi 1992, 36). Most of the members of the group served in the military, and many served in either World War II or the Korean War. Among the twenty-six Old Timers who returned a self-administered questionnaire (explained in more detail in chapter 3), the average time lived in Ann Arbor is 57.8 years (st.dev. = 19.31 years). They have known one another for many years: about a quarter of the group has known one another since childhood. Many of them went to grade school and high school together, have lived their entire lives in Ann Arbor, married into one another's families, played sports together, and still attend church together. Of the twenty-six who responded to the questionnaire, twenty knew at least one other person before they started spending their mornings at the corner store.

These overlaps have consequences, and these consequences stand at the heart of this book. Partly because of these shared acquaintances and experiences, the Old Timers think of themselves as a group. When an unfamiliar person is mentioned in the conversation, a common question is whether he or she is "one of us." This group identity is a key component of the perspective through which they communicate about politics.

I selected this case on the basis of a desire to study, in depth and over a long period of time, the processes of understanding politics that happen among the members of a naturally occurring group of people. I selected additional cases to test the conclusions I reached through these observations. Not only were the Old Timers an accessible group that met regularly and commonly spoke about public affairs of their own volition, but they are in some respects an ideal type. They bring to mind the prototypical group of white-haired men who have gathered around a cracker barrel in a general store to hash out local public affairs. They embody our romanticized vision of the local political discussion group. I hoped to get beyond nostalgia to the actual processes, to investigate the validity of our assumptions about such interaction and discover what actually occurs when people talk together about politics.

The other groups were chosen for the study for the following reasons. As my observations progressed, it became obvious that the Old Timers' interpretations of the world and of politics were made by contrasting themselves with other people, often other people within the corner store. To understand the dynamics in that room, I needed to know more about the interactions among the other people, especially the group composed primarily of African Americans. I supplemented these cases with observations of the group of elderly white retired men and women who meet later in the morning and also the group of elderly women who met weekly in the church craft guild.[9] The later-morning group afforded a chance to observe a very similar yet gender-mixed group, and the guild offered a chance to observe a gender-homogenous but female group meeting in the same town—of a similar age, class status, racial, and ethnic background to the Old Timers.

Thus these groups were not chosen simultaneously at the beginning of the study. Instead, the case selection evolved as the study progressed. I intended the observations of the Old Timers to serve as preliminary research. I was planning to use what I learned from several months of observation to generate questions that I would later test with survey data. I did eventually use survey data (of both national samples and of the Old Timers) to round out my understanding of processes of group political interpretation. But the behaviors and communication I observed quickly suggested that such interaction deserved careful, sustained, systematic scrutiny. And so I took advantage of what participant observation could teach us about the political implications of informal talk.

Several choices about the case selection require further elaboration. First, I chose to study elderly and primarily white people because they were accessible to me. Their meeting spots were not far from my home and places of work. I was easily able to join their gatherings and also observe the settings in which they met at other hours of the day and across all seasons. The similarity of my race to that of the Old Timers and the women in the guild also facilitated access to their groups. Because it was not my intention to collect evidence about the frequency of political discussion in general but rather to learn about the nature of such discussion when it does occur, their ability to gather to talk, because of their relatively abundant free time, was beneficial to my study and not a source of bias. I wanted to know, when people do engage in informal political conversation, how do they do it?

To be sure, the talk among the Old Timers and the other groups studied here is not typical of informal political conversations that take place within all groups or associations. The point of analyzing several groups in depth is not to generalize about the topics discussed by a broad array of groups. Instead, the conversations I observed in these groups serve as opportunities to investigate and theorize the process of making sense of politics through public discussion across multiple events.[10] More cases would enhance this study and improve my ability to generalize conclusions about processes of making sense of politics. I chose to err on the side of more accurately capturing the process in a limited number of groups than observing a wide array of groups in only limited depth. By observing these groups over time in their natural settings, I have been able to observe informal political talk as a process through which individuals construct meaning and construct their place in the political world. This depth has allowed me to illuminate the ways in which social context and political understanding are connected and to theorize a process of political understanding on the group level.

Why study informal talk in face-to-face settings? I could have chosen to study the process of public discussion as it occurs in a different type of place. For example, I could have observed talk in families, or on the Internet. I chose to develop an explanation of the processes of informal talk by studying the Old Timers and the other groups because they were accessible, but more importantly, because many people concerned with democracy expect informal interaction in associations[11] to perform important functions in a democracy. Current concern with levels of social capital, or the capacity of people in a community to solve public problems together, points to interaction in associations as an important basis of this resource (e.g., Putnam 2000). Yet in order to understand how we might rekindle it—if it has in fact dwindled (Skocpol and Fiorina 1999; Ladd 1999)—and to know whether interaction in associations should be the focus of attempts to invigorate democracy, we need to know what takes place within such associations.

In addition, I chose to study political talk in informal groups meeting in person because, contrary to the prevailing image of ordinary citizens as un-interested, unknowledgeable, and disconnected from politics, many people *do* talk casually about politics in these settings. Data from the 1990 Citizen Participation study (Verba et al. 1990) are illustrative. Of the 2,517 respon-dents in that study, when weighted for nonresponse and oversampling, 72 percent report having attended one of nineteen types of association meet-ings or events in the year preceding the interview.[12] Of those, 72 percent report that "people at these meetings sometimes chat informally about pol-itics or government." In other words, roughly one in two people in 1990 was part of a group that talked about politics. It appears that casual political conversation among members of the public is a common part of everyday life.

Implications for Our Time

The importance of the processes that take place during informal interaction was especially obvious during the historical moment in which this study took place. As I observed the Old Timers and the others, the Lewinsky scan-dal threatened to oust President Clinton from office. Then, the presidential election of 2000 generated one of the most divisive results in American his-tory. These events would be interpreted in starkly divergent ways by different people. Were these cases of justice served? Or cases of democracy denied? The answer, of course, depends on how one looks at them. Often, interpretation coincided with partisanship, but evidence of additional divides, especially along the lines of race, suggested that the people of the United States were far from unified in their interpretation of public affairs.

And then, just nine months later, September 11 blasted into our lives. Here, suddenly, was an occasion in which unity rather than difference made the headlines. Yet the sudden awareness of one's attachment to the nation as a whole was not entirely the creation of political leaders. It took only mo-ments that morning—before leaders had altered the balance between civil liberties and national security or provided a framework for understanding the events of that day—for people in the United States to notice that, col-lectively, our lives had changed. These two events, the presidential election of 2000 and the events of September 11, 2001, illustrate that our views of the world are intertwined with our conception of who constitutes our "we." Moreover, they underscore that these notions of "we" are not static and that people can collectively broaden narrow conceptions of community to encompass others previously considered outsiders. Unfortunately, however, the spate of hate crimes and threats to civil liberties in the months following the terrorist attacks remind us that even the most seemingly unifying events brand some people as outsiders as strongly as they celebrate people labeled "one of us."

In this book, I study systematically what these events brought to the fore, that despite unifying events such as 9/11, people in the United States live in many separate worlds and that these experiences have implications for how they understand political events. In particular, this study of casual interaction within voluntary associations reveals several things. First, much of political behavior is rooted in social rather than political processes.[13] Social identities are integral to political understanding, yet they are clearly not defined entirely in the political realm, defined as the realm of public officials and government institutions. Instead, an important part of their production is done by ordinary people engaging in ordinary talk.

Second, scholars and pundits alike expect that the important determinants of public opinion are the statements public officials and journalists make about politics. However, elite-driven effects cannot be understood without attention to socially rooted processes. Politicians' appeals to social group attachments work because members of the mass public are continually doing the work of defining themselves as particular kinds of people.

Third, through casual interaction, people accomplish the civically desirable work of connecting themselves to politics. This in itself is reason enough to pay attention to these everyday processes. But the dark side of this interaction requires attention as well. Despite the ways in which such talk builds network ties or social capital, it incurs civic costs, too. Such interaction clarifies attachments to specific social groups and reinforces the boundaries of "us" and "them," producing collective understandings that are not necessarily democratic goods.

Finally, casual interaction has implications for the models we use to describe democracy. Typically, democracy is conceptualized in one of two prevailing models: liberal individualism or civic republicanism. Liberal individualism conceptualizes people as asocial actors who can bracket their social identities when engaging in interaction. However, the evidence presented in this book shows that when people talk casually, their social identities are central to the interaction. Civic republicanism, on the other hand, views social identities and a sense of community as existing prior to interaction and presumes that people act in the name of the community. The conversations studied here show that this model also falls short because it does not acknowledge the way definitions of community are created through the course of interactions.

This study challenges the elite-driven focus of the field of public opinion and the optimism of calls for more social capital. It gives unprecedented attention to the socially rooted perspectives that people use to communicate about politics and provides a frank analysis of the things that happen within voluntary associations, especially when the topic turns to race. It is the first study by a political scientist of informal political talk as it occurs in natural settings, among groups that ordinary citizens have formed themselves. In a corner store and in a craft guild, I was able to watch groups of people clarify in-groups and out-groups and scrutinize how they collectively use these tools to make sense of political events.

I use the observations of the Old Timers and the other groups to theorize two interrelated processes: the clarification of identity and the interpretation of politics. To be clear, this is a study of the act of *collective* talk about politics. The unit of analysis in most of the analyses in this book is the conversation. That is, I analyze two dependent variables: (1) the processes underlying whether and how a group develops a collective perspective rooted in social identity, and (2) the way groups communicate about and make sense of political issues through these lenses. The purpose is not to investigate whether the people a person spends time with affect his or her preferences. To reiterate, the goal is to investigate and theorize how small groups of people collectively create contexts for understanding and how they use these perspectives to make sense of politics.

A Focus on Conversation Content, Not Network Ties

Previous work on political understanding has been unable to observe how groups of people clarify perspectives rooted in their perceptions of who they are and use these lenses to make sense of politics because of the methodologies chosen to investigate interpersonal political communication. Nevertheless, evidence abounds that important parts of the act of political interpretation take place through bottom-up, in addition to elite-driven or top-down, means. A long tradition of work has provided abundant evidence that people use their own experience, not just elite-provided information, in interpreting political affairs. Robert Lane (1962) demonstrated that the fifteen working-class men from New Haven, Connecticut, whom he interviewed frequently relied on personal experience to make sense of issues and vote choices. Subsequent "constructionist" approaches to political communication (Gamson 1988; Crigler 1998) have affirmed the view that people rely on a combination of top-down and bottom-up resources to *construct* their own interpretation of public affairs.[14]

Even before Lane, the Columbia School voting studies (Lazarsfeld, Berelson, and Gaudet 1944; Berelson, Lazarsfeld, and McPhee 1954) recognized the importance of individuals' social experience. These studies used surveys of people in particular cities to examine the information they relied on to arrive at vote choices. Retrospective reports through panel studies of the content of informal political talk suggested that vote decisions were not simply dictated by campaign messages but were influenced in large part by interpersonal interaction, especially with "opinion leaders" or the more politically attentive members of social networks (Lazarsfeld, Berelson, and Gaudet 1944).[15]

None of these studies, however, provide evidence of how this process works. These as well as later works grant that interpersonal interaction is an important input to political opinions, but they do not investigate what goes on in this interaction. Take, for example, *Personal Influence*. In this book, Katz and Lazarsfeld studied more than eight hundred women in Decatur, Illinois, to find out where they obtained their opinions about movies, household products, fashion, and public affairs. They investigated who was influencing whom and what characterized the opinion leaders. They tracked the reasons their respondents gave for changing their opinions, including with whom they had talked. Then they conducted follow-up interviews with the people who were alleged influencers to verify this persuasion. In this way, the study revealed when persuasion had occurred and which people within the community were the "relay points" between mass media and members of the public.

The authors ascribed a special function to group interaction: the results of such interaction are something other than the aggregation of the individual members' opinions. They asserted that social interaction is not only integral to individuals' political attitudes but is a behavior through which people collectively create meaning together. Nevertheless, the authors did not investigate the content of these interactions directly.

The tradition of looking at the existence of interaction rather than at its *content* has persisted within the rubric of structural or network analysis. Such work theorizes that interpersonal influence is the result of one of two basic mechanisms, neither of which requires an analysis of the content of the exchanges. Influence is achieved either through cohesion, in which case only attention to the extent of network overlap and frequency of interaction is necessary, or through people occupying similar locations within a social network, in which case only attention to who is interacting with whom is needed. The latter is known as "structural equivalence," or the condition of actors not necessarily having ties to each other but having ties to identical third parties (Burt 1992, 42). As Knoke posits, structural equivalence produces similar attitudes because "structurally equivalent actors communicate with the same set of third parties, [and therefore] they come to similar understandings—not as a result of dealing directly with one another, but because of their common external reference group" (1990b, 12). This theoretical approach has justified a lack of attention to what actually goes on when people talk about politics.

Seeing the Work of Social Identity

Interaction is not always necessary for the social context to affect perceptions. For example, one can pick up information about the balance of partisanship in one's neighborhood just from exposure to bumper stickers and yard signs (Huckfeldt and Sprague 1992). Huckfeldt (1984) grants that talks with people met by chance in stores and in one's neighborhood are likely important sources of information (414), but cautions against attributing too much of the effects of social context to interpersonal interaction:

> Intimate social interaction cannot account for all of the social context's effects, however. Some effects due to population composition are obviously *not* the result of social interaction at an intimate level. When the presence of blacks provokes racial hostilities among whites, it is not because whites and blacks associate at an interpersonal level and develop antagonisms. Social interaction which stimulates hostility, exclusion, or intimidation is certainly at an impersonal level and represents a significantly different process. It might well be argued that hostility occurs because intimate contacts do *not* occur. (Huckfeldt 1984, 401–2)

However, this stance too readily dismisses social interaction. Although the racial composition of a context does appear to be related to political stances independent of the level of social interaction (Taylor 2000; see also Oliver and Mendelberg 2000),[16] interpersonal communication is at work.[17] When the presence of blacks provokes racial hostilities among whites, whites and blacks may not be interacting, but whites and whites most certainly are. Huckfeldt's own work shows that identification with different social groups is an important intervening variable in the effect of the social context. An analysis of a 1966 survey of white males living in Detroit neighborhoods revealed that the greater the proportion of working-class residents (defined by occupation) in a respondent's neighborhood, the more likely he was to identify with the Democratic Party. Conversely, the more middle-class residents, the lower the likelihood of identifying with the Democrats. This held for men who had middle-class occupations, whether or not they *identified* as working or middle class. It also held for men who had working-class occupations who identified as middle class. However, this pattern did not exist among men with working-class jobs who *identified* as working class. That is to say, for a man who identified as working class, living in a middle-class neighborhood did not diminish the likelihood that he identified with the Democratic Party. In this way, social identity intervened in the effect of social context on political identity (Huckfeldt 1984).

Therefore, although much of the importance of social context for political behavior can be observed without ever watching social interaction directly,[18] a more thorough understanding of the link between demographics such as race and the interpretation of politics requires attention to social identities and their origin in social interaction.

This is a potentially controversial claim. Arguably the most venerated study of political understanding, Robert Lane's *Political Ideology* (1962), found little role for social identities. Lane believed social identities were important psychological linkages between individuals and politics and argued that the absence of such ties works against the operation of a coherent political ideology and political participation (1962, 399). However, he concluded that social identities had played at best a minor role in his fifteen subjects' interpretations of politics (381–99). They were more likely to use "I" instead of "we" in their responses to his questions (223).

However, in contrast to Lane's conclusions, subsequent studies that used focus groups have suggested a larger role for social identities in political understanding. Gamson's 1992 study of political talk within focus groups about major public issues is one example. In the presence of a group of people, the participants' claims about who was "us" and who was "them" guided the way they framed or interpreted the issues. Likewise, Hart and Jarvis (1998) observed a discussion group within a deliberative poll, the 1996 National Issues Convention, and found that the participants used collective identities in their comments. This was especially the case with respect to talk about international issues, as the participants used "we" to make statements such as "We need a strong military presence in Asia" (7) and "We should get involved because power corrupts and absolute power corrupts absolutely" (8). Notably, both of these studies suggesting an important role for social identities were conducted in group settings.

It is possible that Lane's inability to see the work of social identity resulted from his choice of method. Lane had probed the political thoughts of his respondents in one-on-one interviews in which the men were isolated from peers and from familiar social settings that might have activated the salience of social identities.[19] In such conditions, in which the respondents were speaking with a person of higher status and higher academic credentials and were doing so in a "special office" seven miles from their neighborhood (7), the most salient social comparison tool was not "how are 'we' alike?" but "how are you and I different?" Had Lane interviewed *groups* of working-class people, would he have seen more use of "us" or "we"?[20]

The Compass of Casual Interaction

Lane did not find that his subjects actively identified with social groups. However, he argued that social self-placements were a key resource that people relied on to understand politics. The men of New Haven were apparently without solid political orientations, but Lane concluded that they certainly had a good grip on social life. They seemed to have a belief system "held together by the adhesions of reality. . . . They know the here and now. They know human behavior and how to make their own behavior fit into the scheme of things they have inherited; that is, they know and rarely fumble their social codes" (1962, 380). Thus, the men in Lane's study were not incapable of forming political interpretations. They were equipped with ideas about appropriate behavior for people like themselves.

   •   Another famous observer of American political behavior, Walter Lippmann, acknowledged the role of social resources for making sense of politics but treated them as reason to derogate the average citizen, not as a reason to look more closely at how these perspectives work. "Only the insider can make decisions, not because he is inherently a better man but because he is so placed that he can understand and act. The outsider is necessarily ignorant, usually irrelevant and often meddlesome, because he is trying to navigate the ship from dry land" (Lippmann 1930 [1925], 150).

   Lippmann thought the "outsider"—the ordinary citizen—was meddlesome because he or she saw politics through a perspective tainted by social experience. He argued that people make sense of public affairs through shortcuts obtained through exposure to "social sets," culture, and the "moral codes" therein (1947 [1922]). Lippmann discounted these perspectives as foggy lenses that resulted in distortions of reality.[21] The resulting view of grassroots public opinion—as the product of feeble minds—has allowed us to overlook what ordinary people say to one another. But is it sufficient to discount perspectives as bundles of stereotypes or "prejudices" resulting from a lack of information? Or should we take these perspectives seriously and investigate how people use them to connect themselves with the world around them, including the political world?

This study recognizes that Lippmann's metaphor of members of the public as "outsiders" or skippers on dry land may be apt for politics. In the unfamiliar land of public affairs, members of the public often lack coherent political ideologies and the compass of information. However, they are not left stranded alone. The processes observable in informal political talk suggest that people are equipped with perspectives that are anchored in their social contexts and their personal experience.

As people relate to other people within their social contexts, they confront public affairs as members of communities that they have collectively defined. Because these processes are largely the function of self-selection on the basis of perceived likeness and shared experience, they are hard to notice unless we investigate interaction over time within groups that people have formed themselves.

Contemporary concerns among political scientists about deliberation and social capital require us to account for these processes. If we believe that communication among citizens is essential for a healthy democracy, and if we believe that civic interaction paves the way for solving public problems together, then we need to understand how people do (or do not) connect with one another through the medium of public issues. What tools do people use to communicate with one another? Can members of our increasingly heterogeneous communities solve public problems together? At least partial answers to these questions can be found by treating citizens as people with social biases that may very well complicate their ability to jointly occupy any civic forum.

Scholars who have investigated the effect of social context by measuring it as the distribution of preferences and the existence of network ties have drawn attention to processes of interpersonal conversations but, because of their methodology, they have not been able to study these processes directly and have not been able to uncover how social identity operates within specific contexts. At the same time, neither Lane nor subsequent constructionist approaches have investigated communication within groups in actual social contexts (but have instead used in-depth interviews and focus groups) and have therefore been unable to see the work of social identity. This study brings together both of these traditions in an investigation of informal political talk among people within existing social networks.

Observing these processes makes clear aspects of civic life that are not simply individual-level phenomena, expressed through polls or ballots. In the ways people choose to interact (or not) with one another, they create and reproduce ideas about who constitutes their community, whom they feel responsible for, and thus the kinds of policies they support (Wong 2002) and the way they spend their time. Citizenship is partly rooted in the individual and partly in the community, but an additional dimension of citizenship springs from the interpersonal interaction that bridges the two.

Brief Outline of the Book

Listening to and observing the informal conversations of groups of ordinary citizens provides a window into these collective acts of citizenship. Chapter 2 builds on existing research in political understanding, particularly studies of framing, to develop a model of group-level political interpretation. Prevailing studies of framing effects assume that members of the public are already familiar with the frames used by political professionals, but they do not examine the processes by which these perspectives are acquired. I argue that the concept of identity-based perspectives helps us understand and appreciate the bottom-up components of political interpretation.

Chapter 3 uses the observations of the men at the corner store and the women in the craft guild to provide a descriptive overview of the nature of their talk and demonstrate that this is a social behavior with political implications. I set the stage for the heart of the empirical analysis in this study by providing the conceptual model derived through the combined methods of inductive observations and deductive survey analysis.

Chapter 4 presents empirical evidence from participant observation and national sample survey data of the processes through which small groups of people create contexts of understanding and the conditions that foster such processes. Specifically, observations of when and how groups of people clarify shared identities suggest that the store of overlapping acquaintances and experiences that group members share as well as characteristics of the physical setting in which they meet influence the extent to which they clarify collective identities. National sample survey data is used to investigate this process on the individual level and analyze whether and in what conditions participants in voluntary associations clarify identity through informal group talk.

Chapter 5 analyzes how the social identities communicated in group contexts are used by the members to talk about politics. Data from the participant observations show how groups use these identities as tools of understanding and how these processes vary across group conditions. In a group in which the participants regularly communicate about shared social identities, the perspectives informed by these identities operate to suggest and regulate the appropriate categories for interpreting public affairs. In contexts in which there is no strong sense of shared identity, individuals rely on their own social identities to distinguish their views from those of others. With the use of national sample survey data and previous studies using participant observation, I generalize the claim that participating in associations characterized by perceptions of likeness enables people to think about politics using the lens of social identity.

Further evidence of the existence as well as the shape of the process of using social identities within a group context to understand political issues is provided by an investigation of the role of the mass media in chapter 6. In this analysis, I compare the content of the news the Old Timers used with their interpretations of it. The results reiterate the claim of previous research that elite framing does matter, but they also show that, through conversations, people transform and even circumvent these frames by applying their identity-based perspectives to supplement the information provided by the news stories.

Chapter 7 provides a final illustration of the way in which small groups of people interpret politics with socially rooted perspectives through an analysis of interpretations of a major political event, the aftermath of the 2000 presidential election. I analyze conversations about the outcome among the Old Timers and among the group of African Americans who sit on the other side of the store. In particular, I focus on the implications of their different interpretations for their perceptions of trust in government. The investigation reveals that the information people use to update their attitudes toward government is not a given but is, instead, perceived through identity-based perspectives. These analyses show how the perspectives people use to communicate coincide with very different interpretations of the same event. In addition, the chapter demonstrates that explaining political interpretations on the basis of partisanship is insufficient for understanding how two people can view the very same event in starkly divergent ways. I conclude that our theories of the dynamics of attitudes such as political trust can be enhanced by attention to socially rooted perspectives.

In the final chapter, I sum up and address the implications of this study for political science and American politics. I explain implications for future research on racial attitudes, framing, social context, political socialization, and social identity. I explain how the analyses conducted here suggest a model of civic life that differs from the two prevailing conceptions: liberal individualism and civic republicanism. In informal talk, people are neither devoid of social attachments (instead, they rely on them) nor acting on behalf of a predetermined common good. Conceptions of "the common good" are constantly worked out as they interact together.

Most important, I conclude that the public's part of public discussion is consequential for citizen politics, but not in a way often recognized by democratic theory or work on social capital. Although it can foster trust, it can also clarify social identities and reinforce exclusion, challenging claims that more discussion and interaction are the answers to the decline of civic life. I relate this conclusion to the tradeoff between community and exclusion as well as the violation of civil liberties in the months following the 9/11 terrorist attacks and ask, Where do we go from here? I propose the use of communitywide intergroup dialogue programs as one route toward breaking down barriers of understanding that arise from social interaction in a segregated society.

CHAPTER 2

The Role of Identity-Based Perspectives

in Making Sense of Politics

Leading models of political understanding posit that people interpret politics through the frames used by elites. The concept of frames is ubiquitous because it acknowledges a simple yet powerful fact of communication: in a world with seemingly infinite amounts of information, all messages are packaged in ways that emphasize particular aspects of the issues.[1] They are "interpretive packages" that give meaning to an issue because they suggest which information should be used to think about it (Gamson and Modigliani 1989, 3). The same basic concept has been called many things: "central organizing ideas" (Gamson and Modigliani 1989); "frames of reference" (Zaller 1992, 13; Lau 1986, 112; Katz and Lazarsfeld 1955, 79); "pictures in the head" (Lippmann 1947 [1922]); "attention frames" (Lasswell and Kaplan 1950, 26–38); or "interpretive structures" for understanding (Kinder and Sanders 1996, 164).

It is widely acknowledged that the way elites frame an issue influences how it is understood.[2] What is not recognized, however, is that ordinary folks interpret political information, including elite-driven frames, through perspectives that are shaped by their social identities. Elite-provided frames are successful in getting people to view political issues in certain ways because these frames resonate with the perspectives people have used to think and communicate about politics in their own lives.

Understanding Is about Categorization

Models of understanding generally agree that interpretation is fundamentally about categorization.[3] Simply put, to make sense of the world, people carve it up into manageable parts. The organization of these parts in memory is often referred to as schema-based cognition. A schema is a knowledge structure or a framework of thoughts related to a given topic.[4] It consists of a category label, and attributes, examples, and affect related to that category, all organized in a hierarchical fashion. Schemas operate like folders in a file drawer—those that are available in memory serve as the categories under which new information is stored. When thinking about a topic, people are more likely to retrieve information from schemata that are clearly relevant to that topic. To continue the file drawer analogy, the more people think about a particular domain, the better organized their filing system will become. That is, they have more folders, more hierarchical organization of these folders, more associations among these folders, and a greater likelihood that they will notice inconsistencies within and across these folders.[5]

When people try to make sense of an event, they type it as an instance of a given category, thereby calling up information that has been stored in the schema relevant to that category.[6] A key influence on interpretation occurs when the schemas that have been called up provide information that fills in the blanks for information not provided by the message or survey question. For example, in a mid-1970s study of attitudes toward presidential candidates Jimmy Carter and Gerald Ford, people who had well-developed schemas about specific issues, groups, parties, or personalities were more likely to use information related to these knowledge structures when asked about their attitudes toward Carter or Ford (Lau 1986). Likewise, when people are provided with information about the party affiliation of hypothetical candidates, they infer information about the candidates' issue stances, even when that specific policy information has not been provided (Rahn 1993).

Are Categories Elite-Driven?

Although both the dominant work on framing and the model advanced in this book build upon this general theory of information processing, they emphasize two different answers to the question of where these categories come from. There is general agreement that people pick up the schemata they use for making evaluations from their information environments. Richard Lau explains, "People are not born with any particular political schema, however; these schemata develop through experience with the political world. If most political information involves party, issues, groups, or individual candidate personalities (and it is my impression that it does), then individual cognitive structures must mirror this information environment" (1986, 114). However, prevailing models of opinion assume that these information environments are a function of elite discourse. "They [ordinary citizens] have little control over this environment; it is set by politicians, world events, and the media" (Lau 1986, 96).

Indeed, scholars have been able to explain the main shifts in American mass opinion on the basis of elite rhetoric. For this reason, the origins of the categories people use to interpret politics are typically attributed to elites and the mass media.[7] This elite-driven view is most famously outlined in Zaller's *The Nature and Origins of Mass Opinion* (1992), as Lee (2002, chap. 1) asserts. Zaller posits that the way elites talk about issues affects how members of the public both evaluate and understand political topics. Although Zaller does not investigate understanding directly, his model suggests that elites influence individuals' interpretations of politics in the following manner. Elites provide suggestions, or "cueing messages," about how a given issue connects with individuals' prior predispositions. People are expected to resist messages that run counter to their priors or "predispositions," but only as a function of these cueing messages (44). Under Zaller's model, these messages or frames can be derived from interpersonal conversation as well as elite discourse.[8] These messages suggest to the public how information fits with their prior preferences (in his model, political ideology serves as a proxy for preferences.) In other words, these frames are expected to operate like interpretive packages. Frames focus attention on chosen portions of an issue, which calls up particular schemata and therefore affects which information gets processed (Entmann 1989).

Like many other contemporary public opinion scholars, Zaller argues that the way political information is organized in individuals' minds depends on the frames provided by elite rhetoric. The people who are most "aware" of elite rhetoric are best equipped with these frames.[9] In other words, this tradition posits that unless people are given a road map by elites, they are ill equipped to make sense of the world of politics.

The claim that citizens do not make sense of politics on their own, independent of the maps elites provide, is normatively unappealing, but it is hard to ignore the mass of empirical evidence in its favor (Zaller 1992, 45). Most prominently, there is Converse's evidence, published in 1964, which annihilated support for the belief that ordinary citizens think about politics on the basis of a coherent ideological belief system.[10]

Subsequent work has argued that people reason on the basis of core beliefs, rather than liberal-conservative ideology. Even this work, however, argues for a strong role for elites. The content of beliefs, such as support for equality of opportunity, economic individualism, and free enterprise, is assumed to trickle down from elites, transmitted directly and indirectly by "the political rhetoric and politics of the society" and "maintained over time by the persistence of institutions and policies" (Feldman 1988, 418).

Scholars generally agree that forming political judgments on the basis of core beliefs happens because elites provide the road maps to make it happen. The tension between many beliefs in American political culture, such as that between individualism and egalitarianism, causes policy ambivalence (Feldman and Zaller 1992). The presumption is that elites provide the clarity that causes a particular value to win out.

Various studies demonstrate the difficulty people have with connecting their preexisting beliefs and views with political concerns in the absence of elite guidance. For example, in a study of individuals' interpretations of four policy issues in the Pittsburgh area, Lau et al. (1991) found that only when knowledge structures that individuals commonly and readily use clearly match an interpretation did their prior beliefs matter for evaluation. When this match does not occur, or when only one interpretation was made available, the individuals in their experimental settings made choices that did not correspond to their prior political beliefs.

More evidence of the relative inability of people to evaluate politics by using beliefs to aid interpretation comes from work by Shah and colleagues. They have shown that individuals' values influence their interpretations of media messages (Shah, Domke, and Wackman 1996, 1997; Domke, Shah, and Wackman 1998). They argue that values, ethics, and morals function like heuristics or cues and help people tie political issues to their sense of selves.[11] However, their work suggests that these prior beliefs are more likely to matter for their interpretations of politics (and hence their political evaluations) when elite-driven messages point out the relevance of these beliefs. In an experimental test of the effects of different media frames on undergraduates' and also evangelical Christians' interpretations of candidates' stands on health care, they found that evangelical Christians were especially likely to interpret candidates' positions through ethical as opposed to materialist frames (Shah et al. 1996). In addition, when people were encouraged by the frame of the message to interpret health care stances in ethical terms, the individuals' own ethical beliefs had a larger influence on their choice of candidate (Domke et al. 1998).

The research by Shah and his colleagues underscores the undeniable importance of elite rhetoric. However, it also implies that assuming people are unable to think about politics in the absence of elite-provided guidance overlooks an important fact. Elite frames activate particular ways of understanding a political issue because ordinary citizens already have these frames in their store of tools for making sense of the world. Frames are cultural resources. We teach these things to each other. Political actors are able to use frames in strategic ways because people give them meaning through the course of everyday interaction.

The success of frames in persuading people to think about an issue in a particular way depends on whether they resonate with perspectives that the audience can readily recognize. As Nelson explains, "[F]raming theory argues that social movement leaders and other political elites attempt to mobilize support by relating their claim or cause to a *familiar* socio-political frame of reference. Thus, opponents of affirmative action will frame that policy as 'reverse discrimination' in an attempt to link a purportedly benign policy to a despised social practice" (1999, 5, emphasis added). Likewise, the frames in which elites commonly convey social welfare information continue to prevail because they resonate with common themes in the political culture (Gamson and Lasch 1983). Frames work when they are *familiar.* And this familiarity is not acquired by individuals watching the news in isolation. Instead, it is transmitted in part through social interaction. People are immersed in social contexts in which they ask each other if they saw a certain story, wonder aloud about the implications of an event, and, more fundamentally, suggest to each other and reinforce certain ways of interpreting current events. Frames are ways of making sense of issues that people pass on to, and hash out with, one another.

This is an aspect of framing effects that researchers using a cognitive perspective only rarely acknowledge. Sniderman and Theriault (1999) argue that the term "frame" has evolved to suggest that interpretations of issues exist "out there" and does not acknowledge the source of these interpretations and the manner in which they are constructed.[12] The result, they suggest, is that political scientists' research on framing effects is predisposed to support an elite-driven model.[13]

Of course, part of the familiarity of frames stems from exposure to the mass media and other sources of elite discourse. The mass media are responsible for the outlines of many categories that we use to think about politics and other topics. If they were not, why specifically would race be an important signifier even to people in homogeneously white American towns? Why would people's evaluations of politics be influenced by perceptions of the conditions and opinions of people they have never met (Mutz 1998)? Moreover, some of the *content* of these categories can be traced to mass media portrayals as well. There are notable central tendencies in whites' negative stereotypes of African Americans that could not have arisen spontaneously from a multitude of isolated "realities."[14] Finally, a top-down model can also partially explain how these categories are connected to specific policies. Gilens (1999) argues that the tendency of the mass media to typify poor people as African Americans explains the relevance of race to attitudes toward welfare, and white Americans' opposition to it.

The Bottom-Up Component of Framing Effects

The evidence that elite rhetoric influences which frames people use to understand politics is undeniable. However, several studies suggest a dual top-down and bottom-up process. Neuman, Just, and Crigler (1992), with the aid of surveys, in-depth interviews, content analysis, and experiments, provide evidence that making sense of the news is not entirely a function of elite discourse. Specifically, they looked for the ways in which their in-depth interview respondents conceptualize and interpret public issues and compared these interpretations to those offered by the media. They found that both the mass media and their respondents tended to talk about the issues in one of five frames: "economic themes, divisions of protagonists into 'us' and 'them,' perceptions of control by powerful others, a sense of the human impact of issues, and the application of moral values" (62). They did find a large degree of overlap between the frames used by the media and the frames invoked by their respondents, and concluded, in accord with the elite-driven model, that the frames provided by the media "helped subjects to determine the personal relevance of the issue, to provide linkages among issues, and to formulate arguments from which opinion could be drawn" (62). However, they found their subjects interpreting the news in ways that suggest a much more active process than a simple top-down model implies.

They conclude that their respondents did not "slavishly follow the framing of issues presented in the mass media. Rather, people frame issues in a more visceral and moralistic (and sometimes racist and xenophobic) style. They actively filter, sort, and reorganize information in personally meaningful ways in the process of constructing an understanding of public issues" (77). This work suggests that although members of the public think through public affairs using the frames provided by the mass media, this is not sufficient evidence that their interpretation of issues is beholden to elites' interpretations. The fact that any given frame encapsulates a variety of stances, as Gamson and Modigliani (1989, 3) point out, implies that within these general narratives, individuals *construct* their own meanings and make sense of politics on their own terms.

A further challenge to an elite-driven model of understanding is that it cannot adequately explain why two people can interpret the same media story in very different ways. Even when exposed to identical stimuli, how individuals think about an event is in large part determined by the way they view the world. Evidence of this is easy to come by. We pick it up in daily conversation when friends or family disagree with our "take" on a movie or our view of the implications of an election. More concrete evidence comes from Gross's work on evaluations of the 1992 Los Angeles riots. Through experiments, Gross (2000) researched judgments about the riots and found that differences in the explanations subjects gave for rioters' behavior could be traced to differences in their levels of racial prejudice.

These differences in interpretation are not a simple matter of differences in predispositions defined as preferences. Instead, the divergence is a function of the use of different categories and considerations in interpretation. To demonstrate, consider the systematic evidence that has been collected on variations in interpretations of the Clarence Thomas hearings (Sapiro and Soss 1999). In 1991, the U.S. Senate held contentious hearings debating the confirmation of Clarence Thomas to the U.S. Supreme Court. A former coworker, Anita Hill, had accused Thomas, the chairman of the Equal Employment Opportunity Commission, of sexually harassing her while serving as her supervisor. The hearings became a major news event. Sapiro and Soss found that members of the public interpreted the event in a variety of ways and that these interpretations varied systematically according to the characteristics of the person evaluating Thomas or Hill. Importantly, these interpretations differed in systematic ways by social category. Among Hill supporters, whites and blacks used different sets of considerations to think about her. This was not true among Thomas supporters. Instead, the most striking differences in their interpretations appeared along the lines of gender. Male Thomas supporters used a more complex structure of considerations than did female Thomas supporters. Strong Hill supporters also displayed gendered differences, as men and women in this group appeared to rely on different reasons for support.

This study suggests that members of different social groups interpret the same political event in different ways. But notice that these patterns are not deterministic.[15] Neither all whites nor even all white women looked on this event in the same way. Differences in interpretations within social groups varied according to whether they leaned toward Hill or Thomas. How does this happen? Sapiro and Soss conclude that "meanings vary systematically across social dimensions defined by general faultlines in American politics, by the substance of events themselves, by the stories that journalists and other leaders tell, and by the degree to which people attend to these stories" (308). In their view, though certain social groups may be more likely to favor a particular response to an issue, their interpretations are filtered through elite-driven messages.

However, even *without* elite suggestions about how to interpret an event, interpretations often diverge along demographic, especially racial, lines.[16] Take, for example, Kuklinski and Hurley's (1994) experiment on source cues and persuasion. In their experiment, they randomly assigned 152 blacks and 151 whites to a paper-and-pencil-administered questionnaire. Within the questionnaire, each subject was given the following item:

> We would like to get your reaction to a statement that —— recently
> made. He was quoted in the *New York Times* as saying that
> "African-Americans must stop making excuses and rely much more on
> themselves to get ahead in society." Please indicate how much you agree
> or disagree with —— 's statement.

The name of the speaker was changed across conditions: it was listed as either Jesse Jackson, Clarence Thomas, Ted Kennedy, or George H. W. Bush. They found that when the statement was attributed to Jackson or Thomas, the black respondents were more likely to agree. On a 5-point scale of agreement in which 5 is strong agreement, blacks given the names of Jackson and Thomas averaged scores of 4.11 and 3.79, respectively, while blacks given the names of Kennedy and Bush averaged scores of 3.32 and 2.97.[17]

The act of making sense of political information is conducted with the tool of social identity. It was the race of the speaker—not the speaker's ideology—that mattered for these interpretations. If it had been ideology, we would have expected approval of the statement to be similar in the Thomas and Bush conditions and the Jackson and Kennedy conditions (conservatives and liberals, respectively). But it was not; instead, responses were clumped by the race of the speaker. Moreover, it was not just the race of the speaker that mattered. *The race of the speaker mattered as a function of the race of the respondent.* The patterns among whites were discernibly different from those among blacks. Whites were less affected by the name of the speaker.[18]

Fifteen years earlier, Sapiro (1981–82) demonstrated corroborating results with respect to gender. She randomly assigned undergraduates to read a speech given by one of two hypothetical U.S. senators, *John* Baker or *Joan* Baker. The speech was identical, and dealt with poverty, unemployment, and economic growth. But Sapiro asked the subjects to rate the senator's competence on a wide range of issues. Through this simple manipulation, she demonstrated that people make sense of politicians with the aid of social group categories, but, more importantly, they use themselves as reference points. Men and women judged John's competence on the environment very similarly, but they disagreed on Joan's competence: 15 percent of men, and 50 percent of women, thought she would be competent on the environment. Like Kuklinksi and Hurley's experiment, the gender of the candidate mattered most notably as a function of the gender of the respondent. The shape of the message—whether the senator is portrayed as a man or a woman—matters for interpretation, but so too does the interpreter's place in the social world.

Making Use of the Concept of Perspective

The concept of frame neatly encapsulates the fact that interpretation is done through categorization and that which categories a message invokes influence how it is understood. However, "frame" does not adequately acknowledge that even if two people are given the same message, they may interpret it in two different ways because they see it through different lenses.

It is the concept of perspective that allows us to account for the role of social experience in the act of political understanding. A variety of bodies of research suggest that the perspectives people use to make sense of public affairs are rooted in social identities developed through social interaction. Moreover, they suggest that differences in political interpretation across members of society arise from social interaction among people of specific social locations. By social location, I mean individuals' position in society with respect to characteristics that signify relative status, such as race, gender, and class.

Consider the feminist conception of "standpoint." The sexual division of labor endows women with a different set of experiences than men, which have consequences for the different ways men and women look at the world (Hartsock 1998). Knowledge therefore depends on where one stands in the social world "because every knower is grounded in his or her own particular identities, including gender, race, and class" (Press and Cole 1999, x).

Work by Kristin Luker (1984) on abortion activists in California demonstrates that this grounding is the result of interaction within specific social contexts. Her work shows that members of pro-life and pro-choice groups understand the issue of abortion through strikingly different "world views." It is not level of income, education, or religious affiliation that creates these values. Instead, it is the different social contexts that these demographics characterize that generate the activists' worldviews. Luker shows that the entire social context in which these activists live their lives reinforces their divergent interpretations. The women come from different socioeconomic backgrounds, enter into marriages and occupations with different expectations and goals, and have established social networks that resonate with and reinforce their pro-choice or pro-life perspectives.

Similar mechanisms account for the distinctiveness of the lenses through which African Americans view the political world. Dawson (2001) argues that African-American ideologies are distinct from mainstream liberalism and include variations ranging from "activist egalitarians" to "black conservatism."[19] He states that African Americans' embrace of the idea of autonomy combined with physical, social, and political separation have caused these subpublic ideologies to develop. Thus, African Americans' perspectives differ from those of whites partly because of social structure: the combination of social location, spatial location (residing and working in segregated and often isolated geographic spaces), and exposure to black "counterpublics" or information networks.

Cultural studies of the mass media and society point out that the act of seeing the world from the standpoint of a particular position in society hinges not just on social structure but on active processes of social identification. Such studies show that people of certain social locations engage in "oppositional processing," rejecting the dominant perspective and replacing it with their own frame of interpretation (Morley 1980; Liebes and Katz 1990). How this works depends on the viewers' identities. For example, Press and Cole (1999) argue that prime-time television shows about abortion tend to portray the topic in a mainstream, middle-class manner in which the typical abortion seeker is a poor, often nonwhite woman. They find that lower-income women who identify as "working class" rather than "middle class" readily argue that the shows do not represent the reality they have experienced in their own lives.

Additional evidence that variations in perspectives derive from experience in different social locations stems from Gamson's work on political talk. As noted earlier, he did discover a tendency to rely on collective identities, but, importantly, the tendency to do so differed across groups depending on their demographic makeup. Groups in which people had similar backgrounds were more likely to use their shared collective identities. This was especially the case for groups composed entirely of African Americans "in spite of" media discourse (108).[20] For example, the media content he analyzed as part of the study did not put the issues of troubled industry and the Arab-Israeli conflict in adversarial terms, but the participants in his study occasionally did.

More recently, Lee (2002) has documented the social group basis of public opinion with respect to the civil rights movement. Whether or not group-based considerations mattered for individuals' stance on civil rights policies depended on whether people were part of the activated mass public

(African Americans, southern whites, and later on in the 1960s, northern white liberals).[21] Thus, Lee suggests that opinion is a function of more than which elites individuals pay attention to. His work also shows that deciding which elites to identify with is an ongoing process. In his massive analysis of letters mailed to the presidents in office during the civil rights struggle, he found various cases of people admitting to a change in party affiliation because of the events of the movement.

Put differently, what causes people to pay attention to different elites? When faced with the possibility of subscribing to *The Nation* or the *National Review*, what explains which magazine a person buys? The choice is a function of individuals' self-concepts, which are larger than party identification. Moreover, evidence that two people interpret the same message in divergent ways suggests that individuals' perspectives also influence how the information presented in a given magazine is perceived.

Therefore, part of the explanation for the interpretive lenses people use does lie in the information environments in which they are steeped.[22] But people are not blank pages upon which the news of the day is imprinted. They develop and clarify perspectives of understanding in an active, ongoing process in their daily life as social beings. Thus, the concept of perspective enables us to recognize that political understanding is not performed by millions of isolated individuals but by people who have ways of knowing and thinking that they acquire by living within society.

The Centrality of Social Identity in Perspectives

I submit that social identities occupy a central role in the perspectives people use to think about public affairs. They are not simply another consideration that people take into account when making sense of the world around them. Instead, identities color the lens through which other considerations and factors in opinion—things such as interests, attachments to political parties, and political values—are understood.[23]

The word "identity" can be used to convey either "individuality" or "sameness."[24] Individuals' identities accordingly comprise both the way they see themselves as individuals (personal identity) and as members of social groups (social identity) (Turner et al. 1987). It is the latter type of identity that is of interest here. In this study, I define social identities as knowledge structures that are developed when people categorize themselves and others as types of people (Tajfel 1969) and compare themselves to others for clues about how they should think and act (Brewer and Miller 1984).[25] In more detail, to reassure themselves that their view of the world is a good one, people compare themselves with others they think they are like (Festinger 1954). Through social interaction, people evaluate themselves in comparison with individuals, as well as with social norms of behavior (Pettigrew 1967) and reference groups (Kelley 1952). The process of face-to-face interaction with members of a small group is related to the process of identifying with a larger-scale social group.[26] As people compare themselves with others in their immediate surroundings, they learn what they perceive to be the appropriate norms of behavior for "someone like me." At times this identity can be restricted to the group ("the Old Timers"), but it can also take on large-scale connotations ("Ann Arborites," "Americans"). We can see social identity at work when people think of themselves in terms of "we" and "us" as opposed to "I" and "me" (Turner et al. 1994). When social identities are relevant to a given situation, people respond in ways that are appropriate to that perception of themselves (Tajfel and Turner 1979; Turner et al. 1994). The effect of social identities on attitudes and actions is powerful. Experiments show that people strongly prefer their own group even when their own "group" is a construction of researchers that has only minimal consequence (Tajfel et al. 1971; Brewer 1979).[27]

A variety of work within political science has argued that social identities guide political thought, despite Lane's claims to the contrary. Whether people identify with women has been shown to influence how they justify their evaluations of candidates and their perceptions of the Democratic and Republican Parties (Conover 1984, 1988). Other work, which focuses on evaluation as opposed to understanding, also poses a role for social identity. The degree to which African Americans perceive a linked fate with other African Americans influences their political choices (Dawson 1994). The more people identify with a social group with which they believe they share interests, the more likely they are to think and behave in the political realm in ways that are distinct from nongroup members (Campbell et al. 1960). And this use of identities is not just the work of Lippmann's "feeble minds." For example, among people identifying with Catholics during the 1950s, it was the more politically informed who were likely to support Catholic candidates (Converse and Campbell 1968).

Often, political scientists allude to the centrality of social identity but do not mention the concept explicitly. Take, for example, the following statement by Henry Brady and Paul Sniderman:

> Why, then, are many in the mass public able to attribute accurately attitudes to Democrats and Republicans, to blacks and whites, even to liberals and conservatives? Liberals and conservatives (and Democrats

and Republicans) have, and emphasize, political identities, identities, moreover, that have been developed in contradistinction to one another (liberals vs. conservatives, Democrats vs. Republicans). Because they are competitors, there are incentives—certainly there is permission—for a person who likes liberals to dislike conservatives, and the other way around. What allows citizens to simplify political calculations efficiently is this two-sided, "us vs. them" character of politics; the more attached they are to their side—and the more opposed they are to the other—the more they appreciate the differences between the issue positions of the two sides. What counts, then, is not how people feel toward groups, one by one; rather it is how they feel toward *pairs* of opposing groups. (1985, 1075)

When the authors state, "What allows citizens to simplify political cal-culation efficiently is this two-sided, 'us vs. them' character of politics.... What counts . . . is how [people] feel toward *pairs* of opposing groups," they are pointing out the work of social identity.[28]

Stated another way, perceptions of groups enter political thinking as pieces of information that are rooted in citizens' self-concepts. Kinder's work on the racial basis of opinion provides evidence of this. His work argues that whites' attitudes toward African-American candidates (Sears and Kinder 1971) and race policies such as fair employment legislation, school desegregation, and affirmative action (Kinder and Sanders 1996)[29] are rooted in their atti-tudes toward blacks *acquired as whites in a racist society.* Moreover, his work with Thomas Nelson (Nelson and Kinder 1996) demonstrates that individu-als' attitudes toward policies depend on their attitudes toward the recipient group and on their position relative to that group. With experiments, they showed that when policy information was framed so that it clearly delimited the recipient group, attitudes toward that group mattered more than when such a frame was not used for the way subjects evaluated the policy.

But again, it is not simply the packaging of the message that matters. These effects depend on the race of the subject. For example, among whites who were exposed to information about spending on the poor that empha-sized that such programs "give away money to people who don't really need the help," their stances were more closely related to their attitudes toward the poor than they were when the information emphasized "given the huge budget deficit, we simply can't afford it." However, among nonwhites, the relationship was the opposite: attitudes toward the poor were less important for policy stances when "people who don't really need the help" was empha-sized. Nelson and Kinder conclude, "While this striking reversal defies easy explanation, it does suggest that framing strategies that appeal to negative social stereotypes will not be universally effective" (1065). It also suggests that framing effects hinge on the audience members' own social identity—their attachments to in-groups and out-groups.

In a later project, Kinder and Winter (2001) tested this prediction. They modeled racial divides in opinion in two policy domains: issues directly related to race, such as affirmative action and equal employment opportunity, and social welfare issues, such as spending on education and government provision of health insurance. They tested three hypotheses for the origins of this divide: social class, social identity, and adherence to different political principles. They found different results in each domain. For racial issues, the divide in opinion could be explained by differences in political principles and social identity (measured by closeness to in-groups, feelings toward out-groups, and racial resentment). However, for social welfare issues, social identity had little if any affect. Instead, social class and political principles explained the differences.

But if political principles are exerting an effect, does this mean social identities are not? I argue that social identities do not operate separately from principles. Identities function as links between one's social location and one's view of the world. Indeed, Kinder and Winter (2001) leave open this possibility. They argue that blacks and whites adhere to different political principles (e.g., "the idea of limited government appears to be more crystallized and potent for whites than for blacks" [2001, 450]). The relationship between race and principle supports the possibility that social identities and political principles interact with each other.

The Kinder and Winter study did not conceptualize social identity as a central component of citizens' perspectives. Other studies have similarly treated social identity as one consideration, not as part of the interpretive framework people use that constrains other politically relevant considerations. For example, Mutz and Mondak (1997) examined whether—and how—perceptions of the well-being of various social groups (women, blacks, Hispanics, poor people, the well-to-do, working men and women, and the middle class) affected votes for Reagan in 1984. They tested three possible routes: group membership, group identity, and social comparison.[30] They found little evidence supporting any of these mechanisms. Instead, they found perceptions of inequality were driving vote choice.

Mutz (1998) summarizes these results this way: "Overall, these results suggest that it is not the direction of change that individuals perceive in any given economic group that matters most; instead, the central issue is whether the groups are perceived to have fared the same, or with some benefiting or suffering more than others" (139). But is group identity really not at work here? Consider the way Mutz and Mondak conceptualize the mechanism of social identity. Following Campbell et al. (1960), they theorize that groups operate as proxies for self-interest (1997, 286). In this framework, identity is assumed to influence which information is considered relevant to the vote, which then in turn influences that vote. However, if social identities are central parts of citizens' perspectives, there is reason to think the process is somewhat different. Group identity influences decisions about which information is relevant, but, more fundamentally, it influences *how that information is perceived*—which then influences the vote.

The evidence that Mutz and Mondak (1997) present with respect to perceptions of inequality is consistent with this view. When people judge the economic well-being of social groups in society, how do they make these calculations? Entirely on the basis of the mass media? Or do they root their evaluations in their sense of where they fit in the social world? Mutz and Mondak argue that social comparison works as if people make calculations of their personal economic status and the well-being of members of a social group and then use the distance between the two to inform their votes. But the theory of social judgments put forth by Brewer and Miller (1984) mentioned earlier holds that social identities are intertwined with the act of social comparison. That is, individuals categorize themselves as given types of people, develop identities and anti-identities, and use the resulting cognitive structures in making judgments (including, presumably, vote choices). A claim that social comparison is driving behavior is necessarily a claim that social identity is also at work.

* * *

Previous research generally conceives the process of understanding politics as an act of categorization. Prevailing models of public opinion posit that the categories or, relatedly, frames that people use to interpret public affairs are bestowed on them by elites, despite constructionist work that suggests that bottom-up processes involving social identities are at work as well. Reviving the concept of perspective allows us to acknowledge that people are influenced by the categories elites provide but that they are continually defining these categories through experience in their own social contexts.

Although elite-driven frames induce some categories to be more accessible than others, what these categories *mean* differs significantly across people in different social locations. Moreover, the categories that people apply are a function of their perspectives, which are rooted in experience within particular social locations. We can imagine, for example, that the way a white man married to a woman in the Army Reserve makes sense of war with Iraq is different from the way an Arab-American restaurant owner in Dearborn, Michigan, interprets it. Knowing how the war is framed by the news media is not enough. To observe how it is that people interpret politics through identity-based perspectives, we need to study interaction within actual social contexts.

CHAPTER 3

The Social Practice of Informal Political Talk

> Dave: I was in the mood for English muffins last night. I like English muffins. Went to the store to get some. We were out. The wife usually has them around the house. So I went to the store for them. You know how much they cost? $2.49!
>
> Stu: How many were in there?
>
> Dave: Six, I think.
>
> Harold: Right, probably six.
>
> Dave: I don't know how people do it these days. I don't know how some families survive.
>
> Stu: Well, they're making a lot more now than we used to, Dave.
>
> Harold: Yeah, but some of them don't make very much and they have two or three kids to feed. That's hard.
>
> Dave: The problem is, the divide between those on top and those on the bottom is growing.
>
> Stu: I don't know about that . . .
>
> Harold: It is getting bigger.
>
> Dave: Disappearing middle class. More and more people on the top and on the bottom.
>
> Stu: I would disagree. I think the middle class is growing, getting larger, more prosperous.
>
> Harold: I would agree with that. I think the problem is that the ones on the bottom are getting worse off—that part is growing. The heavies are getting better off, but so is the middle class. It's the ones on the bottom that are hurting.
>
> Stu: I don't know. They aren't all that bad off. I volunteer at the Peace Neighborhood Center . . . The families that are down and out now don't have it nearly as bad as the families that were down and out twenty-five years ago.
>
> Harold: Not in this town anyway.
>
> Stu: That's right, not in [this town].
>
> Dave: Well, look at Ypsilanti, Detroit.
>
> Stu: They're all right here. Right here. This *is* Ypsilanti and Detroit.
>
> Dave: Well, I don't know about that.

O̲n this particular morning, the Old Timers in the corner store found their way from English muffins to the growing gap between rich and poor and then to their perceptions of an increasing African-American population in Ann Arbor. This is the act of people making sense of politics together. This conversation is notable for its organic nature. No researcher induced it. No government institution or agency stimulated it for decision-making purposes. Instead, Stu, Dave, and Harold were engaging in a dialogue with political implications, but as a by-product of their social interaction. Through the medium of political talk, they relate to one another. In so doing, they develop the conceptual resources—the social-identity-based perspectives—that structure how they interpret subsequent issues.

To be clear, the "development" taking place in these groups is not the wholesale adoption of new identities but the clarification of identities. Although identities such as partisan identification tend to crystallize in one's second or third decades of life (Jennings 1989) and then persist across much of the life span (Jennings and Markus 1984), what it *means* to be a Republican, a white person, or a male is not a given, and it is not entirely defined in a person's youth. Norms of behavior, such as ideas about how women should behave, are negotiated in practice (West and Zimmerman 1987). In their interactions with others, people do not necessarily change the labels they give to themselves (e.g., Republican, middle class, pro-union, Ann Arborite); they *give meaning* to what it means to be a person like themselves. This process of updating and modifying identities is what I am referring to by the terms "development" or "clarification."

Gathering Because "My Wife Wanted Me Out of the House": Public Discussion as a By-Product of Social Interaction

To understand the processes that occur during informal political talk, it helps to know the pretexts under which it occurs. Much political interaction occurs not among people who make a point to specifically talk about politics but emerges instead from the social processes of people chatting with one another. When people report with whom they talk about politics, they tend to mention the people they are most likely to interact with about anything. Spouses and coworkers usually top the lists (Beck 1991; Huckfeldt and Sprague 1995, chaps. 6, 10). Such evidence suggests that political discussion arises out of the opportunity to talk in general, not as a result of seeking out people with whom to talk about politics.

Observations of the talk among the groups in this study verify this. The women at the guild claim their primary motivations for being in the group are fellowship and the desire to raise money for the church. During one meeting, a member of the church administration consulted the women about how to ensure the future of the group. Membership had been dwindling because of the declining number of women in the church who have free time during the day. "What brings you to this group? What do you get out of it?" she asked. "Fellowship," a woman named Maureen answered. "I'd say fellowship and crafts. I think we are all here wanting to do something for the church." The other women nodded their heads in agreement.

Likewise, most of the people who meet regularly in the corner store, including the Old Timers, the mixed-gender group that meets later in the morning, and the small-table regulars, profess that their motivation for being a part of the conversations is for social interaction or "a good way to start off the day." There is additional evidence about the Old Timers' motivations from surveys I administered to them in December 1998 and January 1999.[1] In the questionnaire, I asked, in an open-ended format, "Why did you first start spending your mornings here?" None of the explanations dealt with politics, except perhaps one respondent who reported spending time at the store to "discuss problems." But if the other respondents' answers are any clue, 'problems' probably meant social relationships rather than current events. The other answers revealed social needs, such as spending time at the store "to talk and enjoy the people," "meet new friends," "talk to relatives," or "keep in contact with friends." Other answers showed a need for some kind of activity in retirement, such as going to the store "to start the day and the engine with stimulation of coffee, conversation, newspaper," "get out of the way of the cleaning lady," "wife wanted me out of the house," or simply "being retired gave me time" and "I missed day to day work relationships and discussions."

None of the people I observed claim that they gather for the sake of politics. At the corner store, if any one topic motivates their participation, it is sports, especially the exploits of teams from the University of Michigan. One occasional patron, speaking about the Old Timers, said, "That's all they talk about—sports." And one Old Timer once asked the group, "What would we talk about if we didn't talk about sports?" And if sports is not front and center in the talk, it is family. One Old Timer observed, "You come in here, see people you know, talk about sports, family."

Given their many other daily concerns, it is not unreasonable that the people I observed are not preoccupied with politics (Downs 1957). Despite the fact that most residents of the United States are citizens, that identity hardly predominates in their behavior or their self-identification. Before being citizens charged with the duty of being informed about politics, they are parents, retirees, employees, employers, homeowners, renters, and so forth.

Although politics is not central to their groups, talk about politics does occasionally arise out of talk about other things. Political topics among the various groups ranged from the Clinton sex scandals to local parking fees, from military action in the Persian Gulf to economic inequality. However, a comparison of the Old Timers and the guild is instructive. These two groups differ markedly in the amount of time they talk about politics. The women in the guild tend to evade political topics, an issue that will be analyzed in more detail in chapter 5. They do not know one another or their political dispositions very well, and thus they tend to avoid politics for fear of disrupting the air of politeness (MacKuen 1990; Eliasoph 1998).[2] In addition, several members conveyed through their comments that it is inappropriate for them to talk about politics, and thus the members tend to mention political topics with some trepidation.

In contrast, the Old Timers typically move from topic to topic with ease. They openly acknowledge that part of what they do involves occasionally mulling over political issues together. One morning, upon arrival at the corner store, a man asked, "What's new?" Instead of the other Old Timers responding "not much," they listed out everything we had talked about so far: "football, flying [in World War II], Saddam [Hussein] . . ."

They also recognize that others notice the political implications of their gatherings. In their eyes, the place has become "everybody's soapbox." One man talked about how he had known the current mayor for years; when she was first contemplating running for office, he had joked about how she ought to come down to the corner store to campaign. She accepted his offer and "ever since then it's become the soapbox." The local congresswoman at the time, Lynn Rivers, had also started scheduling visits to the store in recent years.

The Frequency of the Old Timers' Political Talk

Over the course of the first twenty months of my observations, I spent 105 mornings with the Old Timers. Explicitly political conversations occurred during fifty-eight of those visits. Among the conversations were ones that touched on segregation, the cost of living, decisions to erect World War II memorials, sexual harassment, inner-city education, HMOs, participation on city and county government boards, the ethics of corporate manufacturing in developing countries, politicians' use of the corner store, labor union news and events, and lottery policy. I did not consider conversations about their experience in the military as political unless they talked about military *policy*, and I did not code talk about the lottery as political unless they talked specifically about the government's role in its administration.

The figures reported above suggest that at least several members talk about politics for a moment every other day. This figure might be skewed slightly high for the following reasons: First, there were five to ten days during those twenty months when I stopped by the corner store for relatively short (twenty to thirty minute) visits and did not take extensive notes on the conversations for the very reason that they did not engage in political talk. These visits were not included to arrive at the 58 days out of 105 on which political topics arose. In addition, during the Monica Lewinsky scandal, I purposely spent time with them on the mornings when there were related major events (such as President Clinton's testimony before the grand jury and the release of the Kenneth Starr report) in order to hear them talk about their expectations; I also spent time with them on the mornings *after* such events to listen to their interpretations. Obviously, they were more likely to talk about politics on those days. Also, even their attempts to change the topic—for example, when someone raised their cup of coffee and said, "Here's to Bill Clinton!" and another responded, "Oh, please, I haven't had my breakfast yet . . ."—were coded as political remarks.

A more accurate measure of their propensity to talk about politics is provided by a summary of just the first two months of my observations from mid-October to Thanksgiving 1997, when I spent time with them regularly, four to five days a week (Monday through Saturday). In this period, I did not schedule my visits around current events but around my other morning obligations. During this period, they talked about politics during fourteen of the eighteen mornings I spent with them. (Even though there was a local election that November, on only two of those days did they discuss the taxation measures or city council seats that were on the ballot.) Recall that this was during the time before they knew I was interested in politics, and knew only that I studied "social science." In sum, the Old Timers chatted about politics quite often.

What Constitutes Political Talk?

In practice, what gets defined as a political conversation is itself a product of the interaction. The Old Timers typically describe "politics" as consisting of elections, debates involving Democrats and Republicans, and occasionally elected officials carrying out their duties. They consider politics as controversy and the stuff of people who lack common sense (where "common" is defined by the way the Old Timers think about the world.) Specifically, talking about politics is "opinionated" talk; unless a person holds controversial opinions (opinions that diverge from their own), the conversation is not political.

One morning they were discussing a state law that put restrictions on feeding deer to prevent the transmission of tuberculosis:

> Bill: It's so ridiculous. You can hunt deer and not get TB, but you can't feed them?
> Mack: Oh, it's so political I could puke.
> Bill: That's all it is, is politics.

This law was the product of politics, not common-sense decision making, as far as they were concerned.

On a visit late in my fieldwork, an Old Timer named John asked me, "What is it that you pull away from here? We haven't talked about a whole lot today—what is it that you look for?" I explained that I was interested in political conversation. This was more of an admission than I had yet made during my observations, and John ran with it:

> Yeah, well, I don't think any of us in here are that intense. I mean, we're up there in years, you know, and most of us have been through a lot of crap in our lives. And I tell you, you're uptight twenty-four hours a day [when you're working]. Take him—Bill—I could never have done the job he did—I would have killed somebody, dealing with human relations, listening to gripes all day long. It would have driven me nuts. Now, I don't want that aggravation anymore.

To the Old Timers, politics is about impasse and petty griping. John's interpretation is that they do not talk about politics very much because they are done with bothering themselves with such aggravation. However, his definition of political talk does not include the many conversations that are relevant to public affairs but do not appear as "opinionated" or "gripes" because the members have similar views. In addition, defining political talk as contested *issues* overlooks their many conversations that do the work of defining whose interests are at stake, whose opinions are worth considering, and where they place people like themselves on various issues.

The Old Timers' responses to the questionnaire reveal that they are aware that they talk about politics. All twenty-six of the Old Timers who responded answered "yes" when asked whether they "ever discuss politics with your family or friends."[3] Eleven of them said they talked about politics every day of the week. Almost all of them, twenty-three out of the twenty-six, said they "have discussions about political issues" in "bars, pubs, coffee shops or stores" at least "sometimes" or "often" when asked to note the frequency with which they talk politics in various groups.[4]

However, few of them recognize their group as a political discussion group—as a group in which political talk is a main activity. In the survey, I provided a standard list of groups and associations and asked them to "Please circle the number corresponding to any of the types of groups to which you belong." One option, "informal clubs or groups," which I expected to capture their participation in the group at the corner store, was circled by only seven of the twenty-six Old Timers who responded. Although they see themselves as an entity, they do not see their group in the same sense that they regard "service clubs or groups," "sports teams," and "church-connected groups." Many of them do not recognize themselves as an organized group, perhaps because of the lack of stated commitment.[5] Even though they tend to sit at the tables every morning during the same span of time, they have not "signed up," paid dues, or committed themselves to the activity through any formal means. They may admit that shooting the breeze includes occasional shots about politics, but few if any of them consider these discussions deliberate attempts to address political issues.

The Shape of a Typical Political Conversation

A typical conversation about a political event would go as follows: Eight people are sitting around a table. One person mentions the latest episode in the Clinton impeachment hearings. Three people are within earshot. One man makes a wisecrack about the trouble Clinton is in, another tells a slightly lewd joke about the ordeal, and the others laugh a little and nod their heads. Usually, the conversation will go on like this for a few moments. On a day in which the people involved are tired or worn out by the weather, it will die after this one bad joke. Sometimes, when the topic hits close to home, at least three people urgently want to talk about their own experiences or opinions, and the topic is discussed for half an hour.

Whether political conversations last two minutes or thirty, the transitioning between them and other subjects of life is virtually seamless. One morning, someone sat down with a full cup of coffee and started looking for the cream pitcher. The standard one was not on the table . . .

> Mike: Yeah, Luke said someone might have stolen it for its antique value.
> Alice: Oh, I suppose . . .
> Orville: Like these ashtrays [pointing to the ashtrays that are left on the tables until the afternoon crowd starts arriving, laughing a little because the ashtrays are aged and inexpensive].

> Harold: Oh yes [sarcastically]. Very valuable.
>
> Orville: Someone said they had disappeared.
>
> Mike: Oh, I think they put out those new ones for special occasions . . .
>
> Harold: Special occasions like when Lynn Rivers [the local Democratic member of Congress] or Ingrid Sheldon [the Republican mayor of Ann Arbor] comes down here!
>
> Todd: Could probably have them replaced at the Kiwanis [weekly rummage sale] for a dime.
>
> Harold: Heh, for a dime? They'd probably give them to you!
>
> Mike: I heard on the radio this morning Rivers hadn't decided how she's going to vote on whether to hold impeachment hearings or not. Said she won't decide until the vote.
>
> Harold: Right. Hasn't had all the information yet [sarcastically], has to hear all sides—
>
> Mike: She's not sure which way she's going to vote.

Impeachment votes, the local congresswomen, and cream pitchers: this is the stuff of their conversations. They mix in a variety of things that are relevant to their lives, which sometimes includes politics. Although the bulk of their talk is casual "catching up" and "checking in" with friends and acquaintances, part of it is done through talking about politics. Political topics arise when they fit in with the flow of the conversation and run little risk of offending someone within earshot.

Expecting Collective Identity Processes within Informal Political Talk

We now have evidence that informal political talk is not necessarily conducted for the sake of solving public issues. If that's the case, what does such talk do that matters for politics? One potential outcome is the gathering of facts.

Are the Old Timers seeking political information? Perhaps. Although they do not cite political information as a motivation for being part of the group, they almost certainly do gather news and information about others' viewpoints during the course of informal talk. Recent focus group work on attitudes toward citizenship in the United States and Great Britain shows that people do profess to talk about politics in order to gain more information, to persuade others, or to take a stand (Conover, Searing, and Crewe 2002). However, the Conover, Searing, and Crewe work on citizenship and political talk shows that people also report that they talk politics out of a desire to listen to others to gain understanding, to enhance self-development, to gain recognition, and to enjoy a good life. Conover et al. (2002) conclude from these results that public discussion is the act of *conveying social information:*

> As the focus groups make clear, citizens understand political discussion as an act of "self-expression." There are two senses in which this is true. Most obviously, when we discuss issue concerns, we are required to make known our preferences on those issues. But there is a deeper and more dangerous sense in which political discussion involves self-expression. Some of our preferences are "constitutive" preferences in that they are central to the meaning of a particular identity. Therefore, stating your issue positions can expose more than just your preferences; it sometimes reveals a basic identity, who you are at your core. (56)

The central political implication of informal political talk is not simply the exchange of information about policy stances. Instead, the fundamental, politically relevant act is the communication of information about the kind of people individuals perceive themselves to be and the collective envisioning of group and community boundaries. Casual exchanges allow people to collectively give meaning to their social identities and gain practice in using their identity-based perspectives to interpret public concerns.

This act of giving meaning to concepts such as "one of us," "Ann Arborite," or "American" is a process through which people are jointly creating contexts for further communication that are something other than a mechanical aggregation of individually held political preferences. Support for the idea that groups do create such contexts was provided more than fifty years ago. In an extensive literature review, Katz and Lazarsfeld (1955) discussed much supporting research. This included an experiment on group norms in children's play groups that showed children, in just three to six play sessions, *collectively establishing norms* that were not easily overcome, even by children with leadership abilities (Merei 1952). Another experiment with children that they cited showed eleven year olds acting in accord with adult-induced democratic, authoritarian, or laissez-faire group climates, even when the adult was suddenly removed (Lippitt and White 1952).

Other evidence came from an investigation of a housing community for married veterans who were returning to college that documented the evolution of their friendship groups and subsequent changes in attitudes toward community policies (Festinger, Schachter, and Back 1950). Katz and Lazarsfeld noted that Newcomb (1951) had referred to these norms of behavior as "shared frames of reference" and explained that these frames were a product of individuals interacting together to "*create* a shared way of looking at things or of doing them" (57, their emphasis). They also noted that the Lewinian (e.g., Lewin and Grabbe 1945) concept of "social realities"—the idea that an individual's perception of reality is a function of what is socially accepted as reality—was yet another variation on the claim that people collectively create the contexts in which they interact (Katz and Lazarsfeld 1955, 54).

In subsequent years, research on group dynamics has provided experimental evidence that groups collectively create contexts of behavior even when that context is not induced by a facilitator. When a group of experiment subjects is instructed to argue to consensus, frequently the collective discussion is an exaggeration or "extrematization" of the direction of the average opinion that existed prior to discussion, a phenomenon referred to as "group polarization" (Stoner 1968; Moscovici and Zavalloni 1969). A leading explanation is that members of the group form perceptions of the group identity through discussion, and these perceptions affect outcome decisions.[6] Moreover, it seems to be interaction that fuels the development of a group identity. Polarization is more likely to occur when subjects are asked to debate without procedural rules (Forgas 1977) or allowed to discuss opinions supporting their preferences (Myers and Bishop 1971; Moscovici, Doise, and Dulong 1972; Myers and Lamm 1976).

These various studies demonstrate that when human beings interact with one another, they collectively create the environment, producing *through the interaction* attachments that guide further behavior. Notice how discussion alters the outcome of what might otherwise be called an exchange of information. It is widely acknowledged that J. S. Mill supported deliberation on the grounds that it generates the consideration of more information and thus better decisions. This is reminiscent of Condorcet's jury theorem (Page and Shapiro 1992, 26–27; Kinder and Herzog 1993, 369–72). The theorem, simply put, holds that the larger the number of individual opinions that are incorporated in a decision, the closer to the "truth" that decision will be. As more minds contribute to the decision, the probability that the "correct" decision is made increases, as long as each individual has more than a one-in-two chance of choosing correctly. However, Condorcet's thoughts on decision making directly question the utility of discussion as a route to the truth. One assumption of his theorem is that the individuals taking part in the decision *do not discuss* information. In fact, in proposing a new constitutional scheme to the French government in the late eighteenth century, Condorcet was *vehemently opposed* to deliberative bodies (Baker 1975). "Anyone who has witnessed the deliberations of a body of any size has necessarily observed the fact that the opinion adopted is very often not the real opinion of the greatest number, and that the form of deliberation is consequently one of the principal causes of error, feebleness and incoherence of majority decisions" (Condorcet, as quoted in Baker 1975, 259). Condorcet worried about deliberation because "the form of deliberation" involved something other than a mere exchange of information.

Condorcet recognized what social psychological research validated approximately one and a half centuries later: the product of human interaction is a function of something more than just individually held opinions. Close attention to the discussions among the Old Timers suggests that this additional factor is social attachments.

The behavior of the people within the corner store displays the centrality of social identity in casual conversation. The Old Timers' attachment to a specific portion of the local community is central to how they communicate with one another. Although they place themselves in broad terms (that is, as "middle" and "common"), their conception of this middle ground is voiced in opposition to other social groups in Ann Arbor. This is easily observed in their descriptions of themselves. "We're all middle class folks in here with moderate values. Everybody here except Charlie—he was born in New Jersey—and Jack down there [at the other end of the table] were born and raised in Ann Arbor," an Old Timer once confided. Dave once explained, "These are hard-working guys, believe in strict discipline with their kids. None of this liberal stuff you see up at city council." And none of "this liberal stuff" from the university, either, he continued: "What you get in there is the common touch. None of that philosophy and theorizing [points toward the university], and they aren't destitute poor people who do a lot of bitching. Just common people, middle people."

Notice the nature of these attachments in light of the motivations behind their talk. They are neither interacting primarily as individuals, devoid of social attachments, nor exchanging information to produce the best possible decision. At the same time, this is not discussion on behalf of the greater common good. Their conception of community is a specific one—people like themselves. These social attachments are facilitated by the process of selection into the group. Their sense of community does not encompass all people who reside in the geographic community of Ann Arbor, nor does it encompass everyone who meets regularly in the corner store. A wide array of people pass through the place on any given morning. Businesspeople, professors, city workers, and university students all stop in to buy coffee and donuts. But although the room is small (covering approximately one thousand square feet), there is little mingling across borders of uncertainty. Seldom does a

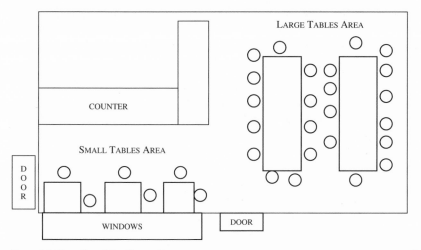

Figure 3.1 Floor Plan of the Corner Store.

conversation take place between people who do not know each other or did not have a mutual friend prior to stepping into the store.

It does not take long to observe that the place is segregated by race and, to a lesser extent, by class and gender. The Old Timers, who are of European descent (except for one Mexican American) sit at the two large tables on one side of the room (see figure 3.1). Along the windows on the other side of the room are three small tables, at which African Americans, blue-collar workers, women, and younger patrons sit. The small-table and the large-table patrons learn about each other by observation more than conversation. On those rare occasions when a non-Old Timer ventures to the large tables without knowing the occupants, he or she sits in silence, obeying the unwritten code of minding one's own place. Typically, such pioneers will bring a paper or a donut with them, in order to buffer the isolation with a little activity.

The most striking display of the way the Old Timers clarify and re-produce the boundaries of their group is a kind of coffee etiquette. The Old Timers serve coffee to each other, but do not fill the cups of the people across the room. It works like this: One Old Timer will get up and help himself to the coffee behind the counter, although everyone else in the store waits in line at the counter to be served. He will pick up the urns, come back to the large tables and walk around, serving "the orange stuff" ("decaf" from the orange-handled pot) or "regular" and then return the pots to the hot plates. But whoever it is, he will not walk the extra ten steps to offer refills to the people sitting at the small tables. He will not do this even though many of the people who sit at the small tables come to the place each day, too. The people at the small tables happen to be African American, female, or retired maintenance workers. Is this racism? sexism? classism? Not necessarily. But in these actions, the Old Timers are reinforcing and clarifying their identity with respect to race and gender and class.

This pattern of behavior speaks volumes about the prevalence of in-group and out-group categories in the corner store. Not only is the Old Timers' talk motivated by social concerns, but socially rooted categories are key inputs to their interactions, as the following chapters will show. By talking with one another, they signal perceptions of who they are and establish definitions of where they fit in the world. In turn, these identity-based perspectives structure their interactions with one another and the content of their discussions.

A Conceptual Model of the Processes

The following chapters demonstrate how people clarify identity-based perspectives and how these perspectives structure talk about politics. In this section I present a conceptual model of these processes. This model was not developed prior to data gathering; it is the result of the combined inductive and deductive methods used in this study. I provide this model near the start of the book rather than at the conclusion to ease the explication of the remaining chapters. As the book progresses, I explain the theoretical basis for the goals for each step of the analyses, the evidence that led toward the conclusions, attempts to observe contrary evidence, and the rationale behind the conclusions that make up this model.

For analytic purposes, the model separates the processes under investigation into two main parts. The first pertains to whether and how a group develops a collective perspective. To conceptualize this, I stipulate the conditions that lead to the clarification of social identity on the individual level, and then, based on these conditions, specify when a group is likely to clarify a collective identity. Thus, the dependent variable of this part of the model is the group perspective created by the interaction among the members. In the second portion, I theorize how a group of people interprets political issues. The dependent variables of this stage are the resources and processes that group participants use to communicate about political issues.

The Development of Social Identity in a Group Context

The development of social identities on the individual level through informal interaction can be conceived of as an updating process driven by prior identities. That is, the development of an individual's social identity during any given visit with a group is a function of the individual's identity prior to the conversations and the information he receives during the conversations.[7] The outcome of the process of clarifying his social identity is more complex than just a weighted average of prior identity and new information, however. His prior identity does combine with the "data" or information gathered through conversations to result in a posterior identity, but his prior identity also influences selection into the group as well as how he perceives the information.

In greater detail, a person has a preexisting social identity before engaging in conversation with a given group of people. Preexisting perspectives influence selection into a group. In voluntary groups, in which people have the opportunity to exit, they are likely to quit, or vote with their feet, if their goals are not met (Hirschman 1970; Warren 2001). If the motivation to join the group is solidary,[8] or a desire for fellowship, then the fit between the kind of person the individual believes himself to be and the kind of people he believes are participating in the group is the main criterion for joining and remaining a member. When the incentive to join a group is purposive (e.g., promoting an ideology or political candidate) or material (e.g., fostering a hobby, improving one's investment strategies, reducing neighborhood crime) then selection will depend on his perception that joining the group is an advantageous way to reach that goal. If given the choice between two groups that appear to convey equal purposive or material rewards, a person will choose the one with the highest perceived fit to his own identity. Thus, all else being equal, people are likely to belong to groups in which they perceive that the other members are people like themselves.

Once a person becomes a member, the effect of the information— broadly defined as conversations, physical behavior, and physical media such as news stories, photographs, or E-mail jokes printed out for sharing—on his or her prior perspective is a function of five key variables. First, the more time a person spends with a given group, the more influence the interaction will have on his identity. Second, the certainty of an individual's prior social identity influences the effect of a given visit with the group. The more certain a person is about his preexisting identity, the less impact the visit will have on his sense of self.[9]

Third, the greater the resonance between one's prior identity and the information conveyed in the group context, the more likely it will be used to update or clarify one's sense of self. In other words, prior identities act as reference points for judging whether or not new information should be discounted. If the ideas a person hears spoken and the signals he perceives through others' physical behavior are largely discrepant from his prior worldviews, they are discounted, or "taken with a large grain of salt." If the comments fall within his "range of acceptability" (Sears and Whitney 1973) he will use them to update his preexisting identity.[10] Thus, communication within informal conversations will have the most effect on clarifying individuals' social identity when the comments resonate with the way they already understand the world.

Fourth, the strength of the signal conveyed by the group about what "one of us" should be like intervenes in the influence of the group interaction on individuals' perspectives. This strength can be conceptualized as the precision, or standard deviation around the central tendency, of the perspective conveyed in the group. Thus, if there is almost unanimous agreement about how "one of us" ought to behave, this will have a more persuasive effect than if the group members disagree about proper behavior.

Fifth, perceptions of the credibility of the other participants about what it means to be a person like oneself intervene in the identity clarification process. Credibility matters because persuasion of preferences is more likely to occur when a source exudes expertise and trustworthiness (Hovland, Janis, and Kelley 1953).[11] This holds with respect to interpretation of a political topic or problem (Druckman 2001a, 2001b). I assume that similar effects hold with respect to persuasion of *perspectives*. Importantly, prior social identities influence these perceptions of credibility: they affect judgments about whether the other participants are people like oneself and thus whether they are knowledgeable sources of information for how "one of us" ought to view the world.

There are several exceptions to this claim about credibility. Speakers that individuals perceive to be different from themselves may also help clarify their identity. If a person appears to be a credible source on an opposing point of view, what he or she says can help confirm or reinforce one's prior perspective. Take, for example, a woman who identifies as a feminist. If she perceives that the other participants are not feminists, and notices that they convey point of view X, this likely reinforces her support for point of view Y.

Also, unexpected perspectives might enhance perceptions of credibility. Sears and Whitney note that sources are especially convincing when they advocate a stance that apparently runs contrary to their interests (1973, 261). If the receiver believes the participants in the conversation are people "like" her (share her perspective), and they unexpectedly convey an opposite worldview, this may be persuasive because it causes her to sit up and take notice.[12]

In addition to the five factors just described, persuasion of perspectives is also a function of how individuals interpret incoming messages. Here again, prior perspectives are important. Prior identities influence the clarification of identity by structuring how people *perceive* the information encountered through interaction. The same information can be interpreted differently by different people. In short, the data are not "given" but are, instead, perceived through the lens of a person's preexisting identity. Prior identities operate as perspectives, or lenses, or "habits of the eye" that influence what information people retain from a given visit.

Given this conceptual model of the individual-level process, we can specify the types of contexts in which these processes will result in the clarification of a shared group perspective. First, the greater the number of overlapping acquaintances and experiences, the more likely it is that people will identify with one another. Second, the more frequently a group meets, the more opportunity they have to recognize similarities. Moreover, groups that are equipped with a mechanism that helps participants recognize similarities are especially likely to clarify a common identity. Therefore, a third factor is the purpose of a group. Groups that exist entirely for the purpose of fellowship are more likely to be composed of people who know each other or perceive likenesses prior to joining. In addition, some groups may be organized for the purpose of focusing on collective identity. Another mechanism is the salience of out-groups. The more salient out-groups are, the more likely it is that group members will recognize a shared in-group identity. Such salience could be a function of the physical presence of out-groups, as well as reminders of out-groups conveyed through the mass media (newspapers on the table, the broadcast of radio or television programs), pictures, bumper stickers, or other decorations in a physical space.

Collective Interpretations of Politics

The preceding model explains how social interaction leads to the clarification of a collective identity, a key component of a group's perspective. The following explanation pertains to how a group of people makes sense of political issues, given the perspectives communicated in the group. The act of understanding can be conceptualized as a process that occurs prior to the act of evaluation or of making choices among policies or candidates (Lau, Smith, and Fiske 1991; Kinder 1998b). In Kinder's terms, when forming opinions, "citizens undertake three generic tasks: they make sense of the carnival of personalities, issues, and events that, moment to moment, comprise the political realm; they decide what is important in politics and what is not; and they evaluate political alternatives—candidates, policy proposals, and more—that are placed before them" (1998b, 168). He notes that although in practice these processes of understanding, judging importance, and evaluation overlap, it is useful to separate them for analytic purposes.

The dependent variables for this portion of the model are the *nature of* resources that the members use to make interpretations and the *process by* which these resources are used to interpret public affairs.

First, it is useful to anticipate *when* we should expect groups to talk about politics. Political talk in American culture tends to be regarded with caution, held separate from casual talk about other topics (Eliasoph 1998). Whether or not individuals will be willing to talk about politics likely depends on the perception that their contributions will be met with friendly rather than hostile responses (MacKuen 1990) and whether they think talking politics is appropriate to the situation (Eliasoph 1998). As MacKuen argues, "Politics probably incorporates more of a sense of morality than many other topics of conversation (say, weather, film, or sport), and thus one would expect that individual choice to engage in *political* discussion should be particularly sensitive to the nature of the social environment" (1990, 94–95). When the purpose of a group is not to reach a decision or a compromise, people tend to avoid potentially controversial topics altogether (Eliasoph 1998; MacKuen 1990). Conflict is also minimized through processes of self-selection. Just as birds of a feather tend to flock together, people tend to talk about politics with perceived like-minded others (Huckfeldt and Sprague 1987, 1995; Beck 1991; Berelson, Lazarsfeld, and McPhee 1954; Lazarsfeld, Berelson, and Gaudet 1944; Marsden 1987).

When a group does talk about politics, what resources do they use?[13] By resources, I mean categories. When a group of people does not commonly express a collective identity, the resources will be a function of the individuals' social identities and their assessments of the kinds of comments that are acceptable in the group. Because shared experience fosters both collective identity development and political talk, political conversations in groups whose members lack shared experiences are relatively rare. Given the smaller amount of political talk among the guild members, who do not have a strong collective identity, I focus on the processes that occur in a group context characterized by a strong collective identity, the Old Timers.

When a group commonly expresses a collective identity, the categories used will be consistent with this perspective.[14] For analytical purposes, I am conceptualizing understanding as occurring prior to evaluation. Evaluation of political issues can be successfully modeled as a function of three main types of considerations: principles, interests, and attitudes toward social groups (Kinder and Sanders 1996, 36–38). Interpretation can be conceptualized as a function of three types of categories, which resemble this typology: values or principles, interests, and social groups.

First, regarding political principles or values, although individuals in a laboratory rely on the stimulus materials for clues about which beliefs are relevant, people chatting over coffee have other resources at their disposal. A group that sees itself as true Ann Arborites who are the last bastion of folks who have "earned their keep" and "make an honest living" is more likely to refer to the political principle of economic individualism than to a belief in a social safety net. In this way, their collective identity suggests which principles are appropriate for people like themselves.

Second, how a group defines its interests is also a function of the members' expression of who they are.[15] For example, one might argue that the Old Timers, given their perception of the relative dearth of patriotism among younger generations in comparison to themselves, have an interest in supporting the education of today's youth. But this potential interest runs contrary to an even more potent part of their identity, their perspective that they are people who have paid their dues and are thus opposed to any tax increase. Therefore, in a discussion about a school tax increase, they are more likely to conceptualize the issue as being about the justice of taxation rather than the improvement of civic life through education.

Finally, perspectives influence which group categories the participants will use to discuss issues. The social identities characterizing these perspectives delineate how they carve up the world into in-groups and out-groups and therefore structure which social group categories they will perceive to be meaningful in making sense of new information.

In most group contexts (characterized by either strong or weak collective identities), the mass media will be the source of at least some suggestions about which categories are useful for understanding a given issue. Whether or not a group will interpret an issue from the perspective presented by the news coverage depends on the five factors of the basic persuasion process outlined in the first portion of this model: the credibility of the media source, the match between the message and the group's perspective, the strength of the group's prior perspective, the strength of the perspective conveyed by the media, and the frequency of exposure to this perspective. First, if a media source is not perceived as credible, the perspectives of the message will be rejected. Second, if a perspective conveyed by the mass media clashes with the group members' perspective, it is also likely to be rejected. However, if the perspective resonates with the group members' sense of themselves, it will either be adopted in its entirety or used as a starting point for interpreting the information. Third, if the group's perspective is such that the members are ambivalent (have relatively weak priors) about how to interpret the issue, they will rely solely on the perspective conveyed by the story. However, if they have a relatively strong prior perspective about the connection between this issue and their sense of self, they will be more likely to "transform" (Just et al. 1996) the media interpretation with more personally relevant categories. Fourth, the more certain or clear the perspective conveyed by the mass media, the greater the likelihood that the group members will use it in their communication. Fifth, a group is more likely to adopt a given interpretation mediated by the mass media the more frequently it is exposed to it.

An additional element of the effect of the group's identity on interpretation is that in a group context characterized by a strong in-group identity, it is likely that there will be efforts to police the boundaries of this identity. When a group's prior perspective is strong, we should expect that comments that contradict this perspective will be silenced.

In sum, this model stipulates when members of a group are likely to clarify collective social identities and how that process occurs. Second, it theorizes the process of collective interpretation of political issues as a function of the group's perspective. When a group has developed a collective identity, it influences interpretation by constraining the categories used to communicate about it.

* * *

In this chapter I have argued that in order to understand the public's part of public discussion, we need a model that recognizes the nature of the social attachments the participants use in light of the motivation behind their talk. The political talk that takes place among the Old Timers and the women's craft guild occurs as a by-product of social interaction. The people observed in this study do not gather to exchange political information or to deliberate on behalf of the common good. However, their interaction is relevant to their lives as citizens. As with other topics, when people talk about political issues they are relating to each other with the aid of social identities. Thus, they are neither interacting entirely as individuals nor as members of the community as a whole. Instead, through their interaction, they are collectively defining who constitutes "one of us."

CHAPTER 4

Clarifying Social Identity through

Group Interaction

Within the first month of my mornings at the corner store, I noticed that the people spending time in the place observed invisible social boundaries. If the volume had somehow been turned off in the room, these divisions still would have been apparent. Their coffee etiquette, in which they served coffee to themselves but not to the other regulars across the room, is one example. There were the Old Timers, the retired men who sat at the large tables, and then there were the other folks (African Americans, younger people, a few women) who sat at the small tables along the window.

These behaviors matter because they are part of the processes that link social locations with the perspectives people use to interpret their world. Rather than being static traits, social identities are psychological connections achieved through the active processes of linking oneself to other people, partly through interpersonal interaction. In a group context, the act of relating to one another as group members structures the content of conversations.

When we conceptualize identity on the level of group interaction, we bridge the individual-level psychological nature of identities and the social processes that create them. Brewer (2001) points out that the concept of social identity has been used in a range of disciplines in a variety of formulations "whenever there is a need for a conceptual bridge between individual and group levels of analysis" (114). Although many of these usages are based in psychology, it is sociological approaches that go beyond conceptualizing social identity as static tools of information processing to regard them as understandings that are continually given meaning through action (Billig 1995; Melucci 1995; Calhoun 1991). As Alberto Melucci states, "Collective identity is an interactive and shared definition produced by several individuals (or groups at a more complex level) and concerned with the orientations of action and the field of opportunities and constraints in which the action takes place. ... [It is] a definition that must be conceived as a process because it is constructed and negotiated through a repeated activation of the relationships that link individuals (or groups)" (1995, 44). As people act together in social movements, or in individual political actions such as in a protest or strike (Beckwith 1998), they develop collective identities. These understandings of who they are and who they are against guide future collective action (Gamson 1992).

It does not take participation in a social movement, or even extended political participation, to develop social identities with political relevance. Just as activists within social movements collectively construct their identity, people doing less dramatic political behaviors, such as informal talk, can also collectively define what it means to be people like themselves in the world. This chapter uses observation and national sample survey data to examine and theorize the processes by which groups of people create contexts of understanding and the conditions under which the clarification of collective identity is more or less likely. The following chapter analyzes specifically how these perspectives influence the categories and considerations brought to bear in the act of collective interpretations of public affairs.

Building Collective Identity on the Basis of Shared Acquaintances and Experience

For a moment, put yourself in the place of an Old Timer. It is a frigid January morning. The vinyl of your car seat crackles as you get in and is still crackling as you climb out after you park in a lot near the corner store. The sidewalks are crusted with white from salt and ice. The windows of the place are steamy from the cold. You grumble under your breath, "Why do I wake up at the crack of dawn to come down here?" Then you open the door and the answer floats out—coffee, cigarette smoke, and, more importantly, the laughter and hellos.

The shouts of things like "Hey, where've you been?" that embrace you as you enter the corner store announce a group belonging that has some history. If you were an Old Timer, chances are you would have a story to tell about most other members of the group. Even to outsiders, there is an obvious sense of group membership among the Old Timers. Over repeated visits with them, it becomes clear that this sense of group membership has developed over time on the basis of shared acquaintances and experiences and many visits that have collectively reinforced and clarified this identity.

Most of the people who sit as Old Timers at the large tables joined the group on the basis of prior acquaintance. One man started coming to the store after he retired "because I know all the guys down here. I decided I would come three or four times a week and visit, have a doughnut on Tuesdays and Thursdays." Most of the Old Timers have long, shared histories together, as relatives and as lifetime residents of Ann Arbor. In addition, almost all of them lived through World War II, and many of them fought in that war. These common experiences have likely had a lasting impact on at least a small set of their views (Jennings 1987) and identities (Stewart and Healy 1989).

This large reserve of overlapping acquaintances and experiences has enabled the development of a small-group identity. They think of themselves as a group, evidenced by the fact that they refer to themselves by the initials of the place ("the X.X. group") or as "Old Timers." In addition, they made membership cards for themselves about fifteen years ago. The cards proclaim: "Bulls of the Corner Store."[1] Below this is a line with "member" written beneath it. Below this are the words "Meeting Daily" and "Exclusive Membership," and in the bottom right corner are the letters "B.S." This stands for "you know, our product," as one of the members blithely informed me.

People outside the group also refer to them as an entity. Around Ann Arbor, when the place is mentioned, it is not uncommon for someone to say, "Oh sure, I know that place. Ever see those guys who hang out in there?"[2]

Part of the work of maintaining their group boundaries is done through their coffee etiquette. Sometimes the race and class relations in the place are put into words. One morning, one Old Timer noted that I had recently spent more time at the large tables than on the other side of the room.

> Pete: We're glad you're sitting over here on this side of the room. You
>   learn a lot more over here than over there in the Dunbar Center.
> Kathy: Dunbar Center?
> Pete: Yeah, you know, the *colored* section.
> Kathy: Why the Dunbar Center?
> Pete: Oh, because that was the name for the old black community
>   center over on North Main [Street].

And on a different morning, pointing to the small tables,

> Charlie: That's the Dunbar Center, you know.
> Kathy: So I've heard.
> Dave: What's that?

Charlie: The Dunbar Center—used to be that the black part of town was
the Dunbar section.

Dave: Oh. Hmmm hmm. [Explaining to me]: There's a black
community center called the Dunbar Center, over on North Main.

Kathy: It's still there?

Dave: Hmmm mm. It was the social center.

Charlie: Ann Street . . .

Dave: Ann Street, between Division and Main, was the social center.
Used to be a lot of Greeks, too.

Charlie: Right. I remember the first day I was in [this city]: October 5,
1945. There was a guy riding his motorcycle around the block
[motions with his hand] on the sidewalk, with a cop chasing him,
trying to catch him . . .

Kathy: No kidding!

Dave: Yep, that was the social center.

Charlie: [Motions to the small tables]: We call that the 'DuMMMbar
Center': D-U-M-B.

Kathy: Why's that, Charlie?

Charlie: All the dumb folks, the outcasts, sit over there.

At the same time that the Old Timers are constituting themselves as
the in-group, the "Outcasts" are giving meaning to their own place in the
relationships there. One man, asked by an Old Timer why he sat at the small
tables, answered simply, "Aw, come on. I can't sit with you heavy hitters."
A small-table regular (a white, retired maintenance worker) differentiates
himself from the Old Timers by making frequent comments about their
wealth: "Shhhhucks! They have more money than they know what to do
with. They got so much money over there. . . . Rich—could light fires with it."

Although the small-table regulars see the large-table regulars as a group,
they rarely have discussions in which they see *themselves* as a distinct social
group. Several factors likely explain this difference. First, the ratio of regulars
at the small tables to the full range of people who sit there is relatively small
compared to that at the large tables. Only four people appeared almost every
day. In addition to these folks, a variety of other people would regularly drop
in, including two brothers, a few women, and several middle-aged white men.
Several other people were daily regulars, but would sit there much earlier in
the day or later in the morning. Thus the people who sat at the small tables
at the same time as the Old Timers constitute a small friendship group more
than a collectivity that they might perceive as a group or association. Second,
few of the patrons who sit at the small tables are lifetime residents of the

area, and the retired men who spend time together on that side of the room appear to have met while "passing time" there. Although among both the Old Timers and the small-table regulars there is an obvious sense of positive affect or camaraderie, the small-table regulars have a smaller base of shared experience from which they can talk about collective perspectives or build a collective identity.

When the topic of group membership arises, it is typically about the "groupness" of the Old Timers. For example, early on in my observations, one of the brothers who occasionally sat at the small tables told me a story about one of the large-table regular's fighting with one of the counter staff. "He actually threw his coffee at him and said, 'You can't treat me like that. I'm a regular!'" Like the small-table regular above who commented on the Old Timers' wealth, any sense of group membership among the people who sit along the window pales in comparison to that displayed by the people at the large tables.

Contrasting Identities among Members of the Guild: The Necessity of Mechanisms of Connection

After spending a little more than one month with the Old Timers, I had concluded that much of the basis for their relations to one another could be attributed to their shared experience as people who had worked in the Ann Arbor area, played sports together, and served in the military. To test this conclusion, I began observing the craft guild, a group similar to the Old Timers in age, class, residence, and race but who, as a function of their gender, did not share these other experiences. The group had approximately thirty members, five or six of whom met once a week. They gathered in a church basement to make crafts to raise money for the church and have lunch together. Observing this group revealed that overlapping experiences and acquaintances can foster collective identity, but in order for this to work, some kind of mechanisms for recognizing these common traits must be in place.

Psychological research shows that communication along the lines of "we" rather than "I" is more likely when the people talking perceive that the differences across groups in the environment are greater than the differences within their own group (Turner et al. 1994). This suggests that having a large base of shared experiences and acquaintances is conducive to talk about collective identity, but it is not sufficient—people need to recognize their intragroup similarities.

What makes these similarities salient? One prominent mechanism in the psychological literature is the presence of out-groups. Tajfel and Turner

(1979) argue that interaction in a group of people is likely to focus on inter-group comparison rather than individual differences when three conditions are met: (1) the participants have internalized their group identity, (2) the situation allows for comparison with other social groups, and (3) members of other social groups are readily available as a relevant base of compari-son (Tajfel and Turner 1979, 41; 1986). With respect to a specific context, Brewer and Miller (1984) conclude that when a large group contains several distinct parts, the differences across them will be salient. But if the group is relatively small, then these differences will be less apparent. Also, when there is a clear minority group, the category that designates this minority status will be salient.[3] Brewer and Brown (1998) note that several other con-ditions affect the salience of social categories: the physical proximity of group members in a setting (p. 556, citing Gaertner et al. 1989), and recent events (p. 557, citing Higgins, Rholes, and Jones 1977). Research on *political* identi-ties, specifically, has supported the claim that contextual information, such as the relative density of members of one's social group within the surround-ing census tract (Lau 1989),[4] and textual and visual information provided in a news article (Huddy 1998) can influence whether or not a person identi-fies with a certain social category. Taken together, these results suggest that a collective identity is more likely to be salient when members of an out-group are present physically or are represented symbolically through such things as newspapers or photographs.

Another key mechanism in fostering the clarification of shared identity is the process of selection to the group. The store of personal experiences is constrained by *perceptions* of shared experiences that people use to self-select into settings and groups. There is widespread evidence of social homophily, or the act of people interacting and associating with others they perceive to be like themselves. For example, perceptions about shared racial background affect individuals' residential selection (Farley, Steeh, Krysan, Jackson, and Reeves 1994). Ideas of how women should behave cumulate to influence the kinds of groups women join (McPherson and Smith-Lovin 1986) and the spaces, such as coffee shops in Greek culture, that they enter (e.g., Cowan 1991).

Selection into voluntary groups is likewise performed on the basis of perceived likeness. If the group is a nonvoluntary collective, ability to self-select is limited. This is the case in the workplace (Mutz and Mondak 1998; Sigelman, Bledsoe, Welch, and Combs 1996). But among voluntary groups, people control whether they enter and whether they exit. If the group gathers primarily for social interaction (as is the case with the groups at the corner store), not for an instrumental purpose, people likely enter on the basis of perceived likeness. If a group forms around a stated function, that is, has an instrumental purpose (as is the case with the guild), people enter on the basis of that hobby, political concern, or professional need, not necessarily on the basis of overlapping acquaintances and experiences.

Therefore, even though the members of the guild do have a base of shared experiences, it is not sufficient to foster a collective identity among them. The vast majority of the members are of the same Protestant faith, members of the particular church in which they meet, have lifestyles that give each of them time to meet in the middle of the day, and like to work on sewing and related crafts. Thus the group is homogenous with respect to religious beliefs, socioeconomic background, age/generation, race, gender, and hobbies. Yet the group is diverse in many respects, especially with respect to gender roles. Two of the women never married or had children, and some of the women worked full time for much of their lives, while others never worked for pay. Among those who did enter the workforce, there is a diversity of occupational backgrounds. There is a former scientist, a retired public school teacher, and several former administrative assistants. In addition, they do not have uniform ties to Ann Arbor. Many of them moved to the area in retirement, after living elsewhere for much of their lives.

On top of relatively few shared experiences, their group and group setting lack mechanisms that might emphasize their similarities more than their differences. First, the group meets only once a week. Although individual members run into each other occasionally at Sunday services, the familiarity this frequency grants is much less than that of the Old Timers, who meet daily. Second, the setting, the church basement, does not provide sources of contrast to out-groups. No other groups or people are there when they gather. Thus, rather than notice how they as a group are distinct from non-group members, they focus on differences among themselves. Unlike the Old Timers, they cannot develop and define their identity by placing themselves (verbally and physically) in contrast to other people in the place.

Why not gender? Why did the women in the guild not talk with one another through the perspective of their experiences as women? Simply put, shared demographics do not equal shared perspectives. Homogeneity with respect to sex—or any other social category—is not sufficient to foster shared identity. As stated above, their experiences as women are *not* identical. They have not all been married, nor have they all raised children. Within a group of people perceived to share a demographic trait (e.g., "women") there are a myriad of individual experiences that have the potential to contribute to a common identity. Without a stimulating mechanism, however, sharing this demographic trait may form the basis for differentiation instead.

Psychological research suggests why gender in particular might not serve as a source of collective identity for a small group. Brewer and Miller explain that across a society as a whole, salient social categories are likely to be those with "convergent boundaries" or differentiation from other groups along a variety of dimensions such as the economic, political, and physical (1984, citing Brewer and Campbell 1976). Arguably, racial categories fit this bill better than gender categories. The identities that people seem to rely on in a given situation are those that fill two opposing needs—the need for affiliation and the need to differentiate oneself from others.[5] Focusing on one's identity as a woman may not provide the optimal balance for many people between belonging to an in-group and separating oneself from out-groups. Since many women live in intimate contact with members of the out-group (men), seeing the world through the lens of a strong attachment to women may not comfortably satisfy the need for affiliation.

Research on consciousness-raising groups underscores that identity with women does not automatically exist—it takes work. What it means to be a woman, and how this relates to politics, is not universal among women (Burns, Schlozman, and Verba 2001). Small group discussions in the women's movement of the latter half of the twentieth century enabled women to recognize the connection between their private lives and political solutions (Freeman 1975, 118). Jo Freeman argues that a key factor in the ability of discussion groups to raise gender consciousness (identity with women that includes political content)[6] was the fact that the groups included only women. However, it was this homogeneity *combined* with selection processes and the explicit goal of talking about shared interests that suggested a common language (124). These combined factors created contexts in which the participants were likely to recognize the similarities across the experiences of others in the group.

Group purpose has also been shown to affect identity processes among people of similar sexual orientations. Lichterman (1999) found that in a lesbian/gay/bisexual/transgendered rights group, in which the relevant out-group was not well defined, the members focused on their differences. They "reflected critically" on their identities as queer people. However, when talking within a different group in which the purpose was to build coalitions across various leftist groups, the same people focused on collective identities. In this context, the relevant out-group *was* well defined: the right or Christian right. (Lichterman gave the group the pseudonym "the Network Against the Right's Agenda.") In this context, the people spoke as if their identity as queers was a given and focused instead on their differentiation from out-groups.

Table 4.1 Factors Affecting Development of Group Identity, Compared across Old Timers and Guild

	Old Timers (Strong group identity)	Craft Guild (Weak group identity)
Shared experiences and acquaintances	Many	Few
Frequency of meetings	Daily	Weekly
Purpose of group (affects selection, and also likelihood of identity talk)	Social	Instrumental
Salience of outgroups	Presence of outgroup members, other reminders (wall decorations, newspapers)	No one else present; some postings pertain to church programs, religious decorations

Without the mechanisms of a group purpose intended to recognize similarities, selection processes predisposing the recognition of likenesses with respect to social categories, or characteristics stimulating the salience of out-groups, the guild women were not in a situation conducive to communicating through and thus developing the lens of a group identity. Unlike the Old Timers, they did not clarify their identities with large-scale social groups like "the middle class" by identifying with each other as "middle people." Instead, they contrasted themselves to one another.

Table 4.1 provides a summary of those group characteristics that are likely to increase the extent to which a group develops a collective identity. Briefly, shared experience and acquaintances lay the basis for recognizing similarity, and the frequency of meetings increases the chances that these similarities will be recognized. The purpose of the group influences the selection processes that result in more or fewer shared experiences and acquaintances and also whether or not the talk in the group will focus on shared social locations. Finally, the physical presence of or physical reminders of the existence of out-groups serve as mechanisms that stimulate talk along the lines of "us" and "them."

Although the members of the guild do not identify with one another, their talk and behavior suggested that social identities were not irrelevant to their interaction. But rather than the setting serving as an opportunity to interpret the world through the lens of "how we are alike," it provided a chance to work out "how should I think about various topics given the kind of person that I am?" Thus their interaction may have helped each individual member clarify her own social identity, although to a lesser extent than in group contexts in which group members reinforce these identities in one another.

I was best able to see the guild members clarifying their social identities with respect to gender. Over the course of my nineteen visits with the guild, the members talked about a variety of topics directly related to behavior they deem appropriate to women. The most common topics dealt with sexuality. For example, one day they were talking about spanking, and then the conversation turned to sexual child abuse. I asked Elnor, a former schoolteacher, "Did you see that a lot when you were a teacher—child abuse?"

> Elnor: No, I didn't see it, and I don't think it took place.
> Eloise: Like that one teacher [recently in the news], having an affair with her student . . .
> Elnor: That's on the western side of the state. [Explaining to the rest of the group] There's a teacher who's been with a student, second child on the way. She's in jail now.
> Kathy: You mean she's pregnant with the kid's kid?
> Elnor: Yes!
> Kathy: Oh my goodness. How old is the kid?
> Elnor: Fourteen.
> Ginnie: Something is not right with that woman.
> Elnor: You know there was a 13-year-old boy on the news who looked like an adult, had the actions of an adult . . . maybe that was the case here.
> Eloise: Still is no excuse.
> Doris: Takes two to tango, you know . . . They have the father in there [in court] now?
> Ginnie: Sickening.

This conversation enabled the women to hear one another's ideas about appropriate female sexual behavior. Other conversations did the same work. In one, they talked about their feelings about nudity and rape. We had been talking about recent student riots at Michigan State University and attempts by police to identify perpetrators with the use of pictures posted on the Internet.

> Eloise: Like that Naked Mile business here [referring to an informal run done in the nude by University of Michigan students on the last day of classes. In recent years, people had taken pictures of the runners and posted them on the Internet.]

Ginnie: What a strange thing. Imagine, having that picture on your record the rest of your life. How embarrassing!

Kathy: That is pretty embarrassing.

Ginnie: It's like these girls, crying rape ... they go to a guy's house ...

Doris: ... after having a couple of drinks with him ...

Ginnie: Right, and then they say he raped them. As far as I'm concerned the police ought to throw the book at them, not the guy. They should know better.

Elnor: We never went out at night alone ...

In this conversation, a consensus emerges; they seem to agree that many of the reports of rape on campus are unfounded or unjustified. But this agreement is temporary and does not carry over to subsequent meetings. When discussing the Lewinsky scandal one day, disagreement about women's sexuality reemerged. Doris said, "Oh goodness, well, we've all sown a few wild oats [like Clinton]. ... We all have, haven't we?" When she looked around the table, they all nodded in affirmation, but tentatively, as if they were not exactly sure what she meant. And on another day, they were talking about the case of a five-day-old boy found abandoned shortly after birth.

Ginnie: You wonder where the parents are when kids act up like that.

Doris: Someone should have spanked that girl! [laughs]

Eloise: I think some of these kids don't know the facts of life—at the age of fourteen ...

Hazel: I sure didn't.

Ginnie: I was a late bloomer. I was really green.

Eloise: Mom gave us a real good book.

Doris: I didn't know anything ... I didn't know. My parents didn't talk about it.

Ginnie: Oh, mine either. I thought if you kissed someone you were pregnant. The first time I did that I almost died. I thought I was going to die!

Doris: But you had fun though, didn't you?!

Ginnie: Not the first time [shakes as if shivering]. When my parents talked about it they said, "Oh, that's the family way."

Kathy: The "family way"? That's how they referred to sex?

Ginnie: That's right.

Doris talks openly about sex and claims a right to do so in this conversation and in others. But when she does, several others usually attempted to change the topic and react to her statements in ways that indicate they think the topic is unsuitable for their luncheon meetings. And yet others think not only should sexual behavior be addressed but it ought to be controlled. Instead of identifying with one another's experiences they are giving testimony about their individual perspectives (Sanders 1997). In this particular social context, they are not developing a group identity but are voicing their own individual definitions of womanhood. By sharing their different views of the way women ought to act, they are clarifying their individual identities.

Beyond Closeness Measures: Observing Collective Identity Processes at Work

The context of a group—including the physical space, the characteristics of the membership, and its purpose—matters because it affects the range of resources people have for connecting to one another. Although the nature of the context in which the guild meets encourages the members to focus on internal differences rather than to relate to one another through the perspective of a common identity, the context of the Old Timers' meetings encourages the development of a group identity.

The presence of out-groups in the corner store at times fosters the eruption of in-group/out-group distinctions. One morning, an African-American man sitting at a small table overheard a white man at the large tables say "nigger." The man from the small tables approached the speaker, as if wanting to start a fight, but the other Old Timers restrained him.

This is an extreme example. The relations among the people who use the corner store are typically neighborly. The people who gather at the large tables are not preoccupied with intentionally denigrating people who are not members of their group of friends. Likewise, the people at the small tables do not show overt resentment toward the Old Timers. However, among the Old Timers, part of communicating with one another and showing an appreciation for their membership in the group is the act of reinforcing their place through talk and behavior that sometimes blatantly discriminates against nonmembers.

This differentiation is often done along racial lines, but the Old Timers clarify boundaries with respect to gender as well. Only women who are accompanied by a male or are direct relatives of one of the Old Timers sit at the tables. Those that do not have these claims to guest status are policed. A member of the church guild reported to me—without realizing I was observing the Old Timers at the corner store—that she once took a seat at the large tables in the store. She was on an errand to buy dry ice there during the Old Timers' gathering time and sat down to wait. The Old Timers went about their conversation for a few minutes, and then one turned to her and said, half-jokingly, "Gee, you must be an aggressive female!" She recalled that the encounter was friendly, but that it sent clear signals about the group's bounds: "They let me know gently that this was a man's group."

"Let[ting] me know gently" is a telling observation with implications for the way public opinion scholars typically study identity. The Old Timers rarely refer to themselves verbally as a group of men. Behaviors such as subtle comments suggesting women do not typically sit at certain tables are aspects of identity processes that are not easily revealed through standard survey-based measures. Typically, social identity is measured with "closeness" measures (Lau 1989; Wong 1998). The measures conceptualize identities as explicit (spoken or directly referred to) labels people give to themselves, and thus they are limited in their utility. They do not capture unspoken conceptions of where people place themselves in the social world.

We can see the discrepancies between the Old Timers' behavior and their responses to closeness measures by looking at their responses to questionnaires that I administered. The closeness measures read: "I am interested in finding out what kinds of people you think are most like you, in their ideas and interests and feelings about things. Please read over the following list and mark the groups you feel particularly close to." The list included poor people, liberals, the elderly, Ann Arborites, blacks, labor unions, feminists, business-people, young people, conservatives, residents of Michigan, Hispanic Americans, women, working-class people, whites, environmentalists, middle-class people, men, Christian fundamentalists, Americans in general, people at your place of worship, and people in your neighborhood. Table 4.2 displays the Old Timers' responses as well as their responses to a similar question asking whether they "felt particularly *not* close to" any of the groups, which I asked in the self-administered questionnaire.

These reported identities convey a group composed of middle- and working-class elderly, conservative, white men who live in Ann Arbor, Michigan, and are somewhat attached to Americans in general. In addition, the group contains few, if any, liberals, union members, Christian fundamentalists, feminists, or people of other races. This is an accurate aggregate picture of the group. However, notice that only 35 percent say that they feel close to "men," while their conversations are often about the proper role of women and men in society.

Although "social identity" is the label social scientists give to psychological attachments with people in similar social circumstances, survey respondents may not as readily label these connections or report that they use

Table 4.2 Identities and Anti-Identities of the Old Timers

Group	Percentage feeling "close to"	Percentage feeling "not close to"
Middle-class people	69	0
Elderly	50	8
Conservatives	50	4
Businesspeople	42	8
Working-class people	42	0
Ann Arborites	39	8
Whites	39	0
Americans	39	4
People in neighborhood	39	12
Residents of Michigan	35	0
Men	35	0
People at place of worship	31	4
Young people	23	12
Women	15	8
Environmentalists	15	35
Poor people	8	27
Labor unions	8	50
Hispanic Americans	8	27
Christian fundamentalists	8	62
Liberals	4	65
Blacks	4	31
Feminists	0	62

Source: Self-administered questionnaire.

them to think about the world through the terms of "feeling close to" a given group.[7] People may identify with groups and put these attachments to use on a more subtle, less conscious, level. This is especially the case among members of dominant social groups (e.g., whites, males, members of the upper middle class). Members of minority groups are more likely to claim "closeness" to social groups of which they are objective members given the relative distinctiveness of their group in the social environment (Lau 1989).[8] For example, in the 1996 American National Election Studies (ANES), 47 percent of men reported feeling close to men, while 65 percent of women felt close to women. In the same manner, while only 44 percent of whites felt close to whites, 79 percent of blacks felt close to blacks.[9] Thus current survey measures of identity are better at capturing group attachments among members of politically marginalized groups than among dominant group members.

Closeness measures are also limited because they tend to portray identity as an either/or proposition with a battery of groups.[10] This is problematic because identities are more akin to a mutable web of interrelated attachments than affiliations that are independent of one another. A case in point is the way in which the perspectives through which women of color view the world are not the sum of their experience as women and experience as people of color but are a function of occupying a qualitatively unique social position (Crenshaw 1989).

Another potential problem with closeness measures suggested by the results of the self-administered questionnaire is that although many of the Old Timers identify as "middle class," their former occupations and their current wealth indicate that the socioeconomic positions they occupy are not good predictors of their affiliation with that label. Of the twenty-six Old Timers who responded to the questionnaire, twenty-one placed themselves in a social class. Nineteen of those people placed themselves as "middle class" (selected from "working class," "middle class," and "upper middle class"). But their wealth, signified through responses to an income question in the self-administered questionnaire, their reports of what they did on their vacations, and the cars (and helicopters, planes, fire engines, and boats) that they own, suggest that many if not most of them have annual incomes well above the actual national "middle" income. In 1998, the middle before-tax household income in the United States was $38,885 (Bureau of the Census 1999). In comparison, self-reports of twenty-one of the Old Timers give an average after-tax income of at least $50,000 per year, even though they are in retirement. Moreover, of the five Old Timers who declined to reveal their income, two are still working full time as small-business owners. To complicate the picture even more, nine of the twenty-six respondents identify with both the middle class and the working class. Closeness measures can tell us that people identify as middle class, but they do not help us see what this identity *means*.[11]

Because class identity is a perception of one's socioeconomic status relative to other people (Jackman and Jackman 1983; Walsh, Jennings, and Stoker, forthcoming), its content is something people continually update. The Old Timers do part of this work through talking about their youth. Most of them grew up in a modest part of town, and several grew up in what they call "Lower Town," or a lower-income neighborhood. To negotiate their class standing, they refer to the "elite" or "cultured" part of town, which consisted of large houses that were home to "professors' kids" when they were growing up.

The public beach, which no longer exists, is a place they describe as a setting in which they noticed class distinctions.

> Pete: That public beach was one of the best things. It was a sad day when they got rid of it. [Turns to Kathy] See, it used to be half blacks and

half whites, because that was in the part of town where the blacks
lived back then. Funny, because we had the beach and the golf
course—us poor kids—and those rich kids on the east side of town
didn't have anything. Their parents wouldn't let them go over to that
beach, no way.

Bill: All professors' kids . . .

Dave: Right, learning how to go to school—we were learning how to get
a job.

Pete: Yeah . . .

Bill: They went on to be academic types, we became tradesmen and
people who worked with our hands.

In this kind of conversation, the Old Timers are drawing the boundaries of
their conception of the middle class with respect to occupation.

Their survey responses reveal other ways in which their objective circumstances do not sufficiently describe the perspectives they use to make
sense of the world. In designing the questionnaire, I borrowed many of the
attitudinal items from the American National Election Studies to enable a
comparison of their political attitudes and behaviors to the nation as a whole.
In addition, I can compare them to a subsample of which they are a part: white
men over fifty with a high school diploma or equivalent, since all of the Old
Timers reported graduating from high school.[12] (See appendix 2 for graphs
and descriptive analyses detailing these comparisons.) The Old Timers are
more conservative and Republican than the nation as a whole, as well as the
subsample. They favor limited government and traditional family ties. Despite their conservatism, their reported tolerance for moral standards resembles that of the nation as a whole and is slightly higher than the demographic
group of which they are a part.

From the outside (compared to the other members of the political communities that they occupy—Ann Arbor, Michigan, the United States), the
group is conservative, elderly, and isolated from the students, younger families, lower-income residents, and people of color that live in the same city.
But from the inside, they are middle America. This comes through in the
way they describe themselves. They are "common people"—middle class,
white, Midwestern men. To them, "common people" are neither liberal nor
extremely conservative; they are hard working, yet focused on their families. They perceive themselves as prototypical Ann Arborites, average Americans. At times they recognize that their perspectives are not representative
of the larger population of Ann Arbor or the United States, but they do so
grudgingly, contrasting themselves with younger generations, or liberals,

and so forth, whom they consider to be "taking over." In a telling demonstration, when I asked them in the survey what comes to mind when they think of "an American" or "an Ann Arborite" they answered by describing themselves, or by noting how other objective occupants of the same political community deviate from this type. The following sample of responses is illustrative:

> "I am sure the city is comprised of all phases of people. I view it from the clients I see. Most of them are conservative, hard-working-class people. The student, in general, falsely liberalizes Ann Arbor."
>
> "A person who believes Ann Arbor is a great place to live, and wants to live in Ann Arbor. One who has attended the local schools, one who has a work history in Ann Arbor and found it good."
>
> "Old timers."
>
> "Not liberal crazies now on the city council, planning commission, school board."

And then there are responses taking note of groups that have "taken over": "liberals"; "academia"; "environmentalists"; Academics, mostly liberal, a little flaky, very little in common with those at the [corner store] who are Ann Arborites, but not in the majority." Their definitions of the real community are subtle: they do not say explicitly that "real" Ann Arborites are "white, middle-class, retired men with conservative values." Instead, a real Ann Arborite is "one of us."[13] They present themselves as the middle and deserving of the title of the common person.

The behavior and the conversations of the Old Timers reveal information that closeness measures cannot. When the Old Timers pour coffee for group members but not others, or tell women, "gently," that they are out of place, they are restricting their membership and setting themselves apart from others. In so doing, they are delimiting who constitutes their community and whom they consider fellow residents of the place.

Their ability to view the world from the standpoint of "middle people like us" is very much a function of their shared history. The following conversation is an example of the way shared experiences and acquaintances, not just shared demographic traits, form the basis of these identity processes. The following exchange took place among a group of Old Timers joined by several women (relatives of the Old Timers) later one morning. This group was diverse with respect to sex but had a vast resource of shared history from which they could draw on to negotiate and reinforce their ideas of the good life.

Skip: Boy, Ann Arbor has really changed. We have lost a lot of good
   things.

Rose and Alice [together]: Oh yeah, yeah.

Skip: It has really changed.

Alice: People used to say "hello" to you; you used to know people when
   you walked around town.

Rose: Hmmm mmm . . .

Skip: Used to play kick ball with a tin can between Thompson and
   Division Streets—the street lights would come on, someone would
   whistle or holler and we'd all say "good night" and go in and go to
   bed. You'd say "hello" to people. If somebody got sick, people would
   be helping out.

Rose: People are just too busy these days.

Skip: Yeah, we've lost a lot of good things. Don't you think so?

Rose and Alice [together]: Oh yeah, yep.

Rose: Now both of them [both parents] are working. I can understand
   why both parents need to work, but now nobody's home, both
   parents are working. The kids are boarded out—never used to be like
   that. In the neighborhood, all the women would be home, we'd
   gather at somebody's house for coffee in the morning. You'd start
   having kids and you'd bring your kids along. It's not like that
   anymore. It's not right.

Skip: When you came home after school, what was the first word out of
   your mouth?

Skip and Rose [together]: "Mom!! Mom, where are you??"

Bob: Oh yeah [referring to Skip]. Well, he'd say, "Hey, what's to eat?"
   [And then, offhandedly], "Oh, Hi Mom!" [Laughs.]

Skip: That's right, you'd call out for Mom. These days, we have more
   latchkey kids than the other kinds. No wonder kids are getting into
   trouble. And we just had another school shooting the other day
   . . . [. . .] . . . [14] The thing is that there's a loss of respect. Young people
   these days don't have respect for their country, for their parents, for
   their teachers—

Alice: . . . and they don't respect old people either.

Skip: That's right. When the national anthem came on when I was
   young, I stood up and saluted. No one made me do it. I just had
   respect. I'll stop my sermon here, but it's just so different.

In talking about the way people ought to behave toward others, these
people are doing a kind of triangulation, in essence saying, "*You* and *I* are

like *this*." Group interaction enables these kinds of linkages, because the act of communicating *with* people requires that individuals relate to one another. Most of the people at the corner store and in the guild follow the conventions of good conversation and try to talk with one another, speaking in such a way that their audience can understand, rather than simply talking for the sake of talking (Grice 1975). To produce satisfactory, sustained interaction that people return for day after day and week after week, people need to either refer to or forge some kind of common language. Even when talking about politics, people tend to convey what they have to say in a package to which their recipients can relate (Polanyi 1989, 46). This can take the form of mutually understood phrases, colloquialisms, or "shared cultural truths" (Polanyi 1989). It can also take the form of mutual acquaintances or common backgrounds. Asking such questions as "Where are you from?" or "What line of work are you in?" is an attempt to establish such common ground by figuring out what a person is like. Are we both Mid-westerners? Do we both work in the public schools? The answers tell people whether they belong to similar social groups and suggest topics for further conversation.

Recognition of similarity can then act as a basis for a small-group identity. Although previous work on the role of social identities in political thinking has focused on large-scale social groups, the relevant group that structures thinking is not always a societywide one (Brewer and Gardner 1996). People are situated within structural locations that are more personal than their status as "blacks" or "men" or "women." Group interaction, by fostering identity with small-scale social groups or associations, can mediate the distance between individuals and larger social groupings.

Over repeated interactions, the Old Timers carve up the world into "us" and "them" and connect themselves to the group as a whole. This act of negotiating ideas of who constitutes "us" perpetuates the interaction as it helps develop modes of appropriate behavior, or norms, that work to make the interaction easier (Festinger, Schachter, and Back 1950; Macy 1990, 1991, 1993). Their group interaction therefore allows them to develop the perspectives of people occupying a shared location in the social world and helps them identify with one another.

Significantly, their perspectives as particular types of people are clarified by emphasizing the ways in which they resemble one another and by pointing out the kind of behavior they do not consider appropriate for a true community member. Although psychological evidence is inconclusive about whether an "other" is necessary for an in-group identity (Gurin, Hatchett, and Jackson 1989; Gurin, Peng, Lopez, and Nagda 2001; Brewer and Brown

1998), the Old Timers often place themselves by pointing out who they are not, including blacks, liberals, and academics. LeMasters, in a study of the lifestyle of a group of "blue-collar elites" who spent time at a Midwestern bar, concluded that the people he observed formed their political opinions more often around what they were *against,* rather than what they were *for* (1975). The same is often true of the Old Timers, who, although slightly more affluent, mirror LeMasters's subjects in generation, region, and ethnic background. Although it may not always be necessary to have an out-group with which to contrast themselves, it is hard to imagine how the Old Timers could claim "we are all just middle people" without considering other people as above and below them in status.

This dynamic is clearly apparent with respect to race. Although they rarely refer to themselves as "whites," they often emphasize that they are not black. African Americans are clearly the most common racial group to which they refer, although they did occasionally speak of Latinos, Asian Americans, Arab Americans, and other ethnic and racial groups. They give meaning to this racial identity by talking about current race relations and by recollecting shared experiences from their youth.

> Dave: Remember how you used to be able to fish for walleye right out of the backwater of Barton Dam? Ahh, walleye . . .
> Pete: And a lot of suckers and carp too. But sure, walleye . . . [. . .]
> . . . There was one time we were fishing off of the public beach in the morning and I caught a huge sucker. Big thing. And there was a black woman down there, and I gave it to her, and she thought she had died and gone to heaven. . . . [. . .] . . .
> Dave: Yeah, I was fishing once on the Huron—mostly for walleye—and I caught a carp. There were some blacks fishing over there, so I went up to a woman and offered it to her. I didn't want it. But she was with a gentleman, if you could call him that, and he let me have it. He accused me of being con-deeee-SCEND-ing, because I was offering her a carp.
> Pete: But that's what they were fishing for!
> Dave: We almost got into a fight [shakes his head].

By relating a specific event, and signifying the different social group memberships while doing so, they define their social identities. More than just calling themselves "white" or calling others "black," they are conveying pictures of what members of these categories are like.

Exceptions to the Process of Clarifying Collective Identity

The process of creating a context of collective identification is far from deterministic. Even in a context of strong group identity these ideas of appropriate behavior are not universally accepted. Even the Old Timers' interactions reveal that they occasionally focus on their differences more than their likenesses. Most of the group grew up in the neighborhood surrounding the store, but some grew up in Lower Town. Sometimes the Old Timers will emphasize this distinction by yelling out "Hey, what do *you* know? You're from Lower Town" to establish the credibility of their "Old Timer" status. At the same time, one or two of the Old Timers will occasionally talk about their ties to Lower Town as a way of giving authenticity to the perspectives they use to discuss public affairs.

For example, on one occasion, Pete was talking about a liberal bias in higher education. To justify his individualist argument, he mentioned that he had grown up in Lower Town. "I quizzed my kids when they came home from school," he said. "They are taught in school these liberal attitudes. Taught in high school and college." He was bewildered by such points of view. "How can you think and be a liberal?" he asked. He said that liberalism simply ignored the fact that people need to take care of themselves. "I grew up on the poor side of town ... and I didn't have anything, but you make your life for yourself."

Pete is not the only member of the group who at times differentiates himself to prove a point. During a large strike by General Motors workers, which affected many jobs in Michigan as well as at GM plants throughout the United States, the Old Timers often talked about labor unions. In these conversations, Dave tended to emphasize his distinctiveness from the others. Although many of them had worked in the auto industry, most of the men had held managerial positions or owned their own businesses. Thus, only a few belonged to labor unions, and only Dave, a former lineman, is vocal about his union affiliation. "Well, I think it's time for me to get going, not much for me to stir up today," Dave said one day as he got up to leave. "You see, there's a bit of a division here. Quite a few of these guys, they're antiunion. Some of these guys, like that guy over there, they say that they're union, but they aren't really. To me, you have to have put in an apprenticeship for four to five years. Those guys, they're just assembly-line people ... but anyway, sometimes I mix things up a little. I haven't had the opportunity today." His comments display that even within a group with a strong sense of membership, such as the Old Timers, communication within it is not always done along the lines of shared identities.

Evidence beyond the Old Timers and the Guild

The foregoing comparison of the Old Timers and the craft guild suggests that people are more likely to clarify a collective identity through association interaction under two conditions: (1) when the members have a large store of overlapping acquaintances and experiences, and (2) when out-groups are present in the setting. Is there evidence beyond these groups that such conditions foster the clarification of identity?

To investigate, I turn to national sample survey data. Several available studies include data on social identity as well as information about participation in associations. However, such studies have not asked whether respondents share overlapping acquaintances and experiences with others in their voluntary associations. Fortunately, one study, the 1990 Citizen Participation Study (Verba, Schlozman, Brady, and Nie 1990), provides a proxy for such a condition—perceptions of group racial and gender homogeneity.[15] I use this as an admittedly noisy indicator of overlapping acquaintances and experiences on the assumption that the more homogenous the group with respect to major social categorizations, the more similar their life experiences.

Conditions of homogeneity matter for social identity processes in the following ways: It is in conditions in which people perceive that others share their race or gender that we should expect them to encounter credible information on "how someone like myself" ought to think, feel, and act. Second, in such conditions, people are more likely to encounter information that resonates with their prior identities. Third, a perception of likeness yields a greater likelihood that an interpretation privately held by any individual member will be perceived as valid for the group as a whole. Therefore, the interpretation is more likely expressed and thus more likely to foster communication about identity. In other words, conditions of heterogeneity can help people articulate their sense of identity, as was evident among members of the guild. However, when people are unsure whether their interpretation resonates with anyone else in the group, they are less likely to express it, hindering the clarification of social identity.[16]

Before examining the effect of group homogeneity, notice the extent of homogeneity across various association types. The 1990 CPS data indicate that most associations are homogeneous, but this homogeneity varies across group type. The CPS collected respondents' perceptions of the racial and gender homogeneity of the group most important to them, if that group was also the one in which they were most active—as opposed to the group to which they donated the most money (see appendix 3 for wording). To indicate the average homogeneity by group type, I averaged these responses across

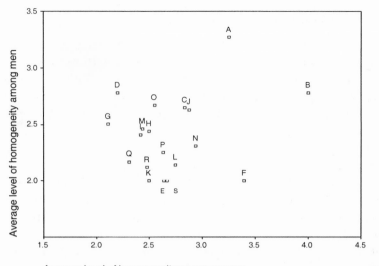

Average level of homogeneity among women

Figure 4.1 Group Gender Homogeneity. (Source: 1990 CPS)
Key: A = Service, fraternal organization; B = Veterans group; C = Religious group; D = Racial/ethnic group; E = Senior citizens' group; F = Women's group; G = Labor union; H = Business/professional group; I = Political issue group; J = Civic group; K = Liberal/conservative group; L = Elections group; M = Youth group; N = Literary group; O = Hobby club, sports or country club; P = Neighborhood group; Q = Health service group; R = Education group; S = Cultural organization

all respondents providing reports about a given group type. Figure 4.1 displays the average gender homogeneity of each group type as reported by men and women, where higher numbers denote higher sex homogeneity (range = 1–4).[17] The chart shows that, like the gender makeup of the Old Timers and the church craft guild, most voluntary associations are segregated by sex.[18] Notice that most group types are characterized by a membership that is on the homogenous half of the scale. The average level of homogeneity reported is at least 2 (gender-mixed) for every group across both men and women. Groups in the upper-right portion of the graph are the most sex segregated. Both women and men who participate in voluntary associations report that they do so primarily with people of the same sex.

Closer inspection of the data suggests that women's groups tend to be more homogenous than men's. In fourteen of the nineteen groups, women reported a higher average degree of sex homogeneity than did men. This is consistent with previous research showing that the associations women belong to tend to be more highly segregated by sex (McPherson and Smith-Lovin 1986). These data also support McPherson and Smith-Lovin's (1986) argument that instrumental groups, such as business or professional groups and public interest or policy groups, tend to be more heterogeneous than expressive groups such as veterans groups, lodges, or hobby groups (67). This homogeneity is partly the result of gender specialization across group types. Jennings (1990) found that among national political party convention delegates, women were more likely to belong to school-related groups, abortion-related groups, women's groups, teachers groups, and public-interest groups than men. Men, however, were more likely to belong to fraternal groups, veterans groups, labor unions, occupational groups, and service groups. His results are displayed in the first column of Table 4.3. Identical analyses among U.S. residents in general are displayed in columns two and three, computed from the 1990 CPS and the 1996 American National Election Study (Rosenstone et al. 1996). Among political party delegates, as well as the nation as a whole, voluntary association participants display considerable sex specialization.

Voluntary associations are also segregated by race. Figure 4.2 plots the average levels of racial homogeneity reported by whites and blacks in their most active groups. Higher scores reflect higher degrees of homogeneity. The plot suggests a high degree of racial segregation across group types for both races.

Further analyses reveal that racial homogeneity is more common than gender homogeneity. Women select into racially homogenous groups even more often than they select into groups homogenous with respect to sex. In the 1990 CPS, among women who reported that their most important group is also their most active group (women for whom measures of group homogeneity are available), 61 percent reported that their group was racially homogenous, while 41 percent said that it was homogenous with respect to sex.[19]

As the guild meetings suggested, however, homogeneity in terms of shared demographics is not enough to produce communication through the lens of collective identity. Some type of mechanism for recognizing likenesses is necessary, such as the presence of out-groups or the purpose of the group. One situation in which the membership is relatively homogenous and the identity is salient is within associations in which the purpose is related to a social category (e.g., "women's groups"). If this is indeed conducive to the development of perspectives rooted in social identity, people who participate in associations whose purpose is explicitly related to a social group of which they are objective members should exhibit higher rates of identity with that group than people who do not participate in groups with that social group purpose. National sample survey data allow us to test for this. To control for the possibility that people who participate in associations are more likely to have strong social identities for spurious reasons, I ran this test only among people who reported participating in associations. I examined this hypothesis

Table 4.3 Sex Specialization in Voluntary Associations

Type of group	1984 Convention Delegate Study			1990 Citizen Participation Study			1996 National Election Study		
	Men		Women	Men		Women	Men		Women
Religious group	48		47	5	<	9	6	<	11
Education group	31	<	39	9	<	15	9	<	14
Women's group	14	<	60	4		2	0		1
Member of a local church, parish or synagogue							40	<	44
Health/service group				5		7	3	<	8
Abortion-related	14	<	40						
Teachers	15	<	25						
Public interest	37	<	55						
Civic group				1		2	1	<	9
Labor union	28	>	23	9	>	3	9	>	4
Service	30	>	18						
Hobby club, sports club, country club				14	>	8	15	>	12
Service/fraternal organization	32	>	12	11		7	6		4
Racial/ethnic group	32	>	30	2		2	3		2
Business/professional group	53	>	43	19	>	12	14	>	7
Veterans group	21	>	4	4	>	1	5	>	2
Elections group				2		2	5	>	1
Youth group				6		8	12		14
Cultural organization				1		2	3		3
Senior citizens group				2		4	3		4
Literary group				3		5	2		3
Neighborhood group				8		7	3		3
Political issue group				3		2	2		2
Lib/con group				2		1	0		0
Self-help group	1		2						
Environmental group	31		30						

Note: Entries are percentage of men or women respondents who report participating in each group type. The first column is taken from Jennings (1990). Several group labels differed slightly. In the Convention Delegate Study labels were "fraternal," "occupational," "school-related," and "church" for those listed here as "service/fraternal," "business professional," "educational," and "religious," respectively. Please see appendix 3 for question wordings in the NES and CPS. Discrepancies are identified in the NES wordings. Following the convention used in Jennings 1990 (p. 232), percentage differences greater than or equal to 5% for the Convention Delegate Study, and greater than or equal to 3% for the other two studies are indicated with < and > signs. Weights were used to compute figures for the 1990 CPS and the 1996 NES. Ns for the CPS ranged from 1,168 to 1,179 for men and from 1,298 to 1,310 for women. In the NES, Ns were 838 for women and 696 for men.

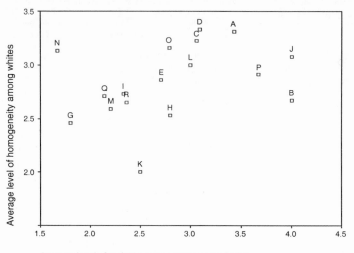

Average level of racial homogeneity among blacks

Figure 4.2 Group Racial Homogeneity. (Source: 1990 CPS)
Key: A = Service, fraternal organization; B = Veterans group; C = Religious group; D = Racial/ethnic group; E = Senior citizens' group; F = Women's group; G = Labor union; H = Business/professional group; I = Political issue group; J = Civic group; K = Liberal/conservative group; L = Elections group; M = Youth group; N = Literary group; O = Hobby club, sports or country club; P = Neighborhood group; Q = Health service group; R = Education group; S = Cultural organization

with 1996 National Election Studies data (Rosenstone et al. 1996) as well as the 1990 CPS data.[20] The results are displayed in table 4.4.

The results suggest that taking part in a group whose purpose invokes social group membership is more clearly related to the clarification of social identity among members of some social groups than others. Women who take part in "organizations mainly interested in issues promoting the rights or the welfare of women" and union members who take part in "labor unions" appear more likely to identify with women and unions, respectively, than people who do not participate in such groups. However, blacks and whites who take part in "groups representing your own particular nationality, or ethnic, or racial group," and elderly people who take part in "organizations for the elderly or senior citizens" are not more likely to identify with their respective social categories than members of those categories who take part in different types of groups.[21]

The small number of cases in the salient group conditions limits the conclusions that can be drawn from this table. However, these results underscore an important factor in the process of identity clarification: the salience of social group categories *in society*. Regardless of the salience of the category in the immediate physical context, voluntary association participation has a

Table 4.4 Relationship between Social Identification and Attending Association Meetings of a Group in which Social Group Is Salient

| | | Mean identification | | |
	Data source	Attend meetings in which identity is salient	Attend meetings, but not in which identity is salient	T-test
Women	1990 CPS	.58	.47	t = 1.869
		(n = 26)	(n = 578)	p = .037
	1996 NES	.90	.67	t = 2.130
		(n = 9)	(n = 544)	p = .031
Blacks	1990 CPS	.49	.50	t = .194
		(n = 48)	(n = 161)	p = .423
	1996 NES	.89	.80	t = .967
		(n = 14)	(n = 107)	p = .173
Union Members	1996 NES	.46	.22	t = 3.428
		(n = 83)	(n = 100)	p = .000
Elderly	1996 NES	.70	.65	t = .594
		(n = 34)	(n = 143)	p = .278
Whites	1996 NES	.28	.50	t = −1.583
		(n = 21)	(n = 848)	p = .074

more obvious effect on identity development with respect to some categories than others. Whether or not African Americans participate in associations, they claim closeness with "blacks" at high rates, as noted earlier in this chapter. Thus, participation in associations has little added effect on whether or not they proclaim an identity with blacks. The high levels of identity with "the elderly" among participants in groups in which that identity is not salient suggests the same dynamic. In contrast, "closeness" to whites once more is an uncommon sentiment, even among whites who profess activity in groups related to their nationality, race, or ethnicity.

In slightly different terms, race is perhaps the most salient social category in political judgment and understanding in American culture, because patterns of social, economic, and political segregation in American society announce and reinforce that African Americans comprise a distinct group (Massey and Denton 1993) at the same time that American elite discourse underscores racial divides (Carmines and Stimson 1989; Mendelberg 2001).

Gender divisions are arguably less prominent than racial divisions in American culture (Gurin 1985). Although women are highly segregated from men in settings such as the workforce (Reskin 1993) and voluntary associations (Jennings 1990; McPherson and Smith-Lovin 1986), they are frequently linked to this out-group (i.e., men) in intimate ways (Jackman 1994;

Ridgeway and Smith-Lovin 1999). Because of this complex social position, many women may not recognize the political relevance of their membership in this social group (Sigel 1996).

Thinking about political issues consciously in terms of one's social class is even less likely than in terms of one's gender or race. This is not to say that social class identity does not matter in American politics. How Americans identify in terms of class is, for example, related to the way they orient themselves to government (Walsh, Jennings, and Stoker, forthcoming). However, overt class conflict is rare among Americans (Jackman 1994, 24–33). The nonsalience of class in American politics is especially apparent when viewed in a comparative perspective (Gerteis and Savage 1998). In addition, other social identities often overwhelm the relevance of class identification to politics. For example, African Americans' racial identities are often more powerful predictors of their policy preferences than are class divisions (Dawson 1994, 192–99). Because the linkage between class location and politics is relatively obscured in American political culture, it makes sense that we see the strongest effect of extra opportunities for interaction—participation in voluntary associations—on an identity related to class, closeness to unions.

Taken together, these results suggest that although the particular contexts of association interaction may matter for whether or not people communicate about collective identity, the broader social and political culture in which they interact has a bearing on these processes as well.

* * *

The characteristics of the broader political environment matter for how people connect themselves to politics, as these results suggest, and as previous research on public opinion, especially framing effects, has shown. However, the observations analyzed in the earlier portion of this chapter underscore that social identities are not entirely the product of elite-driven effects. It takes some work for a group of retired white men living in an idyllic community that has ample resources to perceive the world from the standpoint of people living the "typical" American experience.

Observation of the Old Timers suggests that participation in voluntary associations provides an opportunity for people to clarify their attachments to social groups. When contrasted with the craft guild meetings and tested against survey data evidence, two key factors emerge that influence whether or not people will clarify social identity through their informal interaction. First, overlapping acquaintances and experiences make the clarification of collective identities more likely. And second, for such clarification to occur, some mechanism must operate to give salience to these similarities. When group members do communicate about shared identities, they are giving meaning to tools of understanding. These resulting identities form the basis of perspectives through which they collectively communicate about the world.

Taking part in the conversation is a different act than if the participants were merely listening to the comments of others on a tape recorder. The process of giving meaning to, of constituting, politically relevant identities is an act that is performed in a specific social context through the act of relating to one another. Because they use feedback from one another to clarify and reinforce where they each individually stand, it is the social nature of the act that enables the development of these social attachments.

When people clarify their social identities through informal talk, they are developing basic building blocks of political understanding. This act of "relating 'I' to 'We'" is perhaps the fundamental move of citizenship (Pitkin 1981, 345). When people discuss public issues, they relate their personal and private selves to a collectivity or community (Norton 1988, chap. 1). The struggle over who is in an in-group and who is in an out-group, over who is superior, and how these groups relate are all questions of power, or "cultural politics" (Habell-Pallán 1997, 257). These are questions about how people are connected to others and how they should relate to one another, which are both political and ethical questions (Stoker 1992). And these are questions whose answers do not specify policy preferences but delineate ways of looking at the world—that is, perspectives.

Talking Politics in a Context of Understanding

On a typical August morning, Charlie, a 78-year-old Old Timer, opens the door to the corner store and is greeted by his friends at the two large tables. He takes his fresh copy of the *Detroit Free Press,* places it on a table by one of the few empty chairs, and goes to the counter to get his coffee. A banner headline on the paper reads "IT WAS WRONG." When he returns, he says, mockingly, "He tripped on his zipper." And then after a slight pause, "It's not over. He shouldn't have picked on Kenneth Starr like that."

> Pete: Oh well, what is the press going to write about? 'Course it's not over. Between O.J. and this, they've been covered the last four years. They'd have to have another scandal. It's really embarrassing. They drag a man's sex life out like that. We're the laughing stock of the world.
>
> Alex: Yep, we are.
>
> Pete: Really embarrassing.
>
> ... [...] ...
>
> Kathy: Well, it sure seems that he has a problem.
>
> Pete: Yeah, he likes women!
>
> Kathy: Well, uncontrollably!
>
> Pete: Well, he doesn't pick an appropriate place to do it.
>
> Alex: I expected him to say what he said, I really did.
>
> Kathy: You did?
>
> Alex: Yeah, I expected him to apologize ... [To Kathy]: There are a lot of guys like that in this world, you have to watch out for them. It's a kind of sickness, I really think it is. He was doing it back in Arkansas.... [...] ...
>
> Charlie: He's not worth a blank nickel now.
>
> Alex: That's right, that's right.
>
> Pete: Every time he says something now, people will wonder if he's lying or not.

On the morning after President Bill Clinton admitted to an "inappropriate relationship" with White House intern Monica Lewinsky, the Old Timers sifted through news of the scandal. The Lewinsky ordeal entered their conversations many times in 1998 and 1999, as it likely did for many people. They did not start these exchanges to carefully deliberate about political issues. Therefore, the tools they use to make sense of such events are not rooted in the political world. Because politics is not their central concern, when they *do* give attention to politics, we should not expect that they will use specialized tool kits. Instead, they bring to bear the perspectives and related categories that they use to talk about a wide variety of topics.

In the previous chapter, I showed how interaction among the Old Timers and among the women in the church craft guild allows the members of these groups to develop and define their social identities—their attachments to other people in the world. Both their conversations and their physical behavior allow them to either clarify how they are similar types of people or to differentiate themselves from each other. In this chapter, I show how perspectives rooted in these social identity processes structure the way group members talk about political events.

The Pattern of Political Talk among the Old Timers and Other Groups

One of the first things I noticed about the way the Old Timers and the other groups' members talk about politics is that topics related to the government or politicians arise without any fanfare—they slip in like talk about other subjects. As with other topics, talk about public affairs arises because one or more of the members perceives an issue as relevant to his or her life. For example, at a large table in the corner store, Orville asks Ron about his wife. Ron says, "She's great," that "she's playing tennis," and then . . .

> Orville: She plays tennis?
> Ron: Yep, yep, indoors—at that new facility.
> Orville: Nice place?
> Ron: Oh yes, see your tax dollars at work!
> Paul: Oh, Ron, you can drive on any street in central Ann Arbor and see your tax dollars at work!

From here, they segue into a conversation about local taxes. Once in motion, others enter the conversation because they, too, can see a connection between their personal experiences and the issue of taxation. This is the general pattern of their conversations. An anecdote that fits the flow, or a personal experience with the person or event at hand, is their ticket to jumping in.

One morning, an Old Timer mentioned recent events in the Persian Gulf. Although the conversation began as one man's views about the situation there, Jack transformed it into a discussion of immigration, as he mentioned his own family's experience.

> Charlie: What about that Tariq Aziz?[1]
> Jack: Oh, I know it.
> Charlie: And they show lines of people lying on the ground in Iran . . .
> Jack: He's a real character. It's such a mess over there . . . [. . .] . . . it's ancient grievances. Don't know why they're fighting anymore, like in Ireland.
> Charlie: Not even a potato famine can stop them.
> Jack: Right, my family came over after the last potato was gone. . . . [The conversation turns to immigration.]
> Jack: Pretty soon we're going to be the minority.
> Charlie: That's right.
> Jack: In California, they're going to have a [Mexican-American] governor and two senators, they say . . .
> Charlie: Yep, we'll be in the minority, say 2020.
> [Turning to Kathy]: You'll have to tell us about it, because we'll be gone.
> Jack: Yeah, you think then we'll be able to exercise our rights? Use affirmative action for us? [laughs]

Notice how Charlie brings up the topic of war in the Middle East, Jack chimes in and then relates it to his family, and from there they spin the conversation off in the direction of immigration. Note also how they make use of a shared social identity—"we." They put conflict in the Middle East into focus by looking at it through the lens of their shared place in the world.

This is a typical pattern for the Old Timers. When political topics arise, they use the terms "us" and "we" to relate to one another and to link their individual contributions to the conversation—and at the same time use the categories of these perspectives to create their collective interpretations.

Shared Group Identity and the Frequency of Talk about Politics

Their ability to connect with one another and make sense of public affairs through perspectives may actually facilitate shared talk about politics. A useful point of contrast is the craft guild, where political topics arise much less frequently. Why? Consider three potential explanations, based on the major differences between these two groups: (1) the groups' goals, (2) the gender composition of the membership, and (3) the prominence of a shared group identity. (Recall table 4.1 in chapter 4, which compared the differences between the Old Timers and the members of the guild with respect to characteristics that likely influence whether a group develops a collective identity.)

There is good reason to think that the goals of a group adequately explain the difference in political talk across the Old Timers and the guild. National sample survey data demonstrate this. In the 1990 Citizen Participation Survey, respondents who participated in various types of associations reported whether "people at these meetings sometimes chat informally about politics or government." The proportion of participants who reported hearing such talk provides a measure of the relative level of informal political talk (as differentiated from political topics on a group's meeting agenda) across group types. Table 5.1 displays these results, ordered from most reported to least reported political talk.

The results suggest that people are more likely to encounter political talk when participating in groups that clearly have a political function (the three top-scoring groups have political purposes). Thus, we would expect that the craft guild, whether we classify it as a hobby group, a group affiliated with the members' religion, or a senior-citizen group, would exhibit a relatively low amount of informal talk about politics.

But the goals of the groups do not entirely explain the discrepancy in the amount of political talk between the Old Timers and the guild. The purpose of the Old Timers' group is not political either, and yet they regularly talk about politics.

Consider the second potential explanation: gender. Compared to men, women who take part in associations do report less talk about politics in their groups.[2] According to the 1990 CPS data, 67 percent of women who take part in associations (n = 650) report informal political talk in those groups, and 77 percent of male group participants (n = 643) report such talk. The gender gap in level of reported political talk in associations is especially evident concerning service or fraternal organizations and organizations interested in women's issues. Among participants in these types of groups, a greater proportion of men report informal political chatting than do women.[3]

Of course, this discrepancy is not a function of biology but of socialization. Women in the United States are not born less likely to talk about politics, but they live in an environment that conveys that being interested in politics is not "natural" for women. For example, when women live in

Table 5.1 Level of Informal Political Talk by Association Type

Group Type	Attendees reporting informal political Talk (%)	N reporting attending meeting of this type of group in past year
Liberal or conservative political group	100	4
Organization active in elections	99	51
Political issue organization	97	63
Labor union	84	147
Nonpartisan or civic organization	82	39
Veterans organization	81	57
Business or professional organization	77	370
Racial or ethnic organization	75	40
Organization interested in women's issues	74	32
Neighborhood association	70	187
Literary, art, or discussion group	68	93
Senior citizen group	67	72
Service, fraternal organization	66	219
Educational organization	66	295
Group affiliated with R's religion	56	184
Hobby or sports club	54	264
Cultural organization	50	22
Health service organization	49	133
Youth group	35	168

Source: 1990 CPS.

a state in which few women hold office as, or have recently run for, governor, the House of Representatives, or the U.S. Senate, they are less likely to be interested in politics, have knowledge about politics, or perceive that they can have an impact on the political process (Burns, Schlozman, and Verba 2001, chap. 13). However, the level of political interest among the Old Timers is unusual, even for men. We can see this by comparing their responses to the self-administered questionnaire with those of a national sample in the American National Election Study.[4] Ninety-two percent of the Old Timers say they follow what is going on in government "most of the time" or "some of the time" while only 69 percent of the ANES respondents pay that much attention to what is going on in politics.[5] They also follow politics more than white men over fifty with high school diplomas (or more education), 72 percent of whom follow politics "most of the time" or "some of the time."

Their higher-than-average education and the fact that many of them held professional and managerial jobs for most of their lives are characteristics that are correlated with gender and so predispose this group to be more interested in politics. In addition, several of the men have held public office. Several are still consulted (sometimes in the corner store) by local public officials, policemen, and university athletic department officials.[6]

Even if we pin the discrepancy in the levels of political talk across the Old Timers and the guild on different levels of political interest by gender, this explanation is insufficient. The missing factor is the context of understanding, rooted in a shared group identity, that the group collectively creates.

In the guild, for example, I was surprised to learn that Ruby, the treasurer of the group, had been a Labor-Farm candidate for public office. This personal experience never arose during the meetings I attended, only in an aside to me. "I was president of [all kinds] of things, real active in the peace movement [after World War II], in my workers' union . . . We used to meet on folding chairs out in the field. One time I was standing on a dining room chair with no seat, raising my fist like this [she puts her fist in the air, a huge, proud smile on her face]." In a private conversation, Ruby talked about herself and her relation to politics with ease. She had a genuine concern for politics. However, in the context of the group, the members—including Ruby—rarely broached such topics.

A key element in the explanation for the guild's relative lack of political talk is the lack of connections among the members, the lack of a strong collective identity. Ruby's behavior is indicative of a member of a group whose participants are slightly uncomfortable and unfamiliar with each other. As MacKuen (1991) argues, people are more likely to clam up about politics if they perceive that their remarks will not be met with friendly responses. Collective identities can go a long way toward facilitating ideas of what is acceptable to say in a group.

In the guild, the surliness of one particular member, Eloise, means that comments in general are likely to be met with a hostile response. However, the avoidance of political topics within this group is not simply a matter of personality but of the context that the group collectively creates. When a member does attempt to carry on a conversation about politics, she offers her comments in a private conversation, or, if she makes them in the larger group, she usually gets no response.

When political topics do arise in the guild, the bulk of the comments convey that it is inappropriate to speak of oneself as an activist in that context. When "activist" is used as a category for talking about a topic, it is only as a tool for designating "them," not "us." For example, several weeks before Ruby's revelation of her Labor-Farm candidacy, the women had been discussing a recent riot in Ann Arbor that had taken place during a Ku Klux Klan rally. A women's activist group from Detroit had violently protested the presence of the Klan.

> Doris: So has anyone been downtown to see the damage from the
>   riot . . . the rally this past weekend?
> Kathy: I have—not much damage, really not a lot of damage.
> Doris: So it was okay?
> Elnor: Only a few broken windows in the Larcom building [City Hall].
> Eloise: They pulled a fence down too.
> Elnor: Well, that was just put up for the rally.
> Kathy: Just a temporary fence . . .
> Nan: Must have cost the city a lot.
> Eloise: Big expense.
> Elnor: I think they should split the cost between the KKK and that
>   group of women from Detroit that come out and stir up all the
>   trouble. What are they called? Starts with an "n" . . . "NAY-rock" or
>   something like that.
> Ginnie: They come to the city meetings . . . They have it now so that
>   they can only talk for five minutes, which is good. They used to come
>   in there and take over the thing. And those women are so belligerent.

In this conversation, several women in the guild made it clear that they thought the behavior of "those women" was inappropriate. Their comments conveyed that radical protest was unacceptable behavior for women. In such a context, it is not surprising that Ruby talked about her own radical politics only in private. If she had offered up her experience as a leftist activist, she would have opened herself to the same kinds of criticism that the others had made about present-day radical women.

As Eliasoph (1998) has documented, groups often create a culture in which political talk is unwelcome. When talk about politics is perceived as incompatible with the group's goals or interests (as was the case with a group of volunteers she studied), or at odds with the group's identity (such as a "cynical chic" group of people who spent time together at a country-western dance bar), politics is avoided or only talked about "backstage," as Ruby did with me.

The members of a different group in Eliasoph's study who also met at the country-western bar, "the Buffaloes," were afraid to talk about politics. "[T]hey had no framework for sorting through the facts or finding patterns, no one upon whom they could rely in thinking through their own opinions, no place to figure out how all the facts fitted together" (1998, 131–32). In Eliasoph's terms, they did not think of themselves as a public and thus had few tools with which to communicate about politics together.

Without these kinds of resources, the Buffaloes had a difficult time connecting the complexities of their lives with the symbols of modern politics. According to other scholars, this is common for many people. In revisiting Lane's work, Sears and Funk (1991) write, "In short, political dialogue is by its nature coded into abstract semantic terms. But personal experience may be morselized because it is difficult to code the rich complexity of direct personal experience into the simple symbolic terms that can be readily triggered by political symbols" (14). Identity as a public or as a type of collectivity may facilitate the connections between individuals and the political realm. When people have a strong sense of community and a well-recognized similar perspective or outlook on life, talk about politics is easier. In such settings, it is not so much a potential arena for disagreement as an opportunity to reinforce one's ties with the group.

As a final demonstration of the way a shared group identity can promote talk about politics, consider the way the guild talked about parking fees compared to the way the Old Timers discussed this issue. The guild members' conversations reveal the squelching effect that a lack of group identity can have on the process of making sense of politics. When they discuss a topic such as downtown parking, they tend to do so along the lines of "me" versus "you" rather than "us" versus "them." This is typical of the way they treat what are potentially political issues as personal dilemmas rather than as public problems. Eloise, the "chairman" of the group, once brought up the fact that she had hurt her hip getting into her car after a women's club luncheon, and from this began a conversation about parking.

> Eloise: You know, they're talking about parking downtown, and I think that for handicapped people, there ought to be spaces you can park in for free. They're talking about raising the prices of the meters and the garages to $1 per hour. That's just too much for people who are handicapped.
> Kathy: You mean that people who can't walk should have a place to park for free?
> Eloise: That's right.
> Elnor: Well, if you do that then someone will use the space that isn't handicapped. Many times people use those spaces when they're with a handicapped family member, but then they abuse the privilege when they're on their own.

> Eloise: I suppose. But then they ought to make it cheaper.
> Kathy: Well, I think that's a good idea. You should call the city building.
> Eloise: Well, I wrote it down in that survey they sent out. You know, that thing on city spending.
> Kathy: Good for you.
> Eloise: You know, it's hard to get around downtown. It's hard to get around when you're handicapped. But I surely won't go there at all if I can't park there.
> Elnor: I haven't been downtown in about one year.
> Doris: No kidding . . . [in agreement with Elnor.]

Rather than identify with Eloise's predicament, the other women doubted her need to park at all. The women at the guild did not use the topic to recognize a common grievance or a target for potential political action. Instead, as with many topics of conversation within this group, it became yet another forum for declaring their differences in opinion.

We can see a different direction that conversation about such a topic could take by listening to the Old Timers. Witness this discussion about the same topic:

> Charlie: Hey, did you hear they're going to put meters on Fourth and Fifth Streets?
> Kathy: No kidding, I park there!
> Bill: For a buck.
> Kathy: It's going to be a dollar?
> John: Yep, dollar an hour in June.
> Charlie: That council—nuttier than a fruitcake, then they wonder why everybody goes out to [the local mall].
> Bill: Idiots. No wonder there's no downtown . . . [. . .] . . . How long did it take them to decide what to do with that parking structure?
> Kathy: Eight months?
> Mack: So stupid, they waited until *all* the parking structures started to collapse and then impose a millage.
> John: And raise the parking fee . . .
> Mack: Makes no sense.
> Bill: Bunch of idiots.

Among the Old Timers, when the topic of parking comes up, they use it not as an opportunity to differentiate their points of view but as a chance to agree and clarify their identity as a group of regular people governed by a "bunch of idiots." They make sense of this political issue, like many others, through their shared perspective. Rather than avoid political topics or have the conversation lack momentum because the others present cannot relate, the Old Timers communicate about politics through their shared concerns, common battles, and ready agreement.

Social Identity Constrains Political Understanding

Consider now how social identities work to constrain political understanding when groups do talk about politics. In this section, I address the identity-based perspectives that influence collective political understanding by affecting which interests, social groups, and political principles are acceptable to the conversation.

Before presenting evidence about the power of shared identity among the Old Timers, however, it is useful to recognize that not all group members participate equally in the conversations. In every group there are undoubtedly people who dominate the conversation, people who are more timid about stating their views, people who prefer to talk and people who prefer to listen. There may also be people who emerge as opinion leaders, members of the group whom others look to as experts within particular domains of knowledge (Katz and Lazarsfeld 1955). Among the Old Timers, no one clear leader was evident. Baxter was notorious for talking a lot, but many different people initiated political topics.

Who takes the lead in a conversation depends on the specifics of a topic. Even the quieter group members are asked for input if the others recognize that they have related expertise. For example, if the topic deals with events in a nearby town, then the talkers turn to those at the table who have moved there. If it deals with the military, inevitably a veteran gains the floor.

Just as they ask the resident plumbers and mechanics for home and car maintenance advice, they turn to former World War II pilots for an educated guess about whether the United States will engage in military action. During the December 1998 U.S. bombing campaign against military targets in Iraq, some of the Old Timers turned to Charlie, one of the resident veterans.

> Jack: Hey Charlie, are we bombing Iraq again today?
> Charlie: Yep.
> Orville: Yep, as soon as it gets dark over there. Charlie said it's about
>   4:30 there.
> Charlie: Right. Eight hours ahead.

> Jack: So what are we going to do once we're done bombing? Start all
>   over again?
> Charlie: I guess so. Do it all over again.

Most of the Old Timers contributed to a political conversation at some point during my observations. Although certain members tend to sit together, the slight variation in the times at which they arrive results in a shuffling of people at each table from day to day. Although casual observers of the place remark that "they each have their own seat," this is not actually the case. Only one man sits in the same spot every day (unless someone has already taken it, which is rare). Political conversations are therefore not clustered among a select few. They bubble up among all combinations of people and often ripple down the length of a table.

Part of the nondominance of any one member might be a function of the purpose of the group. Because this is a social hour (everyone is there to visit), a strong norm exists against talking too much. Several are notorious talkers, especially Baxter, who one Old Timer likes to characterize as having been "injected with a phonograph needle." When such characters start to go overboard in the length of their comments or in their emphasis on one topic, the others try to change the topic, go visit people at the other large table, or get up to serve a round of coffee.

Dwelling too much on which members do more talking misses something about the nature of the interaction, however. Talking does not constitute all of the important communication in these settings. The mere presence of a person is an important statement of "I want to belong" or "I agree with what is going on here."[7] Even nods of agreement and attentive listening contribute to the collective act of making sense of an issue. When what is going on is basically socializing, there is little reason to stick around if one does not feel his opinion is valued or does not resonate with the group. In contrast, in the guild, disagreement with others' perspectives on the world might be set aside because of the satisfaction of having a social environment in which to make things and contribute to the church.

Social Identities Constrain Definitions of Interest

At the same time that the perspective of a shared identity greases the wheels of political talk, it also constrains the interests that the participants proclaim in their conversations. The Old Timers' collective lens as "common people" serves as a guide for how they ought to think about their interests with respect to new issues.

For example, quick comments such as the following announce the general opinion climate of the group:

> Mike: How's your son doing up north?
> Baxter: Good. Real good. I think part of the reason he moved was he was tired of having the neighborhood kids sent on a bus across town to school. "Bye!" There goes the neighborhood. . . .

One sentence, followed by a round of nods from the others within earshot, serves as a brief indicator of acceptable opinion.

At times, their talk reveals that there are prevailing assumptions about which interests are held by "one of us." The morning after an election that included several ballot initiatives generated by local liberals and environmentalists, Joe walked in and gave the group's assessment, without even wondering whether it *was* the group's assessment.

> Joe: So I see we knocked down 'B,' but not 'A.'
> Orville: 'A' was just a renewal though, right?
> Fred: Yeah, but that's been going on for five years now, going to go perhaps another twenty-five.

Joe commented on the elections, well aware that the group members and people like themselves—"we"—had opposed both of the ballot items.

The way in which the Old Timers' political conversations are made possible by and in turn clarify and reinforce shared perceptions of their place in the community is particularly on display during talk about taxes. One Saturday, the group had been talking about property taxes. Mike explained to me that he was trying to sell his house so that he could move out of town and avoid paying large school taxes. "See this guy, and that guy [pointing to other men sitting around the big tables], and him, and let's see . . . that guy—they are all retired here, and you know how much they pay in school taxes? Thirty-five hundred dollars. Makes no sense. They all worked here, raised their families here . . . ridiculous. [Shakes his head]. They pay that money now and for what? My kids are out of school now." And on another day, Joe explained to a visitor that "we pay such high taxes here. It's unfair. You got all these students here and they vote. As soon as someone wants money for something, they get it on the ballot, and then go get the students to vote."

Taken together, their comments delimit their identity as a group of people who "have paid their dues" and are unfairly forced to bear the burden of students and younger generations. Such expressions of identity structure how they talk about their interests. The following exchange shows how their perspectives as certain people are used to talk about their distaste for taxes. In it, the Old Timers talk about a recent millage that would fund a new science education center.

> Baxter: Ann Arbor voters turned right around on that election. They voted in favor of the parks millage, and even a slight increase, but voted down that building, because it said nothing about paying for staff, upkeep. It was simply, "Oh, this won't cost much."
>
> Harold: Uh huh . . .
>
> [The conversation segues into taxes in general]
>
> Baxter: What I don't like is being an enemy of the IRS. It's "you're guilty until proven innocent." But playing the devil's advocate, can you imagine the stories they've been told? The things people have said to try to trick them? But for the middle guy like myself, for the Great American Taxpayer, I don't like being the enemy.
>
> [Baxter gets up to leave]
>
> Harold: In the building where I live the ladies get all kinds of catalogs, and I'm not just talking Sears and Roebuck. They get catalogs with items in them for fourteen thousand dollars. And no sales tax. That just makes no sense to me. It's not fair that these mail-order outfits don't have to pay sales taxes.
>
> Fred: I was down in Tennessee last week—it's 8 or 9 percent down there. Real high. But property taxes are real low.

In this conversation, the Old Timers place themselves ("middle guys") against out-groups threatening that position. Sometimes the out-group is the government. Often it is the University of Michigan administration. By identifying in this manner, they constrain which attitudes toward what groups are relevant. Their identity-based perspectives structure the way they talk about their interests. Although many Americans might agree that lower taxes are in their interests, the Old Timers attach this claim to their sense of who they are in the world.

Social Identities Constrain Considerations of Group Affect

To illustrate how social identity constrains which out-group attitudes they refer to when communicating about politics, witness the following conversation. It is indicative of the way the Old Timers resent University of Michigan officials for impinging on the way "their" Ann Arbor used to be, for gradually "eating up" parts of the city and removing property from the tax rolls.

One morning, we were talking about various places in town, and some of the Old Timers were talking about where they had lived. The conversation turned to the fact that the university had just bought a piece of property on a corner adjacent to the football stadium.

> Pete: They need that like a hole in the head.
>
> Sherm: Right across from the stadium I think, didn't that belong to [name unintelligible]?
>
> Pete: Sure did. He was holding onto that for thirty years.
>
> Tim: I think they paid about five hundred thousand dollars. There goes another chunk off the tax rolls.
>
> Pete: [Shaking his head, then turning toward Kathy]: They don't pay property taxes, you know. Last year 40 percent of the city was off the tax rolls, belonged to the university; before you know it, it'll be 50 percent.
>
> Kathy: Forty percent?! Wow.
>
> Pete: Yeah, they buy up every piece they can get their hands on.
>
> Bob: No one can say "no" to them. They plunk down a hunk of change like that . . . I think about all the businesses in this town, big important businesses that the U bought. There was that furniture store, four floors, the U bought that up.
> . . . [. . .] . . .
>
> Tim: They plan to buy up Division [Street] eventually.

Their opposition to the "U"-niversity is indicative of a common way they discuss many topics, including political issues: they place themselves by denoting what they are against, or to whom they see themselves in opposition. From their place on "middle" ground, they perceive themselves as political isolates, overpowered by residents of Detroit, university officials, staff, and students, and student-age generations in general. From this position, they use affect against the government, "the bureaucracy," and even the "local crazies on the city council" to talk about politics.

The following is a short exchange that demonstrates the way the Old Timers use their antagonistic orientation toward the government to understand policy:

> Mike: You know when all the problems with Detroit Edison [the local electric company] started? When that pharmacist up near Flint took

> them to court, saying that since they were giving away lightbulbs for
> free he couldn't sell his. And the court agreed, and then the Baby
> Bells broke up, and that was it.
>
> Dave: Well, who's "they"?
>
> Mike: You know, the people who want to deregulate.
>
> Dave: Yes, but who's "they"?
>
> Mike: Well, the government, political officials, I assume.
>
> Dave: Right, it's not "us."
>
> Harold: Right, we the people . . . [motioning around the table with his
> arm]
>
> Dave: That's right, "they" is "they." "Us" is "us." It's not "us."

Their reliance on out-groups as reference points more than their direct
acknowledgment of who they are as a group is not surprising, given their
objective and subjective social positions. Their sense of themselves as middle
people obviates the need to consider exactly how they are unique.

As noted in the previous chapter, given their status as members of dominant social groups—whites, men, and the middle class—their social identities are less likely to be on the tips of their tongues than would be the case
for a group composed of minority group members. Since most of them came
of age before the heightened salience of racial issues that accompanied the
1960s civil rights movement, it makes sense that they do not readily think of
themselves as "whites" (Valentino 1998). When they do address their race,
such references come out awkwardly, as if they are unfamiliar with the act of
perceiving themselves as members of a racial group.[8]

The tone of their exchanges is often light, conveying attitudes through
jokes or joking comments. One-liners or longer joke stories signal to other
group members who the out-groups are and, in doing so, reinforce the outlines of their collective identity.[9] In this way, their perspective of "one of
us" constrains which out-groups are relevant and acceptable when talking
about current events. To illustrate, the day after the city held a school board
election, several people started talking about whether or not they had voted.

> Mort: No, I didn't vote.
>
> Hal: Nah, me either. I don't have kids in school anymore—[laughs]
> I know that's no excuse.
>
> Mort: I don't even know any of the people in it—I didn't even know
> about this library board thing.
>
> Hal: Yeah.
>
> Alex: I vote absentee.

> Mort: Me too, sometimes, especially for president—I don't want to wait
>   in line for an hour. I've done that before, but . . .
> Sam: Yeah, just as long as they don't start teaching Ebonics or
>   something [laughs].

One can imagine many group contexts in which joking about Ebonics would
not be acceptable. Here, such a joking comment falls within the bounds of
their collective identity and in turn reinforces these borders.

As the preceding conversation suggests, affect toward blacks is a common reference point in their conversations about current affairs. These references hinge on their social identities even though they do not refer to themselves as whites. The following conversation exemplifies how this happens—
how their racial identity structures the way they collectively understand a
political issue without the blatant use of terms such as "whites" or "blacks."
The conversation was occasioned by the death of Coleman Young, an African-
American former mayor of Detroit.

> Baxter: They're burying that guy [Young] today, and several weeks ago
>   there was a report that said twenty of their [Detroit's] thirty fire
>   trucks aren't in working order. What did he accomplish? What in the
>   heck did he accomplish? Tell me, Jim, what did he accomplish?
> Jim: Careful, now Baxter, that's a saint you're talking about! Be sure to
>   bless yourself.
> Baxter: What did he accomplish?! He didn't . . . he didn't clean up Belle
>   Isle . . . [. . .] . . .
> Jim: He made his pockets . . . [laughs]
> Harold: Yeah, he lined his pockets.
> Steve: He helped the economy of South Africa by collecting a lot of
>   Kruggerands . . . helped the economy of South Africa. . . .
> Baxter: He stole from his own people, not from us, but from his own
>   people. I'm telling you, what did he accomplish? He's a thief.
> Harold: Well, the thing is, the people he stole from are thieves
>   themselves, so . . .
> Baxter: Like the school board, high-backed leather chairs, when the
>   facilities in the schools . . . [. . .] . . . roofs are leaking. . . . Do you think
>   they [the school board] sit on folding chairs at tables thrown across
>   sawhorses? No way.

In this conversation, Baxter says "He stole from *his own people,* not from *us,*
but from *his own people,*" proclaiming not only his own differentiation from

African-American residents of Detroit but his sense that the other Old Timers share that same identity. In this way, their political conversations convey their racialized ideas about their place in society, all without explicit recognition of their white majority status.

Social Identities Constrain Consideration of Political Principles

One Saturday morning, a political activist entered the corner store. He was campaigning in opposition to the proposition that would fund a new science center. His organization opposed the ballot initiative on the basis of environmental concerns. The young man walked into the store, handed out a bright green flier to one of the Old Timers at the other end of the table, and then placed one on the table in front of Mike. He made a quick speech telling the folks at the large tables to remember to vote ("Make sure you guys vote on Tuesday"). And then the rumbling started.

> Mike: What's this for?
> Activist: The proposition for the Leslie Science Center.
> Jack: Oh yeah, this science center, another gol dang waste of money. Next thing you know they'll be wanting more money to fund the staff at this place. [A variety of voices chime in as Mike starts talking to me.]
> Mike: You'd think with all the bird and nut people [environmentalists] in this town . . . [that a thing like this would never pass].

Exchanges like this make it clear that the group does not look kindly on large amounts of government spending. Their distaste for the government and belief in limited government go hand in hand. Here again, social identity is constraining these considerations. We might say that the principle of favoring limited government spending exists prior to their evaluation of specific policies and government actors. But their conversations suggest that their sense of the kind of people they are is not a product of their belief in limited government but is intertwined with that principle.

This is apparent in the way they refer to the government as an entity that exists separate from citizens. The following conversation illustrates this. In it, Charlie and Orville were discussing their tax returns.

> Charlie: I got a check back from the federal government yesterday.
> [Whistles and cheers from others at the table.]

Charlie: Yep. I send mine in April 15 every year, get a check back three weeks later. I don't know why people . . . [garbled reference to people complaining about the IRS.]

Orville: I won't be getting a check from the federal government. I paid *them*.

Ken: Then you won't be getting a check back!

Orville: But from the state—I filled out this thing for the Homestead Act.

Ken: Oh, you sold your house.

Orville: No, it's for my apartment.

Ken: Oh, I think that's only for homeowners.

Kathy: No, renters too.

Charlie: Oh really?

Kathy: Yeah, I think it's to protect low-income people who have to rent because they can't afford to buy a home.

Charlie: Oh, he's not low-income!! Shoot. When he commits suicide, he'll jump off of his money. If I did that, I'd stub my toe. He fills up an ashtray, then buys another one, and he doesn't even smoke!! [The others at the table laugh.]

Here, as in earlier conversations, they refer to the government as "them." We might expect such an anti-identity not only from the Old Timers but from any group of people that resent paying taxes. But when we look at the way the Old Timers collectively make sense of relatively new issues, we can see how they rely on cues from one another and shared perspectives to understand the topic. For example, one morning Mike and Jake were talking about suburban sprawl and the congestion it was causing in Dexter, a small nearby town. Many of them talk about Dexter as a reflection of the way things used to be in Ann Arbor. Several of them, including Jake, have moved to this town to escape the hustle and bustle of Ann Arbor.

Mike: Dexter. Went through there the other day . . . [shakes his head]

Jake: Yeah, so much traffic in the morning. Traffic backed all the way back to Island Lake Road in the morning.

Mike: Any talk about a bypass?

Jake: Nah, I've been there twenty-six years, and they've been talking about it forever, but no . . . and there are four hundred houses going up in that new subdivision under the viaduct too, and they say one thousand new homes in the next several years.

Mike: Bring in the money, though.

> Jake: Oh, but they just waste it.
>
> Mike: Where does it go? To schools?
>
> Jake: Yeah, most of it just goes to schools. The schools get so much money. [Mike nods his head.]

In this conversation Mike and Jake commiserate about the traffic caused by development. Mike suggests that although the growth causes traffic, it also adds to the tax base. However, Jake points out, consistent with their government-is-too-big perspective, that the revenue is wasted.

They do not mention a social identity directly here, but the way they easily agree about wasted tax money is characteristic of the perspective they have collectively created in which they situate themselves as honest, hard-working Americans exploited by big government. Their comments are indicative of how their identities as "middle people" are intertwined with political principles to create the overall perspective through which they talk about politics.

Generalizing to Other Informal Interactions

Both the men in the corner store and the women in the guild are participating in contexts they have created together, which in turn structure their conversations about politics. The men in the corner store maintain and modify a collective sense of themselves as "middle people," and they rely on this shared identity to talk about politics. In contrast, the context that the guild members have created is one of disagreement and avoidance, not one of shared identity. This suggests that some association contexts are more conducive to the act of using social identity to interpret politics than others. Does this expectation hold for the broader U.S. population?

Because this question implies a dependent variable that is not simply the presence or absence of social identity but rather its use, investigating it requires a focus on the observable implications of the use of identity, rather than individuals' self-reports of their psychological attachments (that is, their responses to closeness measures). If talking with others who have similar social experience enables people to use social identity to interpret politics, then through these interactions individuals are developing connections between their social location and political issues. Therefore, the more people chat about politics in these contexts, the stronger and more certain will be the linkages between their social locations and political opinions. In statistical terms, the expectation is that when we model political attitudes as a function of social location and informal political talk, we should find significant interactions between social location and the amount of social interaction.

Therefore, to investigate the effect of informal talk on using social identity to interpret politics, I make use of party identifications. My intent in these analyses is not to model partisanship but to show how informal talk helps people link up their social locations to political orientations in general. The concern here is not with showing why people are Democrats or Republicans but rather whether talking informally helps people clarify the connection between various social categories and political attitudes. In other words, the dependent variable of interest here is *not* partisan identification but the interaction terms within the models.

To do this, I use ordinary least squares regression to estimate models of party identification specified as a function of the social location variables of race, gender, and the class indicators of annual family income, highest educational degree earned, and membership in a labor union.[10] I also include a measure of liberal-conservative ideology as a control for the direction of opinion to account for the likelihood that using social identity to think about politics can result in different opinions for different people. For example, clarifying the connection between one's sex and party identification may mean stronger Republican ties for some and stronger Democratic ties for others.

I represent exposure to political talk in associations with a count of the number of voluntary associations respondents belong to in which informal political talk occurs, and I include a set of terms representing the interaction between this level of exposure to talk and social location predictor variables. Again, the expectation is that if participating in informal political talk in associations leads to a greater use of social identity to understand politics, then the interaction terms on exposure to political talk by gender, race, income, education, and union membership should be statistically significant.[11] This specification assumes that greater levels of political talk are a function of greater perceived shared experience.

I do not expect that the statistical interaction terms will be universally positive or negative, because the direction of the effect of more participation will vary across specific social-location variables and policies. Specifically, the term on the interaction between blacks and talk should be negative, because the more blacks engage in informal political talk, the more we would expect a tighter linkage to the Democratic Party, given the historical tendency of African Americans to vote Democratic. The term on female by political talk should be negative. Given the tendency in the past two decades for women to vote for the Republican presidential candidates in lower proportions than men (Abramson, Aldrich, and Rohde 1998, 96), we might expect that women who engage in more informal political talk would exhibit stronger linkages with the Democratic Party. Using similar logic, I expect the coefficient on income and talk to be positive (lower-income people tend to vote Democratic [Abramson et al. 1998, 97]), on education and talk to be negative (the more highly educated have tended to vote Democratic in recent years [98]), and on union membership and talk to be negative (union members tend to vote Democratic [98–99]).

Finally, the key test is whether the set of interactions has a statistically significant effect. Although I expect the coefficient on each of the individual interaction terms to be statistically significant, it is the significance of the set of these variables that is the focus of the analyses. By testing the extra explanatory power gained by including the interaction terms, we are testing the proposition that more exposure to talk tightens the linkages between social location and political attitudes (see Hanushek and Jackson 1977, 124–29).

Table 5.2 displays the results of this analysis. Two of the five interaction terms (talk by race and talk by education) are significant and in the expected direction. More importantly, the F test shows that the set of interaction terms has a statistically significant effect on partisanship.[12] Together, these pieces of evidence support the claim that exposure to informal political talk enables stronger connections between one's social location and political attitudes.[13]

However, these analyses do not address the potential reciprocal relationship between informal interaction in voluntary associations and the use of social identity to understand politics. Just as exposure to talk about politics likely enables people to develop a better understanding of the connection between their life circumstances and their party affiliation, people who have clearer conceptions of this linkage are also more likely to engage in talk about politics. Also, voluntary associations account for only a small portion of any given individual's overall interaction. In many other sectors of individuals' lives—at work, at home, with friends—people engage in casual political chatter. Is it the case that casual talk about politics in any setting helps people create stronger linkages between their social location and politics?

To investigate this in a way that attempts to account for potential reciprocal effects between identity and talking about politics, I turn to panel data. The 1965–1997 Political Socialization Study (Jennings and Stoker, forthcoming) enables an investigation of the effect of the overall level of informal political talk in which people engage, and incorporates a nationally representative panel of people who were high school seniors in 1965 and who were reinterviewed in 1973, 1982, and 1997. I use data from the latter three waves of the study, when the respondents aged from approximately twenty-five to

Table 5.2 Party Identification as Function of Social Location and Informal Talk in Associations

Constant	.14***
	(5.47)
Female	−.07***
	(−4.48)
Black	−.22***
	(−8.61)
Family income	.29***
	(3.31)
Education	.16***
	(3.84)
Union membership	−.10***
	(−3.60)
Ideology	.54**
	(18.24)
Informal talk in voluntary associations	.51***
	(3.38)
Female × Informal talk	.19
	(1.78)
Black × Informal talk	−.50**
	(−2.95)
Income × Informal talk	−.19
	(−.42)
Education × Informal talk	−.57*
	(−2.38)
Union membership ×	−.10
Informal talk	(−.63)
N	2,385
St. Error of the Estimate	.32
R square	.23
F test,	4.46**
set of interaction terms	

Source: 1990 CPS.

Note: Dependent variable is 0 to 1 party identification, such that 0 represents strong Democrats and 1 represents strong Republicans. All variables are coded 0 to 1. Entries represent OLS coefficients. T-statistics are in parentheses.

$^*p < .05$ $^{**}p < .01$ $^{***}p < .001$

fifty, because the measure of talk that I am using was not included in the 1965 interview.

The measure of the amount of political talk I use is a measure of whether or not the respondents tried to persuade others how to vote. In using this, I assume that the amount of vote persuasion a person attempts is highly correlated with the overall amount of his or her casual political talk.[14]

Table 5.3 Party Identification as Function of Social Location And Beginning to Persuade Others How to Vote, 1973–1997

Constant	−.14*
	(−2.30)
Female	−.04
	(−1.15)
Black	−.26***
	(−3.99)
Family income	.10
	(1.48)
Education	.16*
	(2.05)
Union membership	−.03
	(−.88)
Ideology	.14***
	(14.06)
Began telling others how to vote by 1997	.07
	(1.19)
Female × Began to persuade	.00
	(.08)
Black × Began to persuade	−.07
	(−.70)
Income × Began to persuade	.13
	(1.25)
Education × Began to persuade	−.31**
	(−2.72)
Union membership × Began to persuade	−.09
	(−1.60)
N	501
St. Error of the Estimate	.26
R square	.40
F test for set of interaction terms	2.14#

Source: 1965–97 PSS.

Note: Dependent variable is 0 to 1 party identification, such that 0 represents strong Democrats and 1 represents strong Republicans. All variables are coded 0 to 1. Entries represent OLS coefficients. T-statistics are in parentheses.

#$p < .10$ *$p < .05$ **$p < .01$ ***$p < .001$

Table 5.3 displays the relationship between vote persuasion and the clarification of identity with respect to politics. These analyses resemble the analyses reported above, computed with the CPS data: this is a model of partisan identification as a function of social location variables, ideology, and a set of interactions. I analyzed the effect of the act of starting, between 1973 and 1997, to persuade others how to vote. To do this, I analyzed responses only among people who reported in 1973 that they had not been engaging in vote persuasion. Thus, the talk variable indicates whether or not they reported trying to persuade others how to vote between 1973 and 1997 (1 if yes, 0 if no). The interaction terms are computed with this variable.

The significant interaction term on education is evidence that, compared to people who claimed not to try to persuade others how to vote in either the 1973 or the 1997 interview, people who had begun persuading others how to vote by 1997 gained more practice in using their social location (with respect to education) to think about politics.

Why is this one statistically significant interaction term important? The main reason stems from the correlation between partisan identification and social location among the younger generations as contrasted with that correlation among their parents. Like most Americans, the respondents in this panel study picked up much of their party identification from their parents (Jennings and Niemi 1968). However, over time the social location of these respondents diverged from that of their parents. Consistent with national trends, the level of union membership fell off across the generations.[15] Also, the level of income achieved by the younger generation is higher than that of the parent generation. But arguably the most notable difference is the level of education: The members of the class of 1965 were much more likely to have obtained a college degree than were their parents.[16]

Therefore, although the younger generation stuck with the party identification of their parents, they had to define what that attachment meant for people of a social location that differed from the one in which they grew up, especially with respect to education. We should expect that people who had the opportunity to work this out through interacting with others would show more clarification of the relationship between education and party identification. And this is what the results indicate.[17]

Another reason that significance of the interaction term on education is important is that income was a stronger predictor of party identification in the political context of the late twentieth century than was education. Therefore, we see a significant interaction on education and not income because it is this aspect of social location for which informal talk is able to do the most work over time. People on the lower ends of the income scale tend to vote Democratic for national office,[18] but the dominance of the Democratic Party among people at the lower ends of the education scale is less clear. There is some evidence that many less-educated whites defected to the Republican Party in presidential contests in the mid-1990s (Teixeira and Rogers 2000).

Finally, the statistical significance of the interaction between exposure to talk and education is especially important in light of the fact that the F test for the set of interaction terms is marginally significant at $p < .10$.

These basic models display the likelihood that people use social identities to understand politics during informal political talk. The results support the conclusion, reached from comparing the Old Timers and the guild, that having a shared identity facilitates political talk. In addition, people use their social identities to make sense of politics. Thus, these results serve as corroborating evidence of the processes observed in the guild and among the Old Timers, processes that are not unique to people in Ann Arbor, or to whites, the elderly, or people of the World War II generation.

Evidence from Previous Participant Observation Studies

To further establish the generalizability of the act of using social identity to interpret politics, I looked to other participant-observation studies of informal group talk. Specifically, I studied the dynamics of groups of people who meet in natural settings of their own volition as reported in four studies, Duneier's *Slim's Table* (1992), LeMasters's *Blue-Collar Aristocrats* (1975), Eliasoph's *Avoiding Politics* (1998), and Liebow's *Tally's Corner* (1967). I chose these studies because they investigated groups composed of people from different social locations than those of the Old Timers and the guild, several with respect to race. In addition, although only the Eliasoph study focused explicitly on political talk, each study addressed how people make sense of public affairs. In examining them, I looked for whether or not the group members used social identity to communicate with one another, especially about politics, and the conditions that appeared to covary with the use of identity.

Duneier (1992) provides ethnographic evidence about the conversations of a group of African-American men who regularly spend time at "Slim's table" in a cafeteria in Chicago. The men appeared to use social identity in a way that is quite similar to the Old Timers. In their conversations, the men contrasted themselves with out-groups in the setting, such as a token white man, African-American boys, middle-class blacks, and people affiliated with the nearby university. Moreover, they use their identification with one another to make sense of what it means to be a working-class black male in today's society. Duneier writes that places such as the diner in which the African-American men met were "important meeting places, playing a role in helping them develop and preserve ways of looking at the world that were drawn from their experiences . . . the integrated cafeteria concentrates a remnant of another world in a new, relatively stable hangout" (62). As with the Old Timers, the informal association Duneier studied was a group in which people made sense of their place in the world, and they did so by relating themselves to the immediate group and then collectively placing the kind of people they are within the world at large. The diner setting, as well as the shared histories among the members, fostered their communications along the lines of "people like us."

Likewise, LeMasters's (1975) study of a group of white, blue- collar patrons in a working-class bar near Madison, Wisconsin, in the early 1960s showed that this "blue collar elite" used their fellow regulars to reaffirm their social identities and at the same time to make sense of news events. When the men in this bar talked about the military, they moved from self to immediate group to larger social groupings when making their comments. Again, this is similar to the behavior seen among the Old Timers and the men at Slim's table. In addition, they talked about people invading their community, and did so by invoking the categories of "us" and "them." They spoke of the local school board as "those bastards" (177), student demonstrators at the University of Wisconsin as "crazy bastards" (181), and claimed that "the women are just like the niggers, trying to take over this town" (182). They made sense of political issues through the lens of people like themselves. And as with the Old Timers, these identities were constantly being reinterpreted. For example, LeMasters writes, "It was apparent at the tavern during the 1968 presidential campaign that student riots were causing the blue-collar workers to move to the political right" (181).

Eliasoph's (1998) work substantiates many of the conclusions drawn from the craft guild. Recall that the members of the guild did not have a large store of overlapping experiences. She found that a lack of shared experience among a group of white suburbanites who spend time at a country-western bar (the "Buffaloes") similarly hindered their ability to talk about political topics. This lack of shared experience left them uncertain about whether they were the same kind of people who shared the same views on topics such as nuclear power. Without overlapping experiences or acquaintances, social identities were not available to them as guidelines. Like the craft guild, even in the face of these obstacles the Buffaloes still tried to place themselves in the world as certain types of people. Eliasoph argues that their use of racist, sexist, and homophobic jokes were examples of such attempts to locate themselves in the world in contrast to out-groups.

One possible difference in identity processes across social groups relates to the place of anti-identities, or ideas of the kinds of people one is not. They seem especially prominent among members of politically dominant groups, as opposed to politically marginalized groups. The joke telling among the Buffaloes that Eliasoph observed, like the joke telling among the Old Timers, worked to place the participants in opposition to out-groups, without directly talking about who composes the in-group. Telling a joke about African Americans says more about who a person is not than who that person is. Just as the term "race" is typically used to refer to people of color, "gender" to signal "women," and "sexual orientation" to stand for "gay, lesbian, bisexual, and/or transgendered people," people at the cross section of dominant groups are not readily recognized as social group members. Instead they are considered the mainstream, or the standard against which others are compared.

It is possible that the social identity processes that take place during informal talk among members of mainstream groups are more often done by clarifying the kinds of people they are *not* like, rather than the kind of people that they *are*. However, this study suggests that some identity processes that other researchers have described as the domain of politically or socially marginalized groups are perhaps common to members of the perceived mainstream as well. Both Duneier in *Slim's Table* (1992) and Liebow in *Tally's Corner* (1967) concluded that a place to hang out serves a critical function for low-income African-American men. Both studies suggest that these meeting places serve as forums for socially marginalized men to feel a sense of self-worth and of belonging in society (especially Liebow 1967, 212–15). But the interaction among the Old Timers suggests that this behavior is not confined to members of low-income and marginalized groups. Indeed, the men at the large tables in the corner store continually remarked that the world was changing rapidly, leaving them and their sense of right and wrong behind.[19] There is some anxiety in every social position. Whether considering the men on Tally's corner, at Slim's table, or at the large tables in the corner store, people in each of these groups find comfort in interaction with friends and are able to make better sense of the world around them by sorting through events together.

To put it a slightly different way, whites have racial identity too. Although members of dominant social groups are less likely to verbalize identity as closeness to, for example, "whites" or "men," race informs whites' conceptions of who they are in society. When the Old Timers discussed in stark terms their distance from "the people of Detroit," they are doing so along the lines of us/them, with whites constituting the "us" and African Americans constituting the "them." Members of marginalized groups are not the only ones that perceive the world through the lens of their social identities.[20] We tend to miss this because the perspective of dominant groups tends not to be regarded as a particular point of view but as the standard way of viewing things.

In addition, just as minorities "turn inward," avoiding dissonant messages as much as possible (Huckfeldt and Sprague 1995, chap. 8; Finifter 1974) and doing oppositional readings of messages from the mass media (Press and Cole 1999), the Old Timers' behavior suggests that members of dominant social groups have a similar tendency. It is their *perceptions* of their place in the world, how they position themselves among other social groups, that matter for their understanding of politics. The men at the store, as white males of middle-class background, are not minorities in the balance of power in any of the political contexts they occupy. And as Republicans in a city governed by a Republican mayor and a state governed by a Republican governor, they are not partisan minorities either.[21] However, even though they see themselves as "average Americans," they perceive that they are oppressed by the government and threatened by local liberals. Thus, they too turn inward and use their group to interpret the surrounding political world.

Exceptions to Talking about Politics through a Common Context of Understanding

The talk among the Old Timers conveys a clear sense of "who we are," but there are occasions when the group does not reflect a consensus. These episodes reveal the mechanisms of social control that influence the political perspectives that structure their conversations.

First, there are times when social identities are nowhere to be seen in their conversations. Several of their discussions about the contenders in the 2000 presidential primaries revealed their preferences without reference to social groups. For example, one day Alex and Baxter were talking about the candidates. I asked them what they thought of John McCain, a contender for the Republican nomination.

> Alex: I don't like that Gore. I just don't like him.
> Baxter: Absolutely.
> Kathy: What do you think of McCain, Baxter?
> Alex: McCain? I don't know for sure, but I know I don't like Gore or
>   Bradley, so it doesn't matter who I favor between McCain and Bush. I
>   just want a winner. The next president is going to appoint one to
>   three Supreme Court justices and they serve for life.

> Alex: You know what they say, this campaign is just too long. It's too
>   long.
> Baxter: That's right. It should be a matter of weeks.
> Alex: Or just six months. Political scientists don't talk about that
>   though, do they?
> Kathy: As a matter of fact they do.

The absence of any social group entity here other than "political scientists" suggests that even in a context of strong group cohesiveness, social identity is best understood as a constraint and not as a constantly present force in the conversations.

Just as the Old Timers do not always make social identity prominent in their talk, they are not always in agreement about which considerations are appropriate for the discussion. Among the Old Timers, when conflict erupts over politics or other topics, it is usually minimized through joshing or acquiescence. If necessary, dissent is also sanctioned.

When a group member challenges accepted bonds and boundaries, he is openly derided. Dave, the self-proclaimed "only union member" in the group, is sometimes chastised for emphasizing this identity. For example, during one morning's conversation about an upcoming gubernatorial election, he crossed an unspoken boundary of appropriate behavior. While most Old Timers were not strong supporters of the incumbent governor, John Engler, Dave was the only one who supported the Democratic challenger, Geoffrey Fieger. Fieger was known for his past experience as a lawyer for euthanasia activist Dr. Jack Kevorkian and for his brash speaking style. Dave's support for him was especially notable, in that many Democrats defected to Engler in this election because of their distaste for Fieger.[22]

> Bill: [Shouting over to the other large table] Hey, Dave, what about that
>   Fieger? He's your man!
> Dave: I'm a union man!
> Arnie and Bill [together]: Oh Dave!
> Dave: Well, that bozo over in Lansing [referring to Engler] . . . I've been
>   union for fifty-six years, not going to quit now.
> Paul: Going to vote for him no matter how wrong he is, right Dave?
> Dave: Right. Solidarity forever! [Raises his fist]
> Bill: Oh Dave, we know you're a bleeding heart liberal.

Rarely do they shout across the room to make a point, but Dave's unorthodox views brought an onslaught of comments. Their policing of his identification with labor unions illustrates that their conversations consist of more than a mere passing of opinions that exist prior to entering the room. Collectively, they negotiate what considerations are acceptable to "people like us" and therefore what interpretations are possible. This strong sense of who is one of us and how such a person should behave serves as a useful guideline for both preventing and dealing with dissent when it does arise.

What happens when dissent does arise in a context such as the guild in which the members are not equipped with a shared perspective? Unfortunately for democrats hopeful about the benefits of debate, dissent was rarely engaged in by this group during my observations. When disagreement appeared to surface, it was not met with challenge or counterpoint but with silence or an abrupt change in topic. With no overriding sense of what the "right" stance was in this context, the members were on shaky ground if they wished to advocate a point of view.

Making Sense of Public Women

In the remainder of this chapter, I illustrate the processes of making sense of politics through identity-based perspectives with respect to two specific topics, female politicians and the 2000 presidential election primary. Just as the Old Timers rarely acknowledge that their group is racially segregated, they seldom openly recognize that their group is homogenous with respect to gender. In all of the many hours I listened to their conversations, they never once referred to themselves as a "group of men." The closest they came to recognizing their gender was in acknowledging my status as a woman.

Their recognition of my gender illustrates how they make sense of public affairs through an identity-based perspective without directly naming the social categories that characterize it. Listening and watching to the way they were simultaneously making sense of me and making sense of the proper place of women in public life revealed their ideas of appropriate behavior for women. I was able to observe, in turn, how their ideas of a "good woman" structure the way they talk about female politicians.

Their questionnaire responses about women's roles provide some background to this issue. In the survey, I asked them to place themselves on a seven-point scale that noted their position on whether they "feel that women should have an equal role with men in running business, industry and government" or "feel that women's place is in the home." With 1 as "equal roles" and 7 as "in the home," no one placed themselves in a more conservative position than a 5. However, only 23 percent (of the twenty-four who answered the question) placed themselves in complete agreement with "equal roles." In contrast, a national sample in the 1997 ANES pilot study showed 43 percent in that most liberal position. Using a more specific comparison, among white men over fifty with high school degrees, 45 percent gave the most liberal response. Another testament to their conservatism with respect to women's roles is that although none of the twenty-six respondents reported feeling close to "feminists," sixteen of them reported feeling "particularly *not* close to" feminists.

Although my presence likely discouraged some of their antifeminist comments, it also stimulated some very clear indications of their view of gender roles. Their conversations revealed a belief that women should marry relatively young, have children, and focus their energies on their families first, and politics later on, if at all. "Are you married?" was a frequent question in the first year of my visits. And my answer of "no" was almost as frequently followed with a "I hope you don't plan on staying that way" or "Hurry up, the clock is ticking."

Their interpretations of women in public life played out not so much from a standpoint of men versus women but from their perceptions of women with whom they are familiar and consider "one of us" versus "those other kinds." They contrast "women nowadays" with women in their lives, such as their wives and mothers. As they talk about what they see as the decline of Ann Arbor, they often hinge it on the disappearance of stay-at-home moms. One man complains about his former boss, emphasizing her gender. Many of them worry out loud about the choices their daughters are making, such as marrying later, not marrying at all, or wanting to get postgraduate degrees. As "common people" and "middle Americans," they convey a sense that the world would benefit if all women took cues from the women in their self-defined community. When their daughters have deviated from this model, it has produced confusion, and in several cases a good bit of anxiety. Notably, the antagonists in such cases are typically not their daughters but liberal professors at the colleges their daughters attended.

In this context, Hillary Rodham Clinton presents a challenge to their understanding of the proper place of women that they actively attempt to figure out together. Her very visible desire to have a prominent role in public life is in itself puzzling to them. But her marriage, displayed and dissected by the mass media during the Monica Lewinsky scandal, presents perhaps a greater challenge to their understanding of the role of wife.[23] They believe that women should undertake marriage to facilitate family life. However, they perceive that Clinton, in contrast, entered into her marriage as another business contract, not as a commitment to fulfill a tried-and-true set of family roles. They were repulsed that her priorities seem to be defined by her ambition rather than by her loyalty to her husband. For example:

> Al: Since [Hillary's] in office . . .
> Tim: But she's not in office.
> Al: Well . . .
> Jake: You know, I just don't think that's right. You can have influence, but to have her hand in things the way she does . . .
> Al: She's a smart person.
> Jake: You know, I think that once they're out of office, she's gone.
> Al: You think so?
> Tim: I don't know.
> Jake: Oh yeah, she's gone. . . . That is all for show.
> Al: Well, I think she knows what she's doing. You know, I think we will never understand—maybe Kathy here will—what that lifestyle is like, what kind of things those people go through. She knew what she was doing when she met him at Yale, she knew where he was headed . . .
> Jake: Yeah, I think so . . .

Hillary Rodham Clinton's marriage is "all for show" and thus is as foreign to them as the rationale for affirmative action. They use each other to make sense of such mysteries; moreover, they use the group-reinforced sense of the way "common people" ought to be. By collectively contrasting what "those kind of women" are like with their perspective on women's roles, they convey that women like Clinton have a lifestyle that is beyond their personal experience and antithetical to the view of the world they share. The conception of who they are, which they define in their daily interactions, allows them to clearly distinguish Hillary Rodham Clinton as a type of person outside their community.

Understanding Elections through the Lens of "People Like Us"

Conversations about elections in particular also stimulate a negotiation of the boundaries between "those people" and "people like us." When talking about candidates, the Old Timers sift through the options not on the basis of issues but through the lens of the kind of people they perceive the candidates to be. Are they people like *us?* Are they people *we* would want to be *our* leaders? They talk about what various candidates stand for based on information picked up from the mass media and surmised from their perceptions of the type of person a candidate is. They comment on whether the candidate is someone that meshes with who they are or represents a type that they are decidedly against.

On the day of the 1998 midterm elections, Tim reviewed the way he had voted that morning, starting with his votes on various ballot issues.

> Tim: I voted for the assisted suicide, for the farming thing [a land use proposal] . . . I had a hard time with the governor's race, though. I voted for [the incumbent governor, John] Engler. Did you vote for Engler?
>
> Alex: Yeah.
>
> Tim: Yeah, after hearing [the challenger, Geoffrey] Fieger last night on TV, I just couldn't. And the [Lynn] Rivers race [for Congress. Rivers was the Democratic incumbent]. I don't know. That guy [her challenger] was from Livonia . . . "Hickey," yeah that's his name. I couldn't vote for someone from Livonia.

Tim did not have to clarify what he meant by opposing someone merely because they live in Livonia. He could easily make that reference on the basis of their previous conversations. Livonia is a city to the east of Ann Arbor, closer to Detroit. On other mornings, I had heard them talk about it as a place on the edge of the urban problems they associate with Detroit. Thus Hickey would not have been an acceptable representative to the Old Timers, because people from Livonia are not people like "them."

When it comes to candidates for president, they also use where a person is from to help figure out whether or not they support him or her and as a proxy for the kind of moral values he or she maintains. In the following conversation, on the first day of the Senate's trial on whether to convict the impeached Bill Clinton, several men approved of a woman or a black candidate, provided that they were a certain kind of person.

> Arnie: So I gotta head home for the Senate trial.
>
> Bill: You're going to go watch that stuff? God, I'd rather die than watch that.
>
> Tim: They still don't know what they're going to do.
>
> Bill: That's what you get when you get one hundred politicians in a room. Bunch of politicians . . .
>
> Kathy: I don't really know what's going to happen. Such a mess.
>
> Bill: Yeah, I don't know . . . I don't want him impeached though.
>
> Arnie: They should do something—impeach him or neuter him.
>
> Kathy: Neuter!! [laughs]

Bill: I don't want him impeached because I don't want that Boy Scout in there. At least Clinton grew up in humble beginnings. This Gore had the silver spoon program. Some of these guys, you know, they've been in there forever. Like this new Speaker [of the House of Representatives, J. Dennis Hastert]. Where the hell did he come from? Probably doesn't have the brains God gave to geese!

Joe: Came from Indiana, I think.

Kathy: I think it's Illinois.

Bill: Maybe the next race will be [Elizabeth] Dole versus Brady . . . I mean [Senator Bill] Bradley. I'd vote for either one. That Bradley is a good guy. Rhodes Scholar, All American athlete. I'd vote for him. Where's he from? Somewhere like . . .

Joe: New Jersey, I think.

Bill: Oh yeah? I thought he was from somewhere out west, like the Dakotas. I know he's a senator from New Jersey, went to Princeton.

Tim: Yeah, he's got that New York-area accent.

Bill: Oh, okay.

Joe: Yeah, Bradley is good. I went to see Cazzie Russell at Cobo Hall when they played Bradley's team—Princeton. I like him. I wish Colin Powell would run.

Bill: Oh I'd vote for Colin Powell. I think this country could use a woman president, or a black—the right person, you know. Wouldn't want someone like [Jesse] Jackson in there. Christ! I'd move to Canada. But Dole, she'd be good. Or Powell, yeah I'd vote for him. I think that'd be good.

Tim: [To Kathy] What's Dole's first name?

Kathy: Elizabeth, or they call her "Liddy."

Joe: That Dole—you know they say that Hillary is smart, but Dole, I think she's got it.

Their approval of various candidates maps onto the way they perceive themselves and the kind of behavior they find admirable. They applaud hard work, and disdain people who they think do not earn their money honestly and through personal initiative.[24] Thus, they disdain people, such as Al Gore, who are in the "silver spoon program." The (distasteful) perception that Bradley is from New Jersey is outweighed by his All-American persona (and the fact that at this point in the campaign they were not aware of his policy stances).[25] They approve of Colin Powell because he is not a "crazy liberal" like Jesse Jackson or the kind of African American who makes them confront issues such as affirmative action, discrimination, diversity, race, and racism.

In the same manner, they approve of Elizabeth Dole because they see her as a woman who has fulfilled her role as dutiful wife and has stepped into the limelight in a manner consistent with that role, at least more honorably than another "crazy liberal," Hillary Rodham Clinton.

These conversations about elections demonstrate that their sense of themselves as "middle Americans" constrains which group-related attitudes are relevant to their interpretations. Likewise, their shared social identities constrain which political principles are relevant considerations.

This behavior stands in contrast to that of the guild members, who do not share a clear sense of who they are and thus do not engage in discussions about whether or not public figures compare to that standard. For example, talk about Hillary Rodham Clinton is short lived. In February 2000, Hillary Rodham Clinton announced her candidacy for the New York Senate. I tried to generate a conversation about this news item,[26] but with little effect. During a guild meeting attended by five women, including myself, I said, "Hey, how about Hillary announcing?"

> Ruby: Yesterday?
> Kathy: Yeah, Sunday afternoon.
> Ruby: Oh yeah.
> Kathy: What do you think about that?
> Dot: Well, I didn't think she was fooling around with this. I wasn't
>   surprised.

And that was the extent of the conversation. There is no clear sense of how Hillary Rodham Clinton should be regarded, no clear stance on her candidacy, even by Ruby, who had herself run for elected office as a Labor-Farm candidate earlier in her life. When the topic of Bill Clinton is touched upon, the women avoid stating their views, rather than jump at the chance to criticize or support him. In a context in which they are not equipped with a perspective rooted in group identity, they enter into conversations about public figures tentatively, if at all.

* * *

Among both the Old Timers and the craft guild, the contexts of understanding that the members collectively create influence the way they interpret political issues. These perspectives work by (1) influencing whether politics is an acceptable topic, and (2) by constraining which principles, interests, and group-directed attitudes are appropriate to the exchange. Through a group identity as "middle Americans," the Old Timers talk about political issues such as taxes, presidential candidates, and women in politics. In the guild, the context is such that conversations about politics rarely arise, despite one member's background as a Labor-Farm candidate for state assembly. Several members condemn activism among women and claim that they are not the types of people that have any political opinions of importance.

The difference in the use of collective vs. individual identities is not explained either by the different purposes of the groups or by gender. The male Old Timers are highly interested in politics, likely, in part, because of the gendered roles they have held. But the ease with which the Old Timers talk about politics is more readily explained by the factors outlined in the previous chapter that facilitate the development of a group identity: shared acquaintances and experiences alongside mechanisms such as the presence of out-groups that increase the salience of these likenesses.

The collective identities that the Old Timers clarify during their meetings are the same tools that they subsequently use to divide up the world and make sense of political events. The Old Timers collectively create a context in which they are, as a group, "common people," and they use this lens to give themselves the authority to confront, and to think about, political issues. With short comments as well as longer discussions,[27] the Old Timers reinforce a perspective as "middle-class people minding their own business."

These notions about who represents the community and the nation in individuals' minds and in their talk may not be offered up for purposes of decision making, but they are political objects nonetheless. Although believing "we are just common people" might seem to be a function of a lack of awareness of public affairs, it is actually a potent political statement that is a refusal to represent the "other" in one's interpretation of political events. As common people, they are the average, and thus have a claim to a status as representative of the public as a whole. Thus placed, they have no obligation to actively consider other points of view or the possibility that their notion of the "common good" is perhaps not universal.

Notice the power of this act, in light of September 11, 2001. Arguably, the terrorist attacks were an affront to all of humanity. However, when people define them as an act against "real Americans," they excuse themselves from recognizing the increasing diversity of the U.S. populace and prevent any affinity with people unlike themselves that a catastrophe such as 9/11 might create. In a group context in which the participants commonly announce identities with one another, this is an indication that they perceive similarities. In this situation, we should expect relatively more talk about politics.

We would not notice these mechanisms of understanding and these building blocks of civic life if we interviewed these people in isolation. Their political values could be measured through survey items, as the results of the self-administered questionnaire suggest. But in the group context, the political principles that are appropriate are delimited by the social identities communicated in the group. Even when the participants separately maintain an individualist view of the world, collective ties play a role in their joint interpretation of politics (see also Gamson 1992, chap. 5). Although the Old Timers espouse conservative values such as individual responsibility and a belief in limited government, they do not comprehend the political world as a realm of individuals.

If our concern is prediction of individuals' opinions, knowing the stances they will take or the candidates they will favor, then measuring partisanship and the shape of the debate among political professionals may be enough. However, assuming that daily interaction does matter for the way individuals interpret politics, we need to understand how people collectively build on attachments such as partisanship to interpret elite debate.

For example, knowing that the Old Timers are a group of conservative Republicans predicts accurately the direction of their opinion of Al Gore. They do not like him, and that is not a surprise. However, knowing their political leanings does not tell us the process by which they will evaluate a set of candidates they might find similarly attractive. When voters first become acquainted with candidates, such as occurs during a primary season, partisanship is not sufficient to interpret the differences across the contenders. The behavior of the Old Timers demonstrates that people can rely on identity-based perspectives to make sense of this information.

These processes also matter because recognizing the correlation between partisanship and vote choice is not, as the saying goes, causation. When the Columbia School scholars noted that social interaction helped people make this link, they were unable to specify the underlying process. The model posited here suggests that identity-based perspectives act as interfaces between politics and one's own social location. Between demographics and vote choice lies the process of people categorizing themselves and others and using social interaction for clues about how people like themselves ought to behave and what they should believe.

Each of the Old Timers may talk about these issues in different ways in other settings of their daily life, depending on with whom they are conversing. People in the United States vary in the extent to which their relationships reinforce each other with respect to political attitudes, specifically vote choice (Zuckerman et al. 1994). Some people may participate in multiple contexts that are characterized by different political leanings.

Nevertheless, the results reported here are important on both individual and collective grounds. First, on the individual level, one benefit of studying groups into which people have selected themselves is that these groups are reflections of the kind of people with whom they choose to spend time, as opposed to groups or contexts in which they spend time on the basis of something other than choice. Thus, even if the various contexts of their lives differ in what gets communicated, knowing what goes on in voluntary associations is an indication of communication that individuals are likely to believe is more consistent with their own sense of self than communication in a context in which they have less control over their entry and exit.[28]

Second, this study does not address whether group discussions influence individuals' privately held interpretations. But such a claim is logical.[29] Even if the men in the corner store associate with the other Old Timers and "people like us" for only an hour a day, they have reflected on political events while being sensitive to the concerns of such people. How different would their political opinions be if each of these Old Timers were to spend an additional hour every day in the "Dunbar Center" across the room or at the black community center across town? And how would they view local politics if they regularly joined the craft guild for tea? We cannot know for sure whether such interaction would reinforce the boundaries they have drawn between themselves and others in the community, or whether it would cause them to modify their interpretations of an "Ann Arborite." But we can surmise that the cumulative effect of participating in the conversations at the corner store influences the overall worldviews with which they confront the political world.

Most importantly, the results of this study matter on a collective level. What goes on within a group is important as a dependent variable in its own right. Much of the public opinion that is consequential for modern democracy is the aggregation of individuals' attitudes, as indeed mass-sample public opinion polls tend to treat it (Blumer 1948). But public opinion also operates as a social fact (MacKuen 1990), or an entity in and of itself.[30] Examining a conversation within a group demonstrates how this entity, or this collective opinion context, is created. Just as the dynamics of a formal decision-making meeting (for example, a staff meeting) can produce decisions one would not anticipate looking at the actors involved individually, so too can groups of citizens collectively produce contexts that are important forces in their own right. The fact that legislators regularly take comments expressed by groups of constituents in cafes and other gathering places in their districts as indicators of public opinion is evidence of the political importance of group talk.

CHAPTER 6

Public Discussion of the Daily News

On any given day, an Old Timer who joins the large tables and asks "What's the news?" can be quite certain to get at least one response. Sometimes "the news" consists of the latest gossip about the University of Michigan sports teams. Oftentimes, though, "the news" is a comment about public affairs. As with other topics, one person's news becomes another person's springboard to join the conversation. Gathered around the large tables, they collectively digest the events of the day.

However, the Old Timers, like most people, have only impersonal connections with most political events. Even if they have tools of interpretation on hand, it often takes a blatant hint for people to apply a relevant knowledge structure in their attempts to figure out a problem (Duncker 1945, chap. 6). Thus elite frames, or the way political professionals package information about public affairs, likely influence the Old Timers' interpretations. This is, as explained earlier, the prevailing assumption among public opinion scholars, especially for conditions in which political leaders generally agree about an issue. In these cases, "individuals can do nothing but follow elites" (Zaller 1992, 8). And when elites disagree or offer several different legitimate stances, individuals still follow elites—they just look to leaders whose views they perceive match their own (Zaller 1992). The bottom line is that opinion scholars expect that elites are responsible for the public's interpretations of politics.

In this study, I have argued that elites do suggest which categories are relevant to a topic, but the meaning attributed to these categories is a function of the identity-based perspectives that people develop partly through social interaction. Just as public discussion among policy professionals popularizes "common frame[s] of reference" and ideas about how individuals should apply those frames when evaluating policy information

(Chong 1996, 201), so too do ordinary people popularize ways of under-standing politics by talking with one another. Through everyday interaction, people teach one another the content of categories of understanding (such as stereotypes), suggest which categories are useful for making sense of the world, and also arm one another with perspectives that enable them to reject some interpretations outright.

The methods used in previous work on the interpretation of news have not been able to observe these processes, although communications schol-ars claim that informal communication with others is essential for making sense of the news (Erbring and Goldenberg 1980, 41).[1] Framing experiments have not captured the role of social interaction in interpreting the news be-cause they have typically not allowed participants to talk to one another[2] and have been conducted over limited periods of time. Focus group approaches have been handicapped in a different way: the settings are artificial and the studies exist over only a limited time frame. The following investigation is uniquely equipped to investigate how understanding the news works when people are in familiar social contexts and are able to rely on communication with others, as well as on the media frames, to make sense of the messages.

In this chapter, I investigate the way public affairs are framed by news coverage and compare this to the perspectives the Old Timers use to talk about those issues.[3] The comparison demonstrates how elite frames are understood through socially rooted perspectives. The investigation enables us to see how people bring political issues into focus through the lens with which they and their fellow participants in the conversation are equipped.

Expectations: Accepting, Ignoring, or Transforming?

This study acknowledges both the top-down and bottom-up processes in-volved in the public's interpretation of the news. Although the bulk of atten-tion has been given to the former part of the process, Just et al. (1996) provide a useful point of departure in a typology of the different modes of bottom-up interpretation that groups of people use.[4] In *Crosstalk,* the authors use focus groups as part of a multimethod approach to investigate how people make sense of and evaluate the 1992 presidential election campaign. Focusing on four cities, they conducted content analysis of the election news coverage available in those cities, administered citywide surveys in each location at three points in the campaign, and conducted in-depth interviews with pan-els of respondents and focus groups. Their intent was to examine how making sense of an election campaign is a process of information exchange among candidates, the mass media, and the public.

In the focus group analysis specifically, they investigated how citizens interpret a variety of media messages including advertisements, horse-race coverage, news analysis, and talk shows. They found that the groups did not always adopt the media messages wholesale (chap. 7). Some groups did display "following" behavior, but other groups ignored the message and changed the topic. Still others engaged in a "transforming" mode of interpretation: the group would initially use the frames that the media message had provided but would then bring in their own personal experiences to reformulate that interpretation.

Just et al. suggest that the groups were most likely to engage in transformative discussion when the topic resonated with their own lives. During the primary season, the groups rarely talked about horse-race stories in this reformulating way. The authors conclude, "Participants in the focus groups seemed to think these stories had little to do with them, and they were unable to connect them with their personal experiences" (168).

An additional finding from the Just et al. (1996) study that is important for the present investigation is that even though the participants acquired more information across the primary and general election periods, they used their personal experiences to interpret the messages more, not less, as the campaign progressed. This is counterintuitive to most assumptions about the role of factual knowledge in political understanding. Political scientists often fall back on evidence provided in studies such as Gamson (1992) and Graber (1988) that people rely on personal experience as a resource for interpreting news to console ourselves that people can and do get by in the political realm even though they have little factual knowledge about politics. However, the Just et al. (1996) results suggest that relying on one's own life is not necessarily a *crutch;* rather, it is an indicator that a person has done the *extra work* of recognizing the relevance of an issue to his or her own circumstances. Perhaps people do not rely on their own lives only as a substitute for "better" information. Instead, it appears that as people make the connections between their own lives and politics, they rely on their personal experience *even more.*

The concept of social identity can help us understand when and how people are likely to use personal experience. The model outlined at the end of chapter 3 anticipated the factors involved. To further elaborate, assume that a group of people is interested in a given public affairs topic.[5] If news coverage uses a frame that is consistent with a group's sense of the kind of people they are (their collective identity), the participants will be likely to interpret the information using that general framework, while filling in the missing blanks with their own experience. In the terms of Just et al. (1996), this is a *transforming* interpretation. However, if a message contradicts the group's view of the world and their place in it, they are likely to *ignore* the frame of the message and provide their own interpretation. Finally, a group of people is likely to *accept* a news interpretation outright when the message resonates with their prior perspective, provided their perspectives are such that they are ambivalent about how the issue relates to their own lives.

Two years of participant observation of the Old Timers and the craft guild had led me to expect that the Old Timers would do little accepting of media frames and more ignoring and transforming. I had two reasons for this expectation. First, analyses of their conversations revealed that they commonly relied on their social identities to communicate about public affairs. The group context was such that there was a strong shared understanding of the kinds of views and interpretations common to "one of us." This suggested that there would be little ambivalence about how an issue related to their lives. Second, they had often remarked about the "liberal media" in their conversations, suggesting that they tended to discount the media's interpretations of events because they often fell outside their range of acceptability.

I also expected that the specific social group categories the Old Timers used to interpret the news would be more consistent with their group perspective than with the media's messages. Specifically, I expected that the groups the Old Timers mentioned would overlap with the political actors named in the news reports, but that they would bring in additional social groups in their interpretation of news events. Given the large role that race played in their interpretations of a wide range of issues, I expected that a common divergence from the media's use of social group categories would occur in the form of the Old Timers bringing in racial groups even when these groups were not mentioned in the news.

Data Collection

The goal of this investigation was to study the media's effects on the Old Timers' interpretation of public affairs. Between October 19, 1999, and February 8, 2000, and between June 6 and July 19, 2000,[6] I observed conversations about specific political events and simultaneously gathered the content of the related news stories to which the participants had been exposed.

I intentionally limited the study in several ways. First, I focused primarily on the Old Timers. My attempts to include the guild in this analysis were complicated by several factors. At this point in the study, membership in the guild had dwindled to approximately four people. In addition, to properly compare the effect of the media on the Old Timers versus the guild, I had to observe their conversations about the same topic on the same day.[7] However, it was difficult to catch conversations in both groups on the same topic, given their different interests (for example, the Old Timers were more inclined to discuss sports-related issues such as the firing the University of Michigan athletic director). In addition, as noted in the preceding chapter, the women in the guild were reluctant to talk about public affairs at all. Also, the topics that both groups did discuss tended to be ongoing stories, such as Y2K preparation or the Elián Gonzalez case, which did not lend themselves to this analysis (for reasons discussed below). Only for one topic, an increase in parking meter rates, was I able to stimulate discussion in both settings shortly enough after the story broke to conduct a valid analysis.

The second intentional limitation was to restrict this study to framing effects. More to the point, this is not an investigation of agenda-setting effects. To properly test agenda-setting effects, I would have had to measure all information to which they had been exposed. That is, I would have had to observe every moment that the Old Timers met together, to measure whether or not they had discussed each issue appearing in the news, and to measure each individual's exposure to all news. This was not feasible. My intent was not to analyze *which* of the media stories they perceived were relevant to their lives but to focus specifically on understanding of stories.

Third, because my intent was to investigate the way in which the people I observed digested news stories together, it was necessary that I focus on breaking news (stories that had appeared shortly before their conversation) rather than ongoing stories. Doing so minimized the extent to which they discussed these topics with people other than the group members prior to conversations I observed. Although I tried to focus only on stories that had first appeared the previous night, this was not always possible. On several occasions, a story broke several days before I was able to observe conversations at the corner store. In addition, to observe their conversations in the most authentic form possible and to avoid making my presence overly disruptive, I attempted to wait until the topic arose naturally, at times choosing to wait a day until stimulating conversation about the topic. Thus, these portions of my participant observation differed from the first two years of the study in that I sometimes intentionally stimulated conversations on specific events.[8]

Although I focused on breaking news, they mentioned, of their own volition, several long-running stories, including plans for a new homeless shelter and the potential for Y2K disasters. In the analysis below, I make use of their conversations about these two topics to supplement the other analyses.

Fourth, I focus the following analyses on the Old Timers' discussions of breaking news about *local* events. Because the attendance at the Old Timers' "meetings" is fluid, changing slightly from day to day and from hour to hour and drawing from a rather large membership of occasional participants, I was unable to collect all of the news to which they each had been exposed. However, the media sources for local stories were limited—namely, the local daily newspaper, the *Ann Arbor News*. The Detroit local television news gave very little attention to Ann Arbor public affairs, not even events concerning the University of Michigan administration or athletics. The limited nature of local news sources enabled me to collect the vast majority of all television coverage and all local newspaper coverage.[9] Because I have the most confidence that the data on local news content is comprehensive, I focused the analyses on that domain.

This focus on local stories and on stories they chose to discuss may bias the analyses in favor of observing bottom-up processes of understanding. It may be on the local level that people are most likely to interpret the news through perspectives that are rooted in their own social context as opposed to the media message. People discussing local news may have firsthand experience with the topic or event and can, therefore, circumvent media interpretations with their own expertise. When talking about higher levels of government, especially national or international, people are less likely to have had direct experience with the issue, and therefore may be more reliant on impersonal others such as journalists for clues about how to understand it (Mutz 1998). The tradeoff between incurring this potential bias and providing a rigorous comparison of the content of the news with the content of conversations is one I intentionally incur in order to provide a detailed analysis of the way naturally formed groups interpret news media messages.

Focusing on local news adds one additional complication to the analyses. It is on the local level that people who create the media messages are most likely to live in the same or similar social contexts as the members of their audience.[10] Therefore, what appear to be elite-driven understandings may in fact be shared, socially rooted understandings. In the following analyses, I take into account the possibility that local news content is reflecting, and not necessarily driving, local opinion.

Method of the Content Analyses

I began the analyses by determining the sources of news that the Old Timers and the members of the guild rely on. I gave them a short questionnaire that asked for the specific television programs, newspapers, radio stations, magazines, and Internet sites they used for local and national news. (Please see appendix 3 for question wording.) They completed these questionnaires in my presence. Of the seventeen Old Timers who filled out this questionnaire, every one of them reported watching both the local and national nightly television news at least two times per week. Ten of them watch ABC news, five watch NBC, and two watch other channels. As for newspapers, the main source is the *Ann Arbor News,* which every one of them reported reading at least two times per week. Five reported reading the *Detroit Free Press,* six *USA Today,* two the *Wall Street Journal,* and one each reported reading the *New York Times, Investor's Daily,* and the *Detroit News.* As for radio, nine of them said they listened to news on the radio at least two times per week, relying on a variety of stations and listening at a variety of times throughout the day. Seven read a newsmagazine on a regular basis, and four reported using the Internet for local or national news. Of the four people who were members of the guild at the time of this study, three reported watching news more than twice a week. Two of them watched ABC local and national news. Three of the four members also read the *Ann Arbor News* on a daily basis. They used the radio "for the weather," and did not read a newsmagazine. Based on the results, I collected the content of both the local and national news sources used by a majority of the respondents within the group of Old Timers and the guild: the ABC local and national evening news and the daily newspaper, the *Ann Arbor News.*[11]

I pursued the data collection in the following fashion. After watching (and recording) the ABC Nightly News, reading the afternoon *Ann Arbor News,* and listening to the morning radio news, I would go to the corner store and observe conversations about public affairs. When the Old Timers brought up a current events topic, I would listen carefully as they proceeded to talk about it in their own terms. When the Old Timers did not start talking about current events, I attempted to start a conversation about one of the most prominent[12] breaking news stories from the recent press coverage, usually the previous day's newscasts or newspaper. Typically, I would mention a topic in a general way (such as "Did you hear about X?") or in a way that asked for the group's interpretation (such as "I don't get what's going on with X. Do you guys?"). I was careful to insert topics in a way that maintained as much authenticity in the conversation as possible. On several occasions, this meant I could not initiate discussion on certain topics. For example, in mid-December 1999, in the midst of the 2000 presidential election primaries, Baxter was talking about his admiration for John McCain. I wanted to stir up a conversation about a campaign finance pact McCain and Bill Bradley had signed the previous day, but did not attempt to do so because the jump would have been overly artificial.

To minimize the possibility that the people I observed had already ex-changed thoughts on a topic before I had arrived in the setting, I took two precautions. First, when I brought up a topic, I listened for comments that indicated they had already addressed the issue, such as "Oh, we already dis-cussed that" or "Where have you been? That's all we've been talking about this morning." In these cases, I would not pursue the topic further. Second, I timed my arrivals so that I sat down between "shifts." The Old Timers would gather at about 8 A.M. every day, replacing the earlier morning crowd. That way, I was able to listen to conversations about a given topic from start to finish.

There are two important limitations to my approach. First, when I posed a topic the Old Timers had not yet mentioned and were uninterested in, their conversations were relatively short, hampering my ability to compare their interpretations with those of the media stories. More importantly, because the topics they did discuss were somehow interesting and salient to them, they likely resonated with their prior perspectives and, therefore, predisposed results in favor of bottom-up processing.

To enable the reader to read the following results while taking into account these potential biases in my presentation of results, I identify which discussions I stimulated. In addition, table A6.1 (in appendix 6) displays all of the conversations about public affairs that I observed during this portion of the study, whether I initiated the topic, and whether a long conversation ensued. The topics listed in the top portion of the table refer to breaking news, while those in the bottom portion dealt with ongoing stories. In total, I observed conversations about twenty-four different current events during this period of the study.

Although the intent was not to investigate agenda setting, some back-ground on the nature of current events at the time is helpful for taking into account the political and historical context in which they were meeting. In the early stage of this analysis (the fall and early winter of 1999), the stories that dominated news coverage included preparation for Y2K disasters (possi-ble malfunctions of banking, transportation, government, or other systems because of the inability of computers to recognize dates on or after 1/1/2000); the danger of terrorist attacks on New Year's Eve (prompted by the discovery that an Algerian terrorist had attempted to drive a carload of bomb-making materials across the Canadian border into Seattle); Hillary Rodham Clinton's announcement of her candidacy for the U.S. Senate; and the Elián Gonzalez case (in which a boy arrived in Florida after attempting to flee Cuba by boat with his mother. His mother had drowned when the boat capsized, but Gonzalez remained afloat and was rescued several days later by fishermen off the coast of Florida. A controversy ensued over whether to return the boy to his father, who remained in Cuba, or to allow him to stay in the United States with relatives who had emigrated to Miami).

On the local level, a controversy over building a new homeless shelter had been brewing when this study began. More recent stories included controversy over a huge plastic "halo" that had been erected around the rim of the venerable University of Michigan football stadium, the firing of the University of Michigan athletic director, the resignation of the local police chief, an increase in parking rates, a scandal involving the president of a local conservative college, and an attempt to pass a local living wage ordinance.

In the second period of the analysis, the summer of 2000, the guild was not in session and therefore I investigated only the conversations among the men in the corner store. On the national level, news coverage was dominated by the presidential campaign, especially Republican nominee George W. Bush's stance on the death penalty and the execution of Gary Graham, a convicted murderer whose sentence was questioned by several death penalty watchdog groups. Graham was a prisoner in the state of Texas, of which Bush was governor at the time. Other national news priorities included gas prices and a rash of sexual assaults in New York City's Central Park by a gang of youths. Prominent local topics included high gas prices, the accidental drowning of a recent high school graduate, and a library fiscal scandal.

The issues for which I was able to capture the news content that the Old Timers had watched and also listen to them talk about these topics within twenty-four hours of the breaking story include the following:

> Forced resignation of the University of Michigan athletic director
> Drowning of recent graduate of a local high school
> A scandal concerning the public library
> A scandal concerning a nearby conservative college
> Increased local parking meter rates
> Automobile corporations' decision to offer same-sex benefits

The last story is a national-level story that had special relevance to people in the Detroit area. The Big Three automobile manufacturers announced that they would be granting health benefits to same-sex partners of their employees. I include it in the analysis even though it was a national news story and therefore may not have captured the news from which all of the Old Timers learned about it, because it was announced late in the news cycle the day before the conversation I observed. I use it with the caveat that although most of the respondents watched ABC's coverage of this story, a few may have watched NBC or CBS nightly news coverage, which I did not analyze.

Comparing the Content of the News with the Content of the Talk

The newspaper stories included in the content analysis were all the articles, editorials, guest editorials, and letters to the editor printed in the *Ann Arbor News* prior to the Old Timers' conversations on the topic.[13] All ABC local and national evening news stories relevant to the topic that had been broadcast prior to the conversation were transcribed as well.

The comparison in this analysis is between the perspectives the Old Timers used to talk about the issues raised in the news and the frames journalists used to package those stories. Recall that I distinguish perspectives from frames because I expect that the viewpoints people bring to bear when talking about the news are broader than one individual issue. Because one of the purposes of this analysis is to test this hypothesis, I do not assume that the interpretive structure that the Old Timers used is substantially different from that used by the news. For this reason, I refer to both the frameworks of understanding among the Old Timers and those conveyed by the news as "frames."

To analyze these frames, I operationalized the concept in three components: the main idea, or central claim about what the issue is about; the stance or argument of the story or conversation; and the actors mentioned. I coded for the first component, the main idea, to capture the core of the frame. This is the claim about what an issue is fundamentally about. For example, take the topic of the firing of the local university athletic director. Main ideas used in the news and conversations included (1) the accountability of local officials; (2) defining reasonable criteria for judging the performance of a public university administrator; (3) upholding the tradition of the institution; and (4) the effectiveness (in securing qualified employees) of affirmative-action hiring policies.

The second element of frames that I coded for is the stance or argument. The arguments used are indicators of the viewpoint that a person or journalist is using to understand a story. For example, when a person responds to an issue concerning assistance to the poor with the argument that such assistance should be reduced *because the poor are undeserving,* this stance reveals that he or she is viewing the issue through his or her attitudes toward the recipient group. Alternatively, an argument that assistance should be reduced *because the budget deficit cannot support further social programs* is evidence that the person is interpreting the issue in terms of fiscal policy.

To illustrate coding for stances, take the athletic director story for example. On this issue, the codes included (1) The athletic director should be fired because, even though he performed well in some respects, he made costly decisions; (2) The new athletic director should be someone with previous connections with the University of Michigan, because that person will be accountable to alumni; (3) The athletic director should not be fired because his firing is a product of decision making at an institution that is becoming beholden to liberal administrators; (4) The athletic director should not be fired because the rash of bad decisions is just coincidence; (5) The athletic director should not be fired because the man is performing well in a tough job; (6) The athletic director should be fired because he was an unqualified hire made through affirmative-action policies.

The third and final coding category pertains to the actors involved in the issue. Which actors an interpretation mentions is an important indicator of the frame because this conveys who the interpreter considers relevant to the story, either as instigators, responsible parties, recipients, or otherwise influenced members of a community. Including this category is particularly necessary for comparing the social groups emphasized by the media and by the Old Timers. I coded for which actors were mentioned (either participants in a controversy or recipients of a policy) and then also specified to whom responsibility was being attributed. I coded for a wide range of actors, including interest groups, institutions, individuals, and social groups. In addition, I coded for both the actors mentioned directly through words and those recognized through pictures.

In many media stories, no actor was attributed with responsibility (consistent with Iyengar 1991). Instead, in most stories, a responsible party was suggested but not explicitly named. For example, when University of Michigan athletic director Tom Goss was forced to resign in February 2000, the local sports columnist wrote that Goss had performed well in a difficult job and that University of Michigan athletics had been increasingly controlled by the president and the Board of Regents. Although the columnist never explicitly named which party was at fault, the implication was that the university administration was to blame for firing a qualified individual. An alternative would have been to blame Goss for mishandling his responsibilities.

When participants in conversations used an impersonal pronoun that clearly referred to a specific actor, I coded the conversation as if that actor had been mentioned. For example, in a discussion of local parking policy, one of the members of the guild made the statement that "If they think they're going to pay for that garage [with this parking rate increase] in the next year, they have another thing coming." In this case, I coded "they" as a reference to city government.[14]

After comparing the content of the news and the conversations with respect to these codes, I reanalyzed my field notes to investigate two things: First, I investigated whether the group members showed signs of discounting the media stories on the basis of lack of credibility or discrepancy from their own perspectives. Second, I investigated whether the group members started with the ideas, stances, and actors the news stories mentioned and then transformed them with their own perspectives, or whether the overlaps were a function of the members explicitly denouncing the frames and categories used by the media.

Results

Tables A6.2 through A6.4 display the correspondence in the main ideas, arguments, and actors (both the objects of blame and actors in general) mentioned by the Old Timers and the media coverage for three of the issues analyzed. The results with respect to these three particular issues are displayed because they are illustrative of the patterns across all six issues.[15] These tables display the general results, which have a great deal of overlap. This similarity in perspectives was more extensive than I had anticipated. The Old Timers did not simply "ignore" the media perspectives; in many cases, they appear to have "accepted" them, as the overlap in main ideas and stances shows. Across all of the stories (including the three not displayed in the appendix), of the nine main ideas communicated by the Old Timers, five had appeared in the media coverage. Five of the twelve stances expressed by the Old Timers had appeared in the news. The implication is that the frames journalists used either influenced the Old Timers, or the Old Timers simultaneously arrived at the same interpretation as the reporters.

However, this is not the entire story. The comparison suggests that the Old Timers "transformed" the media interpretations at times—they used the media frames as a guide but viewed and reformulated them through their own unique perspective. Tables A6.2 (pertaining to the athletic director story) and A6.4 (the automakers' same-sex benefits story) are displayed in the appendix to illustrate cases in which the Old Timers transformed the media frames. Table A6.3 (the Hillsdale College scandal) is included here to note that this transforming did not always occur. On this issue, all of the main ideas, arguments, and actors that the Old Timers mentioned were also mentioned in the media coverage. On no other issue was the redundancy with the media as complete.

To look in detail at cases in which the Old Timers diverged from the media interpretation, we can begin with the firing of the athletic director. In discussing this story, the Old Timers spoke about the issue using some of the main ideas and arguments emphasized by the news, but they elaborated on it from a standpoint rooted in racial identity. They talked about their belief that the athletic director (Tom Goss), an African American, had been hired through affirmative action and had therefore not been qualified for the job in the first place. This argument did not appear in the news coverage to which they reported paying attention.

And this was not the only substantial divergence. Another arose with respect to the same-sex benefits story (table A6.4). Although the news reports framed the issue in terms of the auto manufacturers' attempts to retain qualified personnel, the role of corporations in setting social norms of behavior, and equality of opportunity, the Old Timers focused on it from yet another angle: whether or not the policy is practical. They reflected the media coverage in talking about the issue through the general frame of equality of opportunity, but their distinctly less supportive stances suggest not an "acceptance" of this frame but a transformation of it.

When we look at the actors mentioned in connection with this story, we see further evidence that the Old Timers "transformed" the media frames through their identity-based perspectives. There is little match between media and Old Timer frames in the actors mentioned, much less so than was the case with the main ideas and stances. None of the three actors to whom the Old Timers attributed responsibility had been named by the news coverage. Looking at the other actors the Old Timers talked about (but did not attribute with blame), only ten of the twenty-six they mentioned were also named by the news.

When we look specifically at the social groups among these actors (noted in italics in table 6.4 and defined as actors that were not institutions, individuals, or organizations), only four of the sixteen groups mentioned by the Old Timers had been mentioned in the news stories. This is indicative of a pattern that will become evident shortly, in the detailed analyses of their conversations. When a news story emphasized a social group, the Old Timers typically would use that category in their conversations but would also mention additional groups. This style of interpretation suggests what schema-based theories of cognition predict: perspectives work to fill in the blanks left by the information included in a particular message.

In sum, the Old Timers' conversations suggested that they were persuaded by the overall frames suggested by the news stories, but they made sense of these frameworks through identity-based perspectives that enabled them to supplement and transform the media interpretations with the use of additional social identities.[16]

Evidence of Transforming: Bringing in Race and a Web of Attachments

A close look at the conversations behind these data shows that one of the more common actors not mentioned by the news coverage but used by the Old Timers was African Americans, as expected. For several stories, although the media did not name race as a major element of a story, the Old Timers perceived that it was and reminded one another of its relevance.

The first example concerns the story of a high school student who drowned in a local pond on a June night in 2000 after a graduation party. The story, along with a picture of the 18-year-old man, ran on the front page under a banner headline in the *Ann Arbor News*. From the photograph, it was obvious that the young man was black.

The day after the story ran, the Old Timers were talking about the marshiness of a local airport runway and the need for pumps to divert water away from it and toward a natural aquifer. The topic of the drowning came up, and Bill acknowledged that the man was black.

> Bob: All marsh out there . . . got pumps going twenty-four hours a day.
>   Runs on natural gas—going all the time.
>
> Bill: Oh that's right. That's where that pond out at Stonefield is.
>
> Alex: The one that kid drowned in—
>
> Mike: A kid drowned out there?
>
> Bill: Yeah, a black kid. Eighteen. Just graduated from high school.
>
> Alex: Yesterday, or the night before.
>
> Mike: No kidding.
>
> Bill: Yeah, nice-looking kid. Going to Howard University on a
>   scholarship, played football.
>
> Kathy: At Pioneer [High School].
>
> Mike: What happened?
>
> Bill: Oh, who knows. Probably got a cramp or something. Was the
>   middle of the night, one in the morning, so he probably had a couple
>   of pops in him. Who knows.
>
> Alex: His name was "Hall," so I wonder if he was related to all the Halls
>   around here.
>
> Bill: You mean the silverbacks who used to frequent your place?
>
> Alex: Yeah.
>
> Bill: Probably. Christ, Alex, you probably know all the blacks in
>   Washtenaw County
>
> Alex: Could be. Could be. Watched a lot of that generation grow up . . .

A few minutes later, Wallace at the other large table was talking about the same event.

> Wallace: I know that pond, we know that pond well! [The newspaper]
> said he was out there with a girl but I noticed in the paper they said
> he was swimming with his shorts on. Not like us, you know how we'd
> used to go out there. . . . So who knows what happened . . . [Orville,
> whom he's talking to, makes an indiscernible comment.] Oh geeze, it
> was probably too cold for you but we weren't that smart! Remember
> how there was that rope and we'd get rope burns down you know
> where?!

Here we see empathy in their comments, as they tried to rationalize the accident. They can relate: many of them swam in the same pond as kids. They do not speak negatively about the young man. Yet a strong sense of "us" and "them" remains. On the one hand, this is a person who resembles who they were as kids, and yet he is not one of "them"—he is a member of the African-American community.

They use race as a benchmark in their efforts to relate to the event. In doing so, they are not simply using media-provided tools to interpret the event. Instead, they use the media categories as a point of departure while simultaneously referring to their own social identities as reference points. They bring in additional pieces of information that are unique to their own perspectives on the world.

Another example of the way in which they brought in race to interpret a breaking story involved the athletic director at the University of Michigan. Tom Goss, who had been athletic director for two and a half years, was the first African American to hold that position at the school. In February 2000, the *Ann Arbor News* reported that he was being asked to resign. The news coverage portrayed his requested resignation as the result of a series of missteps and a poor working relationship with President Lee Bollinger. One of these missteps was the approval of the construction of a "halo" around Michigan Stadium. This "halo" was a garish yellow plastic rim around an expansion at the top of the stadium, which is a city landmark that the Old Timers and many others revere. This "halo" was emblazoned with pairs of Wolverine football helmets and one-story-high letters that spelled out "HAIL TO THE VICTORS," "MICHIGAN," and "THE CONQUERING HEROES." Letters to Goss and Bollinger, reported in the *Ann Arbor News,* complained that the halo clashed with the sedate brick and steel foundation of the 72-year-old stadium. Its reception at the corner store was not nearly as nice. The Old Timers hated this addition and were not shy about saying so.

During the summer of 1999, when it was built, an Old Timer named Leonard joined a table one morning and said, with a smirk on his face, "I've been admiring that new stadium addition."

> Dave: Really something, isn't it?
>
> Leonard: It's horrible, really looks bad. And now he's putting football helmets all the way around it. . . .
>
> Kathy: [I wasn't sure who he meant by "he." So after they exchanged a few more comments about it, I asked,] Who do you think is responsible for those decisions, for deciding what color to make that?
>
> Leonard: Oh well, the A.D. [Athletic Director, Tom Goss]. I would be okay with it without the letters . . .
>
> Dave: I had a bad thought, which I am embarrassed to divulge.
>
> Kathy: Oh, let us have it, Dave.
>
> Dave: Well, I thought with those big scoreboards and the schedule showing on the other side, and then this big "halo" with the backlighting behind the letters, the thing looks like Times Square. And well, let's see, Harlem isn't that far from Times Square, so there was probably an overflow effect there.
>
> Kathy: Oh Dave, is Goss from Harlem?
>
> Dave: No! But he looks like it!

When Goss's impending resignation became an issue, the Old Timers, consistent with the news coverage, did recognize the many things that Goss had accomplished during his tenure. Several of them felt that he was being unfairly blamed for several bad decisions, such as the firing of the men's basketball coach. However, as the above conversation shows, they also brought in racial categories to interpret the issue.

Again, this is typical of a general pattern: when race was used to communicate about an issue, they often brought in other out-group categories relevant to their social identities. The following conversation, which occurred two days after the *News* announced that Goss was being urged to step down, illustrates how they used race and other social categories that constitute their perspective.

> John: You missed it, Kath, you missed the fight.
>
> Kathy: The fight?
>
> John: Yeah, yeah, over the Goss thing.
>
> Kathy: In here?
>
> John: Yeah, that's right.

Stu: Ask Baxter why Lou left.

Kathy: Oh geeze . . . I don't know. I'll start another one [fight].

John: Yeah? Good. We like that. Yeah, Baxter, why did Lou leave?

Baxter: Liberal.

John: Huh?

Baxter: Liberal. I called Bollinger a "liberal" and he went off like a
    rocket. Stormed out of here. I said they were firing the wrong guy.

John: Yeah, I think you're right.

Bill: Heck, me too.

Baxter: He said I brought up the black and white thing and I said I didn't
    say that, and he just went off.

Kathy: Do you really think they're going to fire him?

Baxter: [News]paper says there's a news conference today at eleven. It's
    all over the papers.

John: I'll tell you what—if they're wrong, there's one hell of a lawsuit on
    their hands.

. . . [. . .] . . .

Bill: Do you think they'll bring in a Michigan man?

Baxter: Man? Who said anything about a man?

Bill: Oh, yeah. You're probably right.

Baxter: I wouldn't be surprised if they bring in a black Polish woman
    who's also a homosexual.

In this conversation, "the Goss thing" is understood with the use of
racial categories, but their perspective also makes available ideological, ethnic, and sexual reference points as well. As with the high school student's
drowning, mass media primed the relevance of race. However, the Old Timers
collectively elaborate on how race fits the issue and bring in additional elements of their social identities to help this along. Race is a very potent
and salient part of their collective identity, but it is one component of a
more intricate web of attachments. In their conversations, they use it as
an efficient tool to interpret events through their worldview as "normal"
people whose traditional lifestyles are being threatened from a variety of
angles.

When the Big Three auto companies announced that they were extend-
ing employee benefits to same-sex couples, the Old Timers were likely primed
by the coverage to think about the topic in group-centric ways, inasmuch as
the media coverage clearly emphasized the relevance of this story to gays and
lesbians. The coverage was noticeably positive, pointing out that these automobile companies were not by any means the first Fortune 500 companies

to provide same-sex benefits. The national television news story on the day of the decision acknowledged that this policy might be protested by some groups, but did not report any existing opposition. Only one allusion to such opposition was made. ABC reporter Bill Blakemore noted in one sentence that the Southern Baptist Convention had sponsored a boycott of Disney World and Disneyland when the Disney corporation had begun same-sex benefits. He added, downplaying attention to such opposition, that "Such benefits do appear to be a trend."

The frame conveyed by this coverage clashed with the worldview dominant among the Old Timers. Although the members communicated about the issue through the general framework of equality of opportunity, they did so in a resisting way, claiming that the policy was not feasible. They used arguments that directly opposed the positive tone of the news coverage. In addition, although they used the category of gays and lesbians to talk about the issue, they supplemented this interpretation with references to the United Auto Workers and a variety of social categories. They elaborated on sexual orientation as a social category in ways that were clearly not suggested by the coverage.

> Kathy: I have a question for you guys. What do you think of the
>   same-sex benefits the automakers are going to give?
> Bill: [signals down with his thumb]
> Alex: What's this?
> Kathy: The automakers—going to give benefits to same-sex couples . . .
> Bill: I think it's a bad idea. A really bad idea. How are you going to know?
>   I mean, tell me that, how are they going to know? Two guys living
>   together, not gay, they just say, "Hey! I can get you benefits!" How are
>   you going to know?
> . . . [. . .] . . .
> Bill: I tell you—hey, where's our union guy? I mean the union is behind
>   this—Hey, where is he [looking around for Dave]?
> Kathy: Hi, Dave—I'm sorry I got them started . . .
> Dave: What's all this?
> Bill: The same-sex benefits, Dave, you know who's behind that, don't
>   you?
> Dave: Huh?
> Bill: The unions, goddamn it, the *U.A. Dubbyah.*
> Dave: Achhh.
> Bill: Yes they are.
> Frank: I don't understand it.

Bill: Blame it on the Greeks! That's where it all started.

Kathy: What?!

Alex [a Greek American]: Sure, you know the island where all those women were?

Kathy: No, I really don't.

Dave: You mean you've been in school all these years and you don't know that?

Kathy: No, I really don't.

Bill: How come I don't know about this island full of women??!

Alex: Yes. There was this island.

Dave: That's where all the lesbians came from!

Kathy: What?!

Alex: I'm okay with that, I don't care what they do.

Frank: Well, that's understood, but the benefits.

Bill: Yeah, I'm okay with same-sex, just don't institutionalize it.

Frank: That's right.

Bill: You know, they start in on this, and then what? We're going to be paying the slaves back pretty soon, reparations to them, and to the Indians . . . maybe even to the Greeks. Goes back to them . . . back to Marcus Aurelius!

Alex: Oh, I thought you were going to say Alexander the Great!

Bill: Marcus Aurelius, cripes, you guys been going in with one another since way back when. And heck, now you're blowing up people, like that British guy [the previous day the *Ann Arbor News* had reported that a Greek terrorist organization had assassinated a British diplomat].

Alex: [to Kathy] So what are you going to tell your students, how are you going to answer that question?

Kathy: What question is that, Alex?

Alex: The one you asked Dave.

Kathy [I'm still not quite clear what he means]: Well, actually, I'm pretty liberal about this, Alex. I think it makes a lot of sense in a lot of ways. I believe that if two people are in a long-term caring relationship, they ought to be able to take care of one another.

Alex: Oh yeah, yeah, right, but . . .

Bill: Oh, but it's a dumb policy.

Frank: Caring, sure, but . . .

Dave: You gotta be careful about what you say to your students.

Bill: Especially at that place [the University of Wisconsin]; I told her, that's the hotbed of liberalism. Oh, then again, it's probably not any

> different than the U of M . . . but I told her that's where they invented
> Social Security.
>
> Alex: That's right.
>
> Bill: Bunch of goddamn socialists.
>
> Dave: The unions . . .
>
> Bill: Wasn't the unions did Social Security. They invented it right there
> at Wisconsin in 1931. Had nothing to do with unions.
>
> Dave: Well, yes it did . . . union people, collectives . . .
>
> Bill: Unions, just a bunch of trouble . . . This same-sex benefits thing is
> just the goddamn dumbest idea.
>
> Frank: Not a good thing.
>
> Bill: See it in the price of your cars, that's where . . . show up right there.
>
> Kathy: I'm sorry, Dave.
>
> Bill: She got us started. I gotta go. Makes me so mad.
>
> Dave: [to Kathy] You know, if I had my way I'd shoot every last one of
> them. Every gay and lesbian, shoot them all.
>
> Kathy: You would?
>
> Dave: Yes, I would.
>
> Kathy: Why?
>
> Dave: Because they are abnormal . . . to me.

The Old Timers understand the Big Three automobile companies' conferral of same-sex benefits in terms that hinge on social groups. However, the social categories primed by the coverage, those associated with sexual orientation, are only one part of their interpretation. The media's group-centric frame suggested that categories concerning sexual orientation and unions are useful for making sense of this issue, but the Old Timers filled in the missing pieces with other out-groups (e.g., African Americans, Native Americans, liberals, and socialists), with the out-groups being defined with reference to their social identities.

Circumventing the News: Relying on Firsthand Reports

Recall that the expectation that the Old Timers would display more transforming and rejecting modes of interpretation, rather than an accepting mode, was based on the observation that the group members share a collective identity and also commonly announce a perception that media coverage has a liberal bias. Did the Old Timers discount or ignore news frames because they thought the coverage was biased? Across conversations about these five stories, there were no remarks that supported this assumption. None of their comments revealed a perception that the *reporters* had low credibility or were reporting in frames vastly discrepant from their own views. When views were discounted, they were the views of liberal *activists* interviewed for the stories, such as gay rights advocates in the context of the autoworkers benefit story.

Even though the stories were not overtly discounted, I noticed that at times both the Old Timers and one guild member performed a kind of processing that was neither following, ignoring, or transforming, but was perhaps *circumventing*—interpreting the news with information about the event or issue that they had gathered directly (not through the media). This did not occur with the six breaking local stories included in the foregoing analyses but with several ongoing stories. One of the major stories of the winter of 1999–2000 was the possibility of Y2K disasters. In the two weeks leading up to the millennium, there was an average of 1.4 stories per day in the *Ann Arbor News* related to Y2K. Many of these stories dealt with an Algerian man who had been detained at the U.S.–Canadian border in Washington state for attempting to smuggle bomb supplies into the United States. After that event, stories about potential terrorist acts abounded. This was also true of the television coverage. Besides stories about what the federal, state, and local governments were doing to prepare for terrorism or computer glitches, there were multiple stories about "Y2Ks Do's and Don'ts," which gave bulleted lists of advice such as "keep a three-day supply of food, water, and prescription medicine on hand."

Despite the extensive coverage and headlines such as "Hacker Alert" and "Heightened Risk of Terrorism Prompts Warning to Americans," the Old Timers took the impending doom in stride. They discussed various precautions they were taking (making sure to have extra gas, cash, and kerosene on hand before New Year's Eve), but laughed off the dangers of terrorism that officials were warning about through the mass media. They claimed to be preparing, but only by doing the bare minimum. None of them admitted to filling their bathtubs with water or stocking their basements with cans of beans.

When they did admit that they were interested in taking precautionary measures, they did so by referring to personal experience and private conversation, not to news media "do's and don'ts" lists.

> Kathy: I wonder how many bombs are going to go off New Year's Eve.
> Mike: Ach, I try not to pay attention. . . . Do you have your generator all
>   set up?
> Kathy: No. We have a few cans of beans and a couple of bottles of water.

> Bruce: Yeah, we have water too—whisky! We won't be thirsty!
>
> Kathy: Yeah, and you won't be cold either.
>
> Bruce: You know they have a generator up at the dialysis center that goes on so fast you don't even see the lights blink, really amazing.
>
> Mike: I was talking to [a local policeman] the other day, and he said they're going to have cops centered all over Ann Arbor . . . and I was talking to [a man] who works out at Detroit Metro [airport] and I said, "What are they going to have you doing?" And he said he'll be sitting right next to that generator out on Ecorse Road, probably with his finger on the switch, just in case.

Similar references to firsthand information rather than media coverage arose with respect to the renovations to the University of Michigan football stadium. In December 1999, the *Ann Arbor News* ran a story that donations to the university were being hurt by contributors' distaste for the halo. The Old Timers reacted to this without surprise. Consistent with the news reports, they said the fact that the halo was finally coming down "was all about money." Baxter noted, "Yeah, they decided a few days ago. But they've been talking about it for a month now. See, the president was under a lot of pressure. I know of one guy in particular, millions of dollars . . . big donor, gives one hundred million [dollars], went into Bollinger's office and said, 'No more, no more, not until it comes down.' So that's that." The way Baxter discussed the issue was consistent with the news reports, but the consistency was spurious. Instead of the coverage influencing the Old Timers' interpretations, both the journalists and the Old Timers were drawing from firsthand accounts. On this issue, the Old Timers were connected with actors directly involved with the news of the day.

The guild meetings exhibited a similar example of interpreting local events with information obtained firsthand. At the time of this news analysis, the guild membership had changed considerably from the earlier period of observation. Its membership had diminished, and a politically active woman, Dot, had begun attending. At one guild meeting, I brought up a debate over a local homeless shelter plan. Washtenaw County, in which Ann Arbor is located, had been struggling for months to devise a plan for a new shelter. There were three homeless shelters in operation, which proponents argued were in need of expansion and repair. In October 1999, the *News* ran stories saying a new plan was imminent and, as the month progressed, divulging the location of the new facility. The initial story about the plan featured comments opposing the downtown location by a variety of nearby business owners.

When I asked whether any of the women knew about the status of the plan, Dot immediately answered, "I do."

> I was on the committee. They have a site over on East Huron, about a block from the railroad tracks. The men's shelter and the women's shelter and the warming house on Ashley are all in the vicinity. People are saying they don't want the people walking by every day [on their way to breakfast and dinner at the churches in town] but they have been walking that route all this time. It's a very carefully thought out plan. It's a huge building—people need to understand that it is going to cost a lot. Some of the money is coming from the federal government. . . . They planned to have a place so that they can be outside and not on the sidewalk, planned to keep the men and women separate.

Dot was clearly a part of a group of local leaders who were driving the news coverage. This was especially evident in the following comments, which she made a few moments later:

> There was a very good editorial in the Sunday paper. [A person involved with the shelter plan] and I were pleased. She had gone over to talk to [the reporter] after that horrible front page story [about the opposition among members of the business community], and had tried to tell her what was really going on.

Not only did Dot have firsthand information but a close acquaintance had direct contact with members of the press. These examples suggest that when considering the interpretation of local issues, the perspectives of elites or policy professionals are not provided solely by the mass media. They are often contributed by the people interpreting the news stories.

Even when the people in the guild or among the Old Timers were not sitting on local commissions, their knowledge of local events and relationships enabled them to devise policy scenarios that did not appear in the *Ann Arbor News*. For example, one morning the Old Timers brought up the topic of the shelter on their own. As Mike was sitting down, Baxter said, "I got it, Mike, the plan for the homeless shelter. It's done."

> Mike: Oh yeah?
> Baxter: Yep. I got it. Buyer Hospital [a local hospital that was in the process of closing down].
> Harold: Hey sure, why not?

> Baxter: Individual rooms, singles and doubles.
>
> Mike: Hey, you might have something there.
>
> Harold: Sure, dining hall . . .
>
> Baxter: Right. Their own kitchen, dining hall, loading dock to take away trash, big parking lot there, AATA [Ann Arbor Transportation Authority buses] pick up right on Michigan Avenue, lounge for them to sit there and talk with their friends.
>
> Harold: And to smoke and drink.
>
> Mike: Hmmm . . .
>
> Harold: Closes up in March.
>
> Baxter: Why not? It'll be three years before they get this place [the new shelter] ready [pointing in the direction of the new approved site].

Baxter, Harold, and Mike were talking about the scenario of using an old hospital as a homeless shelter (albeit in a tongue-in-cheek sort of way). Their awareness of local events enabled them to interpret the issue in a way that was independent of news perspectives. The Old Timers and Dot at the guild were aware of local events through *both* the mass media and their own social networks.

This process of interpreting with reliance on the frames provided by the mass media in combination with firsthand points of view underscores that local-level politics are especially conducive to "crosstalk" (Just et al. 1996), the construction of meaning that occurs as a by-product of audiences, mass media, and political actors anticipating one another's reactions. Herbst's (1998) research on journalists' attempts to interpret public opinion predicts this dynamic as well. In her conception, the interplay between the mass media and audiences is reciprocal, not unidirectional. Although media coverage provides explanations, frames, and arguments, it also reflects and anticipates the public's understandings (Herbst 1998, chap. 3; see also Herbst 2001, 454). On the local level we can expect that the correspondence between media and audience interpretations will be especially high.[17]

* * *

This comparison of conversations among the Old Timers and the content of the news they use revealed that mass media stories *do* influence the way people make sense of public affairs. Substantial overlap occurred in the main ideas, stances, and actors mentioned by the news stories and the group. However, attention to the content of the conversations revealed that this correspondence speaks to only a portion of the process of making sense of the news.

The Old Timers "transformed" (Just et al. 1996) the news frames by re-
ceiving the news and talking about it through their perspectives as certain
types of people—in other words, their view of the world given their social
identities. Within the general interpretations suggested by the media, the
Old Timers brought in additional categories to aid in the process of interpretation. A notable category in this respect was race. They made use of an entire
web of identities and anti-identities in a way that underscores that such categories are meaningful because they are rooted in individuals' understandings
of their own lives. In addition, the Old Timers did more than simply transform the news interpretations. They sometimes "circumvented" the news by
contributing firsthand information relevant to a story.

The importance of this behavior for our current understanding of the
media's effect on political attitudes is in the group nature of this act. The
reliance on elite-driven models of opinion formation predisposes us to for-
get that the process of interpreting the news is an active one. Unfortunately,
survey-based approaches also cause us to overlook the fact that people commonly perceive and digest the news with others whom they know. Not only
do people individually have ideas about the way the world should work and
the way people ought to behave through which they filter messages from the
mass media, but casual talk about news allows them to clarify and reinforce
these ideas with one another.

I do not, with this data, have concrete evidence of how long a news frame
stuck with the Old Timers or with the members of the guild. The analyses in
this chapter are limited to the way people interpret news stories shortly after
they break. It is telling, however, that conversations that arose about public
affairs during this portion of the observations were either about news stories
that ran the previous afternoon or evening or about ongoing stories—issues
that the media were repeatedly covering throughout these months. In other
words, seldom did an Old Timer bring up a news story that had been reported
a month, or even a week, earlier and then dropped. The exceptions are notable
for reasons I discuss below. That my attempts to bring up an issue that they
had already talked about were often met with "Where've you been?" convey a
group norm against dwelling too much on any given news event. They did not
shy away from talking about politics, but it seems that once they hit general
agreement about the intractability of a problem or consensus about who is
at fault, the typical pattern was to move on to another topic.

Therefore, the difficulty in determining how long media frames endured is partly the result of the purpose of this study and partly of the quick-
ness with which individual stories were left behind in the wake of new events.
Notice, however, that the general perspective endured across media stories.

Whether or not the persuasion that takes place with respect to a frame on a particular story lasts for a long period of time, the identity-based perspectives reinforced in the group endure. In addition, the speed with which the Old Timers elaborated upon the news frames analyzed here shows that the process of making a news interpretation one's own occurs quite rapidly.

Although this is not a study of agenda setting, the conversations analyzed here do support the contention that what gets said on the news drives what people perceive to be important issues. Once an issue is no longer front-page material, much of it is likely forgotten by the mass public. However, the exceptions to the pattern of discussing only recent or ongoing stories are important for our understanding of the role of identity-based perspectives. The news items that individuals or groups perceive as relevant to their lives become a part of the store of material they draw upon to construct their sense of selves. People hang on to news items that are useful for constituting how they see themselves, occasionally mentioning them even when they are not recent stories. For example, when the Old Timers discussed the firing of the athletic director, Dave recalled that when the halo first went up he had associated his dislike of it with his perception of Harlem.

The foregoing is not an investigation of whether these conversations changed the individual Old Timers' opinions that existed between getting the news and hashing it out with the other members. I have resisted drawing conclusions about the effect of these conversations on the policy stances of the individual members, because my goal is to theorize about processes of collective interpretations of events. But it is possible to speculate about the implications of these processes on individual-level evaluations. As stated in chapter 5, identity-based perspectives work to structure discussions about politics by constraining which social groups, values, and interests are relevant to the issue at hand. Becoming a part of such discussions does not mean that a participant necessarily agrees with each particular interpretation spoken, but it does mean that a person is temporarily exposed to such interpretations. This allows an individual to pick up from the conversation a stance consistent with that interpretation. To reiterate but reformulate a scenario given at the end of the previous chapter, how would the Old Timers' thoughts on the Big Three automakers' same-sex benefits be different if they had talked about the issue with several people who strongly supported gay rights? This is no guarantee that exposure to the experiences of people with a different perspective would change their minds. They could easily discount these hypothetical activists' statements as extremely discrepant from their own perspectives. However, because the Old Timers state, verbally and nonverbally, day after day that they identify with one another as the same type of people, it is likely that they do not readily discount what the other Old Timers say and the way they interpret the news. It is therefore likely that when the Old Timers interpret current events in a way that diverges from the frames the news provides, they arrive at opinions that are different from the stance they would adopt if they based it on considerations structured by the media alone.

One final implication of the results reported in this chapter concerns playing the race card. Several scholars have demonstrated in a detailed and rigorous fashion that political elites can influence mass opinion with subtle appeals to racial attitudes (Mendelberg 2001; Valentino 1999; Kinder and Mendelberg 1995). My results corroborate these claims. They also suggest a more pernicious effect of elite-led racism. First, the corroboration: Recall that stories about the high school graduate invoked the category of race not with words but with one small picture of the young man. When a news frame provided a racial category to the public in either a blatant or a subtle fashion, the Old Timers were quick to use it. This underscores the power politicians have to invoke racial attitudes with even subtle cues. But now the more pernicious effect: Whether elites manufacture racial and ethnic categories, or merely capitalize on racial antagonisms already present in the public, the processes among the Old Timers suggest that members of the public are not innocent of the act of delineating in-groups and out-groups. Even when the news frame did not suggest the relevance of race, the Old Timers brought it in as a useful tool of understanding. Political elites may inflame the fires of racism, but ordinary citizens fan the flames among one another. Moreover, they develop the roots of these hatreds in a way that intertwines such attitudes with their identities. Thus, when political elites play the race card, they are not just using preexisting attitudes to their advantage. They are perpetuating and, even more harmfully, deepening the roots of such attitudes. The result is that when and if elites try to reverse these divisions, they have to contend with strong priors that are anchored in individuals' core ideas about the way people ought to relate (or not) with one another in the world.

CHAPTER 7

The Data Are *Not* Given: Perspectives, Political Trust, and the 2000 Elections

> Kathy: Say, five years from now, somebody, like, I don't know, who's ten years old now, says, you know, "What happened in the election of 2000? Everyone says it was this crazy election, and really unusual." How would you explain what happened?
>
> Baxter: I don't think it was unusual.
>
> Tim: I would basically say that it absolutely showed the flaws of our outdated election process. I mean, the politicians . . .
>
> Baxter: Be careful, Tim. Be careful how you make a general statement about that. I think it showed how strong the electoral process *is,* how well it *did* work, with certain, ah, problems that could be fixed, but to say it showed the flaw in the system, that's a rather broad statement.[1]
>
> [Conversation with two of the Old Timers, regulars to the corner store]

> Kathy: You know, five years from now, say you had to explain this election to a kid who is, say, ten years old right now. How would you explain the election of 2000?
>
> Sarah: I'd say it was an *appointment.* I think that's what it was. It was an *appointment,* not an election.
>
> [Conversation with an African-American woman, a regular at the corner store]

My question to Tim and Baxter, as well as my question to Sarah, concerned the same election, the presidential election of 2000 between Republican George W. Bush and Democrat Al Gore.[2] Tim, Baxter, and Sarah spend their mornings in the same small store and experienced the election within the same media environment of Ann Arbor, Michigan.[3] How can it be that Tim, Baxter, and the rest of the Old Timers interpreted the outcome of the election in a way that differed greatly from the way Sarah and her friends interpreted it? Although they may share the same small space every morning, they have noticeably different views of the world.

When the election of 2000 occurred in November, and then dragged on into December, I returned to the corner store for a final investigation of how this works. Throughout my observations, the Old Timers had expressed clear disdain for a variety of politicians, and yet their conversations conveyed an enduring faith in the institutions of government. Here was an event that brought into the open various imperfections of electoral institutions. I wanted to know, how were they making sense of it? At the same time, I wanted to contrast this with how others in the corner store, who were much less vocal about their belief in the fundamental soundness of government institutions, were interpreting the same event. My observations of the group between the fall of 1997 and the late summer of 2000 had led me to conclude that perspectives matter for the way in which people interpret political events.

This chapter demonstrates why the concept of *perspective* is integral to a dynamic theory of political opinion. Explanations of attitude change that rely solely on preferences or attitudes toward particular groups overlook a fundamental part of the updating process: our perspectives influence how we perceive new information. I use observations of attempts to interpret the 2000 election outcome—among the Old Timers and among the African Americans who sit on the other side of the room—as an illustration of how two groups of people who share the same small room morning after morning, yet do not interact, can interpret the same national event quite differently. I draw out the implications of this for our understanding of the way people update their attitudes of trust in government.

Perspectives and Updating Attitudes of Political Trust

We might say that the effect of the election of 2000 on individuals' levels of trust "depends on how you look at it." However, according to some theories of political trust, such subjective interpretations are irrelevant. Take, for example, Hardin's model of the "street-level epistemology of trust," or the way in which ordinary citizens develop their notions of government trust over time (1993). This is a quasi-Bayesian model in which attitudes of trust are updated in response to new information about the motives or interests of government. Decisions to trust are not only based on facts about the interactions an actor has with government but on judgments of whether it is in the interests of the government to behave in ways the actor expects the government to act.[4]

In Hardin's formulation, prior attitudes on whether it is reasonable to trust government actors are updated on the basis of two types of information: (1) the benefits an actor received from trusting the government in the past; and (2) knowledge about whether the government has an incentive to act in ways that are consistent with what the truster expects the government to do. Hardin expects that interpersonal variations in degree of trust arise as a function of previous experience. People who pick up signals early and often that the government should not be trusted will have relatively distrusting priors. Distrusting priors can be overcome with information that suggests it is in the government's interests to act in ways consistent with the truster's expectations.

As all-encompassing as this model is, it misses a crucial part of the updating or learning process. It acknowledges that members of a society likely vary in how much they trust government, but it does not sufficiently account for how these levels of trust persist over time. This limitation results from treating episodes of government performance as given bits of information, not as information that is perceived through preexisting perspectives. According to his account, if two people experience an identical interaction with the government yet come away from it with different levels of trust in government, the reason must be their prior degree of trust. In other words, the pieces of information from that experience—the data—are treated as given.

But the data are not given.[5] Two people complete an identical experience with different notions of trust not just because of their prior levels of trust but because they *interpret that experience* in different ways, structured by their socially rooted perspectives. The strength of individuals' prior attitudes of trust influences *how much* a given experience influences their degree of trust, but prior perspectives influence *how* people think about trust[6] and *what* people learn from a given experience.

Hardin indirectly acknowledges that socially rooted perspectives play a role when he notes that the truster does not need to have direct contact with government actors. The model assumes that an actor may not know how an actor within government will treat him or her specifically. However, "What I can know reasonably well is that the incentives someone in office faces are in the right direction . . . The political officeholder has no particular interest in me, need not even know about me, but may have a strong interest in supporting *people in my position* in relevant ways" (510, emphasis added).

A judgment of who constitutes "people in my position" is a function of one's social identity. However, Hardin does not conceptualize identity as a psychological attachment that influences interpretation. He notes that some theorists argue "that people are more inclined to like those whom they see as like themselves" but then counters, "This may depend on nothing more than that we are merely better at predicting the behavior of those most like ourselves" (512).

However, who constitutes "those most like ourselves" is a subjective judgment. "Likeness" can be defined on a variety of dimensions. A full theory of the dynamics of the connection between citizens and government requires attention to the psychological perspectives with which people define themselves and interpret their interactions with others, including government actors.

I focus on Hardin's account as an example of a rational choice model to demonstrate how such theories discount the role of social identities and the perspectives they inform. Some interest-based accounts of orientations toward government do acknowledge that identities play an important role. In *Consent, Dissent, and Patriotism*, Levi (1997) examines citizens' willingness to obey laws. Her model is one of contingent consent: citizens are more likely to give consent to a government if they perceive that it, as well as other citizens, are acting fairly toward them. She theorizes about aggregate behavior and therefore does not use the concept of identity directly in her model. However, she notes that a focus on individual citizens would require attention to identity. "Whatever rule or norm informs the choice to comply is often shared and constructed by a group of actors who possess a common identity. This may mean shared interests, but it as often means a shared culture—racial, religious, or ethnic based—that may cut across interests" (10). Moreover, she suggests that citizens respond to democratic institutions in a variety of ways, and one source of these various responses is that "not all citizens perceive government in the same way. Not only are there individual variations in beliefs, information, economic incentives, ideologies, and other factors that influence compliance, there are also systematic variations by groups that have distinct experiences with the fairness of government or distinct differences in their standards of fairness" (218). In Levi's formulation, collective identities are a key component in individuals' choices about whether or not to comply. Variations across citizens in attitudes toward the government result from differences in actual experiences as well as differences in perceptions.

The role of identity-based perspectives is especially important when explaining individuals' compliance with the law or their trust in government when they have not had direct experience with law enforcement or other government officials. As Levi points out, doing so requires an examination of individuals' perceptions of the treatment of "people like me"—perceptions rooted in social identity.[7]

Illustrating the Role of Perspectives

I use conversations about the aftermath of the 2000 election to illuminate how prior perspectives are related to the way the groups in the corner store perceived the 2000 election outcome. The comparison of these conversations strongly suggests that information about the election was not given, but was perceived through the perspectives of the different groups' members.

Why is the concept of perspective necessary? Why not just refer to partisan identification? A person's candidate preference can predict his or her interpretation of the outcome of the 2000 election (Sunstein 2001, 5). However, recognizing the correlation between party identification and interpretations is only a partial explanation. Moreover, it says nothing about the nature of the process of interpreting the outcome. Although claims that we can predict interpretations with prior party identification often are based on an *assumption* that this correlation is driven by social interaction with likeminded others (Sunstein 2001, 7), it remains an empirical question what this process looks like.

To be clear, this chapter is not an attempt to understand either all citizens' interpretations of the 2000 election or their posterior perceptions of trust in government. Instead, it uses conversations about the election among two different groups of people to illuminate the role of prior perspectives in the act of interpreting current political events.

The analyses are limited in the following ways. First, I only gathered survey data on trust in government as opposed to trust specifically in electoral institutions and the Supreme Court because I had administered the survey well before it was clear that confidence in electoral institutions would be a pressing issue. Second, I compare the dynamics of trust across two groups that meet in the corner store: the Old Timers and a group of African Americans who sit at the small tables across the room. I attempt to demonstrate the differences in their interpretations of the election of 2000 as a function of the variations in their prior perspectives, but the groups also differ in other ways. Most significantly, the groups have different racial and class compositions. My intention in the investigation was not to ignore these differences but to further uncover how they are intertwined with the perspectives with which they viewed political issues.

Third, since this is a type of natural experiment, I did not control the treatment. Given the ubiquity of the coverage of this event, I am assuming that the people I observed were exposed to similar information about the election through the mass media, although this exposure likely differed in frequency.[8] The intent is to provide as rigorous an examination of the updating process as possible, while fully recognizing the limitations of conducting such a test in a natural environment. The rationale behind the investigation is that when two groups of people, exposed to the same treatment, provide different interpretations of the event, the cause must lie either in the priors with which they approached the message or the process by which they interpreted it, or both. I assume, based on the preceding analyses, that groups do not differ qualitatively in the process by which they use socially rooted perspectives to make sense of politics.

Background of the 2000 Vote Count

The reasons that the 2000 presidential election displayed in full relief the imperfections of U.S. electoral institutions read like a political novel.[9] Announcement of the winner of the election was delayed thirty-six days, from Election Day, November 7, until December 13. On election night, the decision came down to the state of Florida, whose governor was George W. Bush's brother, Jeb Bush. The drama reached a fever pitch as the television networks first began to declare that Al Gore had won Florida even before polls in the panhandle, or western portion, of the state had closed. Then, as more returns came in, the networks reconsidered. Early in the morning (2:15 A.M. eastern standard time), the networks declared that Bush had won the state and thus the election, and Gore called to concede. A little over an hour later, he called back and retracted his concession.

The closeness of the race triggered an automatic recount in Florida. As the recount began, both the Gore and Bush campaigns maneuvered to obtain a favorable outcome. The recount produced a Bush lead of 229 votes. This was not the final decision, however. A large number of voters in Palm Beach County claimed that they had been confused by the "butterfly ballot"—which listed presidential candidates on both the left and right sides of the page and required voters to punch appropriate holes arrayed down the middle—and inadvertently voted for Reform Party candidate Pat Buchanan rather than for their intended candidate, Gore. Based on these complaints, as well as arguments that many Florida absentee ballots should have been omitted from the final count because of improper validation, the Gore campaign asked four counties to recount the ballots by hand.

In response, Bush's lawyers asked for an injunction on November 11. Two days later, a U.S. District Court judge denied their request. However, the Florida Secretary of State, Katherine Harris, effectively declared that the hand count could not be completed by the upcoming filing deadline. Notably, Harris, a Republican, had campaigned for Bush during the election. The Gore team took its case to court, lost the decision, and appealed to the Florida Supreme Court. This court (six of seven justices had been appointed by a Democratic governor) ruled in favor of Gore, calling for a hand count in the four counties. To counter, the Bush team appealed to the Supreme Court of the United States.

The Court, on December 4, remanded the case of *Bush v. Palm Beach County Canvassing Board* back to the state supreme court. Meanwhile, in related cases, the Florida Supreme Court ruled on December 8 that a recount of all uninspected undervotes was to begin immediately. The Bush team appealed the decision to the circuit court and the U.S. Supreme Court. The next day, December 11, in a 5–4 decision, the Supreme Court issued an injunction to stop the recounts, and heard oral arguments in *Bush v Gore*. At 10 P.M. on the 12th, the Supreme Court issued a 5–4 ruling that stated, as Gillman (2001) explains, "The manual recounts authorized by the Florida Supreme Court violate the equal protection clause of the Constitution because the standard for reviewing ballots, which focused on discerning 'the intent of the voter,' allowed for too much variation in the way identical ballots might be evaluated" (xxiii). On December 13, Gore conceded and Bush was declared the winner.[10]

This whirlwind of events provided many reasons for disenchantment with and disconnection from government. Here, for the first time in U.S. history, the U.S. Supreme Court intervened in the outcome of a presidential election. In addition, for only the fourth time in U.S. history, the candidate that won the popular vote did not become president because he lost the electoral vote. The butterfly ballot and the abundant evidence that election counts are not perfect cast doubt on the reliability of voting systems and vote counts. Moreover, several predominantly black communities in Florida appeared to have disproportionately large numbers of undercounted votes. The events resulted in lead stories and front page headlines that revealed the imperfections of the electoral college, state voting procedures, and the Supreme Court. The various legal claims and allegations left many people confused.

As the vote count dragged on, many people turned back to their daily lives, but the public was clearly saturated with news of the election. I used exposure to this information as the "treatment" in my comparison of the way the Old Timers and the African Americans in the corner store interpreted the same event. For four mornings in January 2001,[11] I split my time between the Old Timers and the African Americans who sit at the small tables near the windows. I asked each group open-ended questions about their reaction to the election, the vote count, the court decisions, and their perceptions of trust in government.

Comparing the Old Timers and the African-American Group in the Corner Store

A first glance at the Old Timers' levels of trust in government prior to the election comes from the survey I administered before the primary and general election seasons.[12] While the Old Timers' survey responses cannot directly reveal the way their interpretations of trust in government are colored by their identity-based perspectives, they do provide a benchmark for assessing their attitudes on trust before the election. In general, their responses reiterate their ambivalent trust in the federal government. I compared their responses on several trust-related questions to nationwide data as well as to a subsample of white men over fifty with a high school degree (the demographic subgroup of which they are a part). In response to the question "How much of the time do you think you can trust the government in Washington to do what is right?" the Old Timers offered a mix of responses, with the balance—58 percent—falling on the trusting side. Six felt they could trust the government "just about always," nine responded "most of the time," and eleven chose "only some of the time." This is a relatively high degree of trust. According to the 1996 ANES, only 33 percent of the nation responded "always" or "some of the time" to this question. Thirty-four percent of the Old Timers' demographic subgroup responded this way. Previous research suggests that responses to this question are driven by attitudes toward incumbents and not necessarily by attitudes toward government institutions (Citrin 1974). In that case, the Old Timers' strong distaste for Clinton makes this high level of trust all the more striking.

At the same time, however, the Old Timers were more likely than the nation as a whole to believe that the government "wastes a lot of the money we pay in taxes." Twenty-two of the twenty-six respondents chose this response. Four said that it wastes "some." (None of them felt that the government wastes little money.) By comparison, 60 percent of the nation (and also their specific demographic) felt the government wastes "a lot" of tax money.[13] Also, when asked which level of government the respondent had the least faith in, fourteen of the twenty-three Old Timers said "national." In sum, their survey responses alone present a mixed view of their level of trust in government.

When we look to their conversations, the nature of their levels of trust in government becomes clearer. In the three years preceding the election, in their interactions with me and with each other, the Old Timers displayed a distrust of politicians and yet an enduring loyalty to and pride in the basic machinery of government. This love-hate stance is consistent with the survey evidence that showed a general trust in government to do what is right combined with little faith in national government and a perception that the government wastes the taxpayers' money. Several of the Old Timers had held local elected offices, served on city committees, or been active in local party politics. Despite their distaste for current public officials, and their belief that many election and policy processes are dictated by money, they frequently conveyed a connection to government. For example, they believed that the mayor or Representative Rivers might be back for another coffee klatch any day.

Recall that Dave had once described the government in "us" versus "them" terms ("they is they, us is us. It [the government] is not us"). On a different day, though, he portrayed politicians as fellow human beings: "The people in Washington, they're just people, and where you have just people, you're going to have backstabbing and cheating. They're just in a position to do more of it." Throughout the Lewinsky scandal, the Old Timers continually criticized and ridiculed Bill Clinton, yet they continued to respect the presidency. As Charlie put it, "He's a horse's ass, but he's still the president. He's the one with the power. As long as he's in there, he's the president."

This mix of distrust of individual politicians and yet acceptance of the legitimacy of the process and institutions carried over into their perceptions of voting. On election days, people would readily ask one another whether they had voted; if someone answered no, the others would pester him for an explanation. In the midst of the Lewinsky scandal, Ted, a later-morning regular, started tattling that one Old Timer had voted for Clinton in 1996.

> Ted: Hey! Charlie voted for him! Charlie voted for him!!
> Charlie: Aw, knock it off. . . . You have no voice. You didn't even vote, so just keep your mouth shut!
> Alex: He didn't vote?! Tell Jack!
> Charlie: Jack! Hey, Jack! Ted didn't vote. Did you know that?
> Jack: Oh, I know. I've been working on him [walks over to Ted]. I've been trying to educate him about his duties.
> Charlie [to me]: See, Jack hates it when people don't vote. Says they have no right to complain.

Among the Old Timers, there was an expectation that the members of the group would vote and a belief that doing so mattered. There were some exceptions to this view. Recall the conversation in chapter 5 between Mort, Hal, Alex, and Sam about whether they had voted in a local school election. Even that exchange, however, conveyed a sense that one ought to vote. That conversation, as well as the one just cited, is indicative of a general understanding by members of the group that some civic duties were not a matter of choice but of responsibility.

When distrusting sentiments were expressed, it was typically in the context of explaining "I have been involved in government–I know firsthand," thus conveying strong internal efficacy, or belief in their own ability to influence government, alongside a dose of cynicism.

> You know, I just don't understand it. There are people sitting around like this all over the place, talking about the same kinds of things, and, you

know, about four years ago there was this real strong anti-federal-government sentiment. But we keep reelecting those people. I don't get it, it's as if "It's not my representative." People think their rep is okay, but it's all the other bozos. You know, I used to be a part of government, and I'd have to go to Lansing to testify for various things and some of those guys would be sleeping, some of them would be asking, "What are we talking about?" They didn't have a clue. I shudder to think about it sometimes. Of course, some of them are excellent.

Tim was one of several Old Timers who had experienced government directly. He conveyed a distrust that came not from alienation but from direct involvement in the process.

The Old Timers' Interpretations of the Election

When I asked the Old Timers for their interpretations of the 2000 election, many of them, like Baxter, had a ready response.

> Kathy: So, what did you think of this election?
>
> John: I'm getting ready to move to Florida.
>
> Baxter: It worked fine, just beautifully. The electoral college did what it was supposed to do. Popular vote, electoral college. That's the way it was set up. Look, I voted absentee from northern Michigan and our ballot was just like the one down in Florida. It was clear to me. They sent instructions with it, sent a stylus with it. It said to punch it all the way through and then turn it over and brush off the back side.
>
> Kathy: Did it really?
>
> Baxter: Yes, it did. It said that it would cause a machine malfunction if you did not. It was clear to me.

The next day, Tim and Baxter initially voiced different views, but reached an agreement that the electoral institutions were at root quite sound, as the exchange quoted at the start of this chapter shows. Here is that conversation at length.[14]

> Kathy: Say, five years from now, somebody, like, I don't know, who's ten years old now, says, you know, "What happened in the election of 2000? Everyone says it was this crazy election, and really unusual." How would you explain what happened?
>
> Baxter: I don't think it was unusual.

Tim: I would basically say that it absolutely showed the flaws of our outdated election process. I mean the politicians . . .

Baxter: Be careful, Tim. Be careful how you make a general statement about that. I think it showed how strong the electoral process *is*, how well it *did* work, with certain, ah, problems that could be fixed, but to say it showed the flaw in the system, that's a rather broad statement.

Tim: Okay, the flaw in the system, I mean, relates to . . . We're really inconsistent in how we vote. I mean, a physical lever . . .

Baxter: Oh! Different *ways* to vote.

Tim: We put a hole in a piece of paper, we put a line across . . .

Baxter: Yeah.

Tim: I mean if people move around literally from community to community, they are going to have to vote in different ways.

Baxter: I have voted three or four different ways. Ah, you move every five years statistically, or in other words, 20 percent of the people in this country move every year. Now, I would like to see a number of, a number of changes. I think that the election day should be a national holiday. That's one.

Tim: I do too.

Baxter: I think that the election—that the precincts should open and close simultaneously.

Tim: I think that's fine, too.

Baxter: Ahh, now noon in Maine would be five o'clock in Samoa. I would like to see the national ticket voted on identical devices in every precinct in the country. The local ticket? Then you get two ballots.

As they talked, Tim and Baxter agreed that the problems were a matter of ballots, timing, and national holidays—all imperfections that could be fixed relatively easily. The more difficult issue related not to government institutions but to the press.

Baxter: Another thing, this is tough to do . . . the press has caused one problem after another.[15]

John: We [Kathy and I] were talking about this . . .

Tim: It was premature announcements, predictions . . .

Baxter: Well, if you have simultaneous openings and closings, you would eliminate a great deal of that. Now, in Florida alone, and I didn't know this until the election, the western panhandle of Florida is in the central time zone. And many people felt that there was no sense in voting.

> John: Communications is a real problem. Take the Dredge [*sic*]
>   report[16] ...
> Baxter: Excess communication.
> ... [/..] ...
> Tim: The other thing that the press has no, no feeling about "we
>   screwed up."
> John: Oh no.
> Tim: ... "let's move to the next thing." I mean it has been all year long. I
>   mean the way they just pick up on an issue, or the next problem, and
>   the headlines are in the paper for months. As soon as that's over they
>   pick on something else.

When the Old Timers did indict the government, it was a matter of individual character, not the rules of the game. For example, Tom, an Old Timer who is one of the most outspoken social conservatives, responded to the election this way:

> Kathy: How do you feel about the election?
> Tom: The election? I think it was a disgrace, a shame to this country.
>   Shameful. It was handled so poorly. And Gore hurt this country, this
>   whole country, he really did. He should have gave up the ship. Now
>   I'm a Republican, but I'm not saying this because he is a Democrat. It
>   was wrong what he did.[17]

So for Tom, as for Tim, Baxter, and John in the conversation above, the election was not exactly a point of pride, but it was notable for what they saw as Gore's distasteful behavior, an inconsistency in ballots, and the behavior of members of the press. They did not read the election aftermath as evidence that elections are "fundamentally flawed" in the sense of systematically disenfranchising voters, and they did not see themselves as alienated from the process. To them, the "flaws" were about ballot inconsistency.

Interpretations of the Election on the Other Side of the Room

Just a few feet away, the understanding that the African Americans at the small tables had of the election was fundamentally different:

> Kathy: What do you think? What do you think about this election?
> Larry: Election?! Election?! You mean the *appointment*. This was no
>   election. I mean, if Bush had won fair and square, if he had won, then

okay. But not this way, not this way. The Supreme Court *gave* him the election. They should've sent it back to Florida and said, "This is your state, you deal with it." But they didn't want to do that. They wanted the Supreme Court to decide. Highest court in the land, what are you going to do? If you knew half of what went on in D.C., in the government, you wouldn't believe it. They tell us just enough, they tell us just what they want us to hear.

As Larry spoke, Howard and Sarah nodded their heads. Their interpretation was not that flaws in ballots, personal character, and the way the press performs had contributed to a less-than-optimal outcome. Instead, their perception was that the outcome had been deliberately manufactured.

Is the difference in their interpretation from that of the Old Timers a function of weighting the data differently? Can the variation be conceptualized as the African Americans attributing a larger weight to the role of the Supreme Court than did the Old Timers? If so, why was the Supreme Court's role in the election decision more central to some people than to others? The Old Timers were well aware of the involvement of the Court, yet they chose to view the election as a function of a different set of institutions and people.

Again, the concept of identity-based perspectives can help. Larry, Howard, and Sarah rarely talked about politics,[18] and thus it is difficult to pinpoint their attitudes toward government.[19] However, their interactions did display their perspectives on their own place within the store and hence within society. And their interpretations of the election are consistent with these views.

Consider the way they interacted with others within the corner store.[20] Even though the corner store is a small space, their behavior clearly signaled their perception that they were not a part of the Old Timers' community. Larry, one of the small-table regulars, engages in friendly chatter with many of the Old Timers as they pass by the small tables on their way in or out of the corner store. He had been spending time at the corner store for fifteen years and had established a warm rapport with the owners as well as with many of the Old Timers. However, he never sat at the large tables. Even on mornings when no one was sitting at the small tables and there were at least several free chairs across the room at the Old Timers' tables, he refrained from joining them. Instead, he sat alone near the windows.

Howard and Sarah had an even stronger aversion to the large tables. Their discomfort with the Old Timers was clear when I asked them directly why they never sat at the large tables. One morning, the hinge of the corner door adjacent to the small tables was broken. Howard was enjoying the fact

that no working corner door meant no cold breezes sweeping over his back
because people would use the other door. A white regular, Clarence, who
seemed to know Howard and Sarah well, came over to look at the door.

> Howard: You think you can drag that [door] project out until spring?
> Clarence: You like having that door shut, eh?
> [Howard, Sarah, Larry, and Clarence laugh.]
> Howard: It's a lot warmer, that's for sure. We might have to all pick up
> and go sit over there [points to the large tables].
> Kathy: Why *don't* you go sit over there? Why *don't* you all sit over there
> at those tables?
> Howard: [Gives me an incredulous look.] No way. Are you kidding?
> You're the only one who can sit over there.
> Kathy: Well, it even took me awhile. . . .
> [They laugh]
> Howard: No way. They look at us funny. That's their place. They don't
> allow other people over there.
> Kathy: Do they really look at you funny?
> Howard: Oh, nah . . . but that's *their* place.

My questions were intentionally naïve. The way Howard responded—
with an incredulous look that said the answer was so obvious that it was ridiculous for me to ask—conveyed that central to their sense of themselves was the
understanding that they simply do not sit at the large tables.[21] Their reaction
conveyed a general orientation as relative outsiders within the corner store.

The point here is to note that Howard, Sarah, and Larry's interactions
were characterized by an orientation toward established institutions that differed markedly from that of the Old Timers. While the Old Timers saw the
government as an institution that was designed to serve people like themselves and saw the corner store as their place, Howard, Sarah, and Larry communicated a perception that channels of power operated for other people.
This identity as outsiders in turn permeated their interpretation of the 2000
election and the voting process in general.

> Howard: I don't trust those machines, those voting machines. I don't
> know why they have them. See, I never vote, I've never voted, that's
> why. I wish it were still paper and pencil. You vote now, put your
> ballot in that machine, you have no *idea* how it counts your vote.
> Larry: Chads and all that. They were supposed to clean out those chads
> every year, but there were so many chads in there. Full of those pieces

> of paper. Someone was supposed to clean them out. Why didn't
> they? Someone's getting paid to do that. Hanging chads, two
> threads? No way.
>
> Howard: Those ballots were complicated. They say that kids could do
> those ballots. That's not true, kids couldn't do those ballots. You're
> supposed to know to clean those chads off?

Whereas the Old Timers blamed the ballot mix-ups on uneducated voters, the small-table regulars asserted that the ballots were not voter-friendly. Yet, their proposed remedies were not entirely different from those offered by the Old Timers.

> Larry: I don't know why they don't pass a law that says everybody all
> across the country has to have the same way of voting, the same
> machines. Then the way you vote in Iowa would be the same as the
> way you vote in Utah, not so confusing then.
>
> Sarah: Uh huh.
>
> Howard: Or maybe they should put the top elections, the top offices on
> one ballot, make that the same across the country.

Like the Old Timers, Howard, Sarah, and Larry believed one solution was creating uniform ways of voting in all states. However, unlike the Old Timers, they perceived that the problem was larger than just ballot construction. It also lay in the Supreme Court's behavior.

> Kathy: Do you think they should get rid of the electoral college?
>
> Larry: No, not a problem with the electoral college
>
> [Howard and Sarah are shaking their heads in agreement].
>
> Larry: It would have been okay, would have been okay . . .
>
> Kathy: Just that the courts were involved?[22]
>
> Larry: That's right, this election was decided by the Supreme
> Court—that's not right! [. . .] And all this when his brother is
> governor. They've subpoenaed him now [. . .] We're in for a bad time.
> Now they got rid of Linda Chavez, and next is John Ashcroft. We're
> in for some stormy times. Now you've got a Senate split 50–50, it'll be
> hard to get anything done, be hard to pass any bills.

These comments reveal that although part of the solution they suggest resembles the one offered by the Old Timers, these two groups did not view the election through the same lens. The African Americans exhibit a fundamental distrust of governmental institutions that runs so deep that Howard does not even vote. Whereas Jack chides his fellow Old Timers for not doing their "duty" when they do not turn out to vote, Howard believes he has no guarantee that his ballot will even be counted.

Looking closer at their interpretations, it is clear that although the Old Timers seemed to agree that some kind of standardization of the ballot is necessary, the balance of their ideas for improving the process rested on individual citizens. In the following conversation, the Old Timers talk about the need to educate individual voters. At this point in the conversation, which had arisen because they knew I was interested in their thoughts on the election, Baxter is talking about his expectations that Florida Governor Jeb Bush will seek electoral reform. However, he and John quickly move on to critiquing the ability of the individual voter.

> Baxter: I look to Jeb Bush to really turn that state upside down in the next two or three years, uh, in the way that elections will be run in Florida.[23]
>
> John: Well, I think there's a ripple effect across the United States for that.
>
> Baxter: At the same time, that's the way we voted absentee from northern Michigan. The directions were explicit, including at the end, turn over the ballot, scrape off all extraneous or hanging pieces of paper, and explaining why—because they would affect the machine counting. Now if those people are pushing dimples and pimples . . .
>
> John: You can't . . . wouldn't have done that in the state of Michigan because of the way we run things. Voting is of a different quality here, we don't take those chances. They don't help people as much as . . . I gotta believe they were either a bunch of dumb people who went into that booth or [unintelligible] to start with because they all have been there. . . .
>
> Baxter: Why don't we take it upon ourselves to have the correct copies of voting instructions to see exactly what it does say? Because I can almost repeat word for word what the Michigan instructions were.
>
> John: Yeah, so can I. And from the comments that we heard, they were basically the same thing. Everything in the political arena, in that voting system, is set up to eliminate corruption. The only reason you have a machine count is because people make mistakes, either by design or because they're getting paid.
>
> Baxter: Well, voting is a privilege which I have always appreciated and always exercised. Along with the privilege goes responsibility. You

don't have the privilege to make, what shall we call, stupid mistakes.
You have the privilege of not only exercising your right but to
exercise it properly. I don't mean properly in terms of which party or
which person, but the physical work of exercising that right. Because
it's public, you know how to do it.

John: All right, now listen to what you're saying . . .

Baxter: If somebody said, if you're an old broad that can run five bingo
cards, why can't you run one vote, voting?

John: You're right [laughs] you're right.

. . . [. . .] . . .

Baxter: It's like a driver's license, it's exactly like a driver's license, which
is, I am licensed by the state of Michigan.

John: It's a privilege.

Baxter: It is incumbent upon me to know how to operate that vehicle.
How do I obey the laws of the state and how to obey the laws of
common sense.

John: Not all people do that.

Baxter: Right, get on the road and you'll find that out.

John: I know, I know.

The same issue—confusion over the process of voting—is interpreted
differently by the two groups of people. John and Baxter question the
ability of the voter. In the conversation reported above, Howard, Sarah,
and Larry wonder about the clarity of the ballot. In their interpretations, these two groups are retaining different information from the same
event.

This is not to say that members of either group were unaware of alternative interpretations. However, when such viewpoints were recognized, they
were discounted and categorized in stark us-versus-them terms.

Kathy: Dave, what do you make of this election? What did you think
about it? I've been asking [the rest of] these guys that all week.

Dave: Which part of it, you mean this fraudulent stuff down in Florida?

Kathy: Any part of it, yeah . . . It was, well, it was unusual.

Dave: I think it was horrible. I have no faith in this incoming president
whatsoever. None. I didn't have any in his father. And I'm usually on
the Republican side. But I think we have four years of nothing ahead
of us. Deadlock. Nothing will happen. . . . And then there's this
problem with the blacks.

Kathy: What do you mean?

> Dave: Well, Jesse Jackson, son of a bitch is stirring ... Jesse Jackson is
>   stirring like crazy. The problem is there's no intelligence there. The
>   leaders, there's no intelligence there.
> Kathy: Do you really think that?
> Dave: Yes, I do. Don't get me wrong: I'm not against blacks.
> Kathy: I know ...
> Dave: But the blacks here in Detroit, or take [names a few other cities],
>   they're just doing crazy things. Saying they should be paid for the
>   Civil War or for slavery! That's ridiculous!! What are they thinking?!
>   We have a horrible problem there.

Although Dave acknowledged that many African Americans viewed the events of the election with fury, he did not believe that the election was indicative of systematic disenfranchisement. Others in the group expressed similar ideas: "Well, look at what's happening right now. The blacks now will not give this up. They're going to court again to try to, I don't know what the hell they're going to try to do, but they're gonna do something. But it's gone on now too long." John, like Dave, recognized that some members of the population were greatly concerned about the election process, yet neither of them viewed the election outcome as calling for institutional reform.

A Function of Partisanship?

Much of these interpretations and the differences between the Old Timers and the small-table regulars could be explained as a function of partisan identification. Such an explanation might go as follows: The Old Timers are Republicans, wanted Bush to win, and therefore rationalized the outcome not as the Supreme Court handing it to the Republicans but as a few flaws that could be remedied in the future. The African Americans at the small tables are Democrats, wanted Gore to win, and therefore perceive a fundamental unfairness in the outcome and the system used to decide it.

This explanation for their interpretations is simple and compelling. But it is insufficient. The conversations among the people who sit by the windows are better explained by a perspective of disenfranchisement than by Democratic affiliation. To put it plainly, does party affiliation explain the sentiment "I never vote"? No. Nor does party affiliation provide sufficient explanations for the Old Timers' conversations. At the core of their discussion is an identity as "middle Americans," people whom the system is intended for and people who have risked their lives to protect it. In this conversation in the aftermath of the election, is it their identity as "middle Americans" or their identity as Republicans that drives the following kind of sentiment?

> Baxter: I believe in my government.
>
> Kathy: And why is that?
>
> Baxter: Because the government is me! I get involved, I vote. I am the government.
>
> Kathy: All right, but I don't think many people think that way.
>
> Baxter: What about your students, why do they fear the government?
>
> Kathy: I don't think they fear it, but they just don't trust it to do what is right, to do the right thing.
>
> Baxter: Well, then they ought to get involved. They ought to get involved. No use in complaining. The government is them.
>
> Kathy: I worry, I mean, what should I say to students who are discouraged now, for whom this was their first election?
>
> Baxter: Ach, they've lived through nothing. Being a student, life is so easy. I see these students drive around in these cars, walk around with a phone to their ears. That's the good life. These guys in here, these guys—being a student for them was difficult. During the Depression, putting yourself through school, it was a financial sacrifice, sleepwise—it was not easy. Students these days, they've lived through nothing.
>
> Kathy: Why is it that the people in here [motioning around the two large tables] have so much faith in the government? Do you think they have more faith than younger generations?
>
> Baxter: They've lived through so much—the government and the G.I. bill, they lived through two wars, they believe in the government.

It is not so much partisanship as a perspective as a member of a group of people who are part of what has been called the "long civic generation" (Putnam 2000, 257). The Old Timers are part of a generation that is unique in the way events during their lives, namely the Depression and World War II, imparted an appreciation for civic engagement and the power of the federal government.[24]

To be sure, partisanship *does* matter. If the Florida vote count had been decided in favor of Gore, and an entire Republican-leaning segment of the electorate claimed that they were turned away from the polls or that their votes were not counted, we could expect that Baxter and the other Old Timers would not have as easily dismissed those complaints as they dismissed complaints made by African Americans.

> Kathy: What about the people down in Florida, say the blacks down in Florida?[25] People who believe that they voted, but it doesn't matter because their vote wasn't counted–or people who were turned away at the polls. How should they feel? What do you think of that?
>
> Baxter: Well, first of all, I'm not sure that really happened. I mean I am just not sure that happened . . . there is a problem with what went on in Florida, something not right there, but . . .

If Gore had won, they also might not have dismissed the election as no cause for concern, as they readily did when asked whether the outcome had changed their perception of the government. Some of them dismissed it as nothing unusual.

> Kathy: Has this election changed the way you feel about the government, has it changed your trust in government?
>
> John: No, heck no. This is nothing new. I've been involved in elections just like this before. This is nothing new.

Others discounted it as an aberration. In a different conversation:

> Kathy: Did this election change the way you feel about the government?
>
> Orville: No, this was unusual. This was a special case, very rare. Things like this don't usually happen.
>
> Alex: Yeah. The last time something like this happened, it was a long, long time ago. Who was it, back in the 19th century, late 19th century [when the last election occurred in which someone won the electoral college but lost the popular vote] . . .

Despite the possibility that they would not have readily discounted the outcome had the Democrat won, partisanship is not sufficient to explain their interpretations of this election. The way they made sense of the election was rooted in their identity as old-timer Ann Arborites, folks who had made sacrifices so that the system in which they voted could exist. These views of the world infused their party affiliation.

* * *

In the Old Timers' interpretation, the election of 2000 was an aberration, an indicator not of fundamental injustice in the institution of government but of the occasional glitches in a system run by greedy and incompetent people. The Old Timers concluded that if the election taught them anything, it was to be a more involved, informed citizen:

> Roger: This election was good for one thing, sure taught people a lot, sure taught them about a lot of different things. I didn't know anything about chads and dimples and all that before this election. It taught us a lot. And I tell you what, people say your vote doesn't count? Well, this election sure proved that wrong.
>
> John [as Alex nods]: That's right, that's for sure.

This interpretation was not shared by everyone, not even everyone within the same geographic community, as the comparison to the conversations among the African Americans at the small tables showed. In stark contrast to the Old Timers' conclusions that this was an example of the power of one vote, the African-American regulars lamented that this was instead an example of the pointlessness of voting.

This is not to say that bottom-up processes such as social identification operate independently of top-down processes in influencing levels of political trust. Levels of trust are a function of the actions of members of the government. However, in the space between the behavior of public officials and the perceptions of members of the public are the socially rooted filters with which ordinary citizens view the world. Merely ensuring that people have a string of positive experiences with government will not guarantee that they alter their perceptions of trust in government. To increase levels of trust among historically disenfranchised groups, political actors will have to take actions that clearly convey they are responding to the needs of these groups. Political events are more likely to influence perceptions of trust if political professionals are successful at framing them in a way that resonates with members of the public.[26] The puzzle then becomes, how can officials do this without simultaneously sending signals to other portions of the public that they are ignoring or discounting their interests? The answer lies in the societywide recognition of the power of perspectives. If citizens view politics as a zero-sum game in which government actions to help one group are necessarily actions against another group, then attempts to include those who are disconnected from government will never gain sufficient support. However, if institutions can be designed in a way that encourages people to view public problems through an enlarged view of community in which helping someone else is helping oneself, then our potential to address the concerns of marginalized groups without alienating the mainstream will be enhanced.

CHAPTER 8   **Social Interaction, Political Divides**

Arnie: How is your paper coming along?
Kathy: Pretty well, pretty well. I've just about finished the report I'm
    writing up for you guys on the surveys you filled out.
Arnie: I was telling someone about that the other day. They wondered
    why you wanted to do that [study the Old Timers and give them a
    self-administered survey]. And I said, "Because she wants to study
    the most conservative people in the world!"
Kathy: [laughing] Well, yes, the group is pretty conservative, more
    conservative than the nation in general, but there are different kinds
    of "conservative" . . .
Arnie: You're not going to ruin our image now, are you?

I began this project because I was interested in the nature
of informal political interaction. I believed that spaces for interaction between the government and the home were the key to a more democratic
society, a healthier civic life. Like many previous observers of American politics from Alexis de Tocqueville (1981 [1835]) to Robert Putnam (2000), I
placed a good bit of faith in the act of citizens coming together of their own
volition. Whether believing in the civic life lived together, or more specifically in political talk, I shared the common expectation that "something
special happens in a group."

At the turn of this century, the United States was rocked
by a presidential scandal, a divisive presidential election, and threats of Y2K
disasters and terrorist attacks. In this tumultuous time, observing processes of
collective identification in the Old Timers was in many respects comforting.
Here was a group of people who day after day appreciated one another, relied
on one another, and through their interaction made some sense of the crazy
world out there.

This study has shown that something special can indeed happen in groups. As an honorary member of the Old Timers, I had the chance to experience the warmth that comes from gathering daily with a group of friends who have enduring ties to a community and to one another. This type of benefit from participation in voluntary associations is evident not just to an observer but is valued and protected by the members themselves. For example, when one of the members was considering moving to a nearby town, I asked him, "Will you still come to this place?" His answer made it obvious that I should not have to ask: "Hell, yes! I would take a bus here if I had to."

Members of such groups, in which one's absence is noted and one's presence celebrated with handshakes, smiles, or at least shared coffee, come into close contact with some of the most admirable sides of human behavior. In such groups, there is a sense of trust and mutual respect, interdependence, and shared fate that makes a seat at the large tables in the corner store feel like the safest seat in town.

But Arnie, in the conversation quoted at the beginning of this chapter, touched on a matter that became one of the central preoccupations of this study. Although their group is a source of social trust and good will, it is also a collectivity that maintains a particular perspective. Unity, whether identity with a small group or a large nation, is often accompanied by exclusion of individuals and violation of liberties. In the corner store, sitting at the large tables is safe, but the safety comes at the expense of distancing oneself from outsiders. The Old Timers' trust in one another and their sense of belonging is clearest when they have the opportunity to contrast themselves with an outside group—African Americans, academics, or members of younger generations.

The observations in combination with the national sample survey data and reference to sociological studies of group interaction revealed that the act of clarifying attachments to particular social groups is a very common political behavior of everyday life. Whether in the corner store, the craft guild, or other settings that allow people to talk informally, Americans work out who they will include in the psychological communities that they use to make sense of politics. Part of this is the "good stuff" of maintaining friendships and a sense of place. But part of it is the less-than-honorable thoughts and actions that Americans—regardless of ideological stripe—create and perpetuate through making connections to some groups while actively distancing themselves from others.

That is why, despite Lippmann-esque decrees that the direction of public opinion is largely determined by the gusts of air coming from elites, informal interaction deserves the attention of political scientists. Whatever happens in the daily chatter of people like Baxter and Dave down at the corner store may in fact be puffs of air compared to the jet stream of opinion from the media, elected officials, and policy elites. But by coming down from the stratosphere to stop and observe those seemingly trivial breaths from the Old Timers and the other groups in this study we have seen that the lines of difference and similarity are worked out in casual conversations. The behavior of ordinary citizens clarifies and reinforces, develops and defines, politically relevant social identities. When the Old Timers talk about themselves in contrast to "those people in Detroit" or "the liberal crazies now on the city council," they give meaning to what it means to be a white person in the Detroit metropolitan area and a conservative person in Ann Arbor, respectively. When the women of the craft guild contrast their attitudes on promiscuity with each other, they too are giving meaning to a social identity, identity with women.

These processes pose a problem for our conceptions of democracy, and for our conceptions of the place of citizens within it. There have long been reasons to be skeptical of overly sanguine views of civic interaction. For example, the Columbia School voting studies, as well as more recent social network analyses, clearly convey that like talks to like, especially about politics. This study, however, explains a more troubling phenomenon. Not only do people self-select into associations in which they are not exposed to cross-cutting points of view but in this interaction they reinforce communities of concern that further diminish the potential for future discussion with people of different perspectives.

Main Findings and Implications for Political Behavior Research

To revisit how this happens, let us briefly reconsider the main findings and implications of this study. The basic model of the processes observed in this study, outlined at the end of chapter 3, is that, as members of a group, individuals clarify their social identities through a learning process. These identities form the basis of perspectives through which people communicate about and interpret political events. When out-groups are salient and the purpose of the group causes self-selection to result in a membership with overlapping acquaintances and experiences, the group members are likely to recognize and develop collective identities. When such identities are commonly used in the group's interactions, the resulting perspective in turn influences the members' interpretations of political issues by constraining the categories and considerations they use to communicate.

The comparison of the Old Timers and the women in the craft guild revealed that not all groups are likely to recognize and develop shared social identities. Two main factors appeared to influence the prominence of collective identities in these groups. The first is the store of shared acquaintances and experiences, influenced by the group's purpose. Both of those groups are composed of white, middle-class to upper-middle-class people who live in Ann Arbor, Michigan. However, the purposes of the groups differed. The Old Timers met to socialize, thus they self-selected into the group on the basis of awareness of likenesses. Many of them have lived their entire lives in Ann Arbor; they went to school together, played sports together, and married into one another's families. Although the women of the craft guild joined the group partly for fellowship (and to raise money for the church), their membership is not predicated on previous acquaintance, and thus they do not have a great deal of shared experiences.

The second major contrast between these groups was that in the corner store in which the Old Timers meet, members of out-groups (African Americans, students, younger people, university faculty) were physically present, either as regulars sitting on the other side of the room or as take-out customers. However, when the women in the guild met, they were the only people present in the church basement.

These differences across the groups in their stores of recognizable similarities are accompanied by different roles for social identity in their communication. The Old Timers talk about politics by referring to the immediate group in ways that then connects them to larger-scale social groups. The guild, in contrast, without similar inducements to recognize shared experiences, created a context in which political discussion was uncomfortable and in which intragroup rather than intergroup differences took center stage.

In this study, I have conceptualized identities as a central component of the perspectives with which people view the world. In this formulation, identities interact with interests and principles to influence individuals' interpretations of politics. Chapter 5 analyzed how both the Old Timers and the women in the guild interpret politics through the lens of their identity-based perspectives. Although people in both groups appeared to use their individual social identities to communicate about public affairs, the Old Timers relied on identities that they share with one another to talk about politics. These shared perspectives influenced what considerations arose in their conversations and what kinds of comments were policed or discouraged.

The comparison in chapter 6 of the content of the news to which the Old Timers were exposed with their conversations about those stories demonstrated that these bottom-up processes work in combination with elite-driven frames. The Old Timers used elite-driven frames as starting points for interpreting local breaking news. They then "transformed" (Just et al. 1996) these interpretations by bringing in social categories, especially race, that had not been emphasized by the media. These understandings were anchored in their social identity.

Chapter 7 further illustrated the way in which perspectives are related to political understanding. I compared the Old Timers' interpretations of the outcome of the presidential election of 2000 with the interpretations offered by the African-American regulars who sit on the other side of the corner store. I focused on the implications of these different interpretations for their attitudes of trust in government. The conversations demonstrated that information about a given political event such as the 2000 election is not given but is perceived in ways that are consistent with individuals' broader perspectives of the world. The implication is that theories of the dynamics of political trust ought to take into account the effect of identity-based perspectives on the way citizens perceive government actions.

Implications for Studies of Racial Attitudes

These analyses revealed that perspectives are an integral part of the linkages people make between themselves and politics. Importantly, racial identity was a key component of the context of understanding among the Old Timers. It entered as a tool for talking about local and national politics. When group members brought up the concept of race, this was not done independent of their other interests or principles. Their sense of themselves as not people of color was a part of their overall perspective, which also incorporated individualist principles. These results speak to a key debate among scholars of racism.

Scholars studying racial attitudes disagree about whether social groups play a central role in the way people make sense of politics. The racial resentment approach to racism argues that deep-seated attitudes toward social groups lie at the root of racist opinions (Kinder and Sanders 1996). An example argument is that whites oppose affirmative action because of their attitudes toward African Americans. However, Sniderman and colleagues (Sniderman and Piazza 1993; Sniderman and Carmines 1997) stand behind a different explanation. They claim that it is political principles such as individualism, not resentment toward blacks, that drive opposition to policies such as affirmative action. In reviewing this debate, Hochschild (2000) argues that our understanding of racism need not take an either/or course. She suggests that one way to reconcile the two is to use focus groups or interviews to "parse what people mean when they identify themselves as individualistic, supportive of equality, hesitant about affirmative action, or a member of an 'other' racial or ethnic group" (331). The participant observation used in this study provided even richer data than we could obtain via focus groups. It provided both verbal and behavioral data about what people mean when they identify as members of certain social groups and as people who abide by certain principles. The Old Timers' conversations analyzed here about the 2000 election, Ebonics, and affirmative action, as well as their coffee etiquette in which they exclude African-American regulars on the other side of the room, suggested that both their affect toward blacks and their political principles are intertwined with their definitions of "one of us."[1]

Implications for Framing Research

This study also has implications for current work on framing. Typically, framing research in political science focuses on the cognitive processing of elite discourse, not the social processes of negotiating meaning. Elite discourse can make an issue "easy" (Carmines and Stimson 1980, 1989) by attaching it to a prominent social category toward which people have strong affective attachments, such as race (Kinder and Sanders 1996). More generally, when elites frame an issue in a way that emphasizes affected constituencies, individuals' attitudes on the policy are influenced by their feelings toward the group (Nelson and Kinder 1996).

This is all the more reason to not restrict our attention to elite discourse but to also pay attention to the social processes that reinforce feelings toward particular groups in society, including religious, ideological, gender, and others as well as racial groups. Attaching an issue to a group-centric frame works in part because of the everyday interaction that has made these categories meaningful.

Processes of socially situated interpretation also deserve attention with respect to "hard" issues, or issues that are not interpreted at a gut level (Carmines and Stimson 1980, 1989). On issues that elites have not framed in a group-centric way, informal interaction can help people develop such connections themselves. For example, previous research has shown that although elite discourse on abortion may focus on partisan and religious divides, interpersonal interaction enables people to relate this issue to their racial and class status (Press and Cole 1999). In addition, African Americans have been shown to invoke the category of race even when the media has not emphasized its relevance to a given topic (Gamson 1992, 108). The analysis of interpretation of the news presented in chapter 6 demonstrated that when a media story suggests a perspective, and people adopt it to talk about the issue, they may transform it by drawing further connections between the kind of people they see themselves as and the issue.

To reiterate a major conclusion of this study, framing in terms of social groups is persuasive not because social groups exist out there but because individuals have developed identities and anti-identities with categories of people.[2] Therefore, a full understanding of the formation of opinion ought to acknowledge the interaction of bottom-up and top-down processes. Elite-driven models are useful for explaining shifts in mass opinion, but, in order to explain the potential for and sources of social change, they need to incorporate an understanding of grassroots processes (Lee 2002). We may not be able to forecast important shifts in approval for public policies by measuring only political attitudes or the content of messages spread by the mass media. The work of modifying political divisions is typically incremental, and this study suggests that much of it is likely done inch by inch in conversations among ordinary citizens.

Expanding Our View of Social Context and Citizen Communication

Previous framing research has been unable to conceptualize these bottom-up processes because of a reliance on experiments. Likewise, previous work on political communication among citizens has been unable to fully theorize social context because of the methods employed. Studying interactions within focus groups does enable us to observe how opinions are created through interaction and how social dynamics influence the expression of opinion, but artificial groupings bias observations against seeing the work of social identity. For example, participants in focus groups in such studies are typically not familiar with one another prior to a study (Just et al. 1996); when they are, they do not meet regularly of their own accord (Gamson 1992). In contrast, the Old Timers, by virtue of many years of building and recognizing shared experiences, have gained practice in using their identification with one another and their collective identity with large-scale social groups to make sense of the world around them. Therefore, it should be expected that the participants in focus groups are less likely than those in "natural" groups (such as the Old Timers) to use their identities with that small group as stepping-stones toward larger social identities.

Likewise, in-depth interview approaches are biased against observing the work of social identity in interpretation. Lane argued that social identity played at best a minor role in the political thinking of the working-class men he studied in New Haven. But these men were interviewed by Lane while isolated from familiar objects and, more importantly, familiar people. In such a setting the salient tools for thinking were not perspectives such as "you and I are like this" but *perspectives of individual difference.* In contrast, this study suggests that natural groups are more likely to invoke social groups than are groups or individuals assembled for the purpose of discussing politics for a researcher.

Finally, survey-based studies of contextual effects, such as those of the Columbia School and more recent social network approaches to political attitudes, have conceptualized the context as something that exists—a distribution of opinions or demographics—not something that is created by the members of that context. This matters because when social contexts are conceptualized as perspectives rather than as preferences, we can study "the community" as a political object whose definition is contested. That is why this investigation departs from the voting studies of the Columbia School and more recent social network research (e.g., Huckfeldt and Sprague 1995). Watching the way in which people connect themselves to others around them, the way they collectively negotiate who is an "Ann Arborite," and the way they establish and maintain group boundaries, we could observe how the social context in which political communication occurs is something other than simply the majority opinion.

Implications for Studies of Political Socialization

Taking the time to hear and observe these conversations has also expanded our understanding of political socialization and the concept of identity *development.* For example, although the conversations among the Old Timers quite likely did not persuade any member to *become* a Republican, together the group members were sorting out what it *means to be* a Republican. Moreover, they were figuring out how their partisan identification matters in the context of current events. Although their partisan identification has not changed "ever" according to many of them, what it means to them to be a Republican twenty years ago likely differed from what it means to them today. To press the point further, if development of the Old Timers' identities as "Ann Arborites" was complete before joining the group, where is it that they figure out what constitutes an Ann Arborite in the face of a growing minority and student population? Recognizing that their interaction enabled them to give meaning to social identities moves us beyond the question of the origins of partisan identification to the question of how partisan identification is modified and maintained throughout one's life.

Therefore, another implication of this study is that adulthood socialization does indeed take place (Sigel 1989), but not always by means that are measurable through attitude change. This is important because understanding how people modify identities in order to maintain values and opinions is key to understanding the sources of, barriers to, and potential for social change. For example, knowing how people collectively interpret their partisan identifications might reveal a strategy that would enable a woman candidate to make a successful run for the presidency. The absence of a woman in the Oval Office to date cannot be explained by women politicians' policy stances or party identification. It is at least partly a matter of the public's interpretation of the appropriateness of a woman holding that office. How this works—how people within the public define the appropriateness of voting women in to office—is just as essential for understanding the emergence of women political leaders as studying the campaign messages that help them win.

Emphasizing the Importance of Social Identity as Opposed to Demographics

The process of identity definition observed in this study also underscores that social group categories are only the touchstones for individuals' understanding of the political world, not explanations of political behavior. Observing that people of a higher income tend to vote differently than people of a lower income is a description, not an explanation. It is social identity, not social groups, that drives group-relevant thinking and action. It is not a given that people of similar social locations will think or act in similar ways. Similarities arise when people do the work of affiliating themselves psychologically with people of similar demographics. By categorizing themselves as certain kinds of people, they use others of that category as models of appropriate behavior. In other words, this study illustrates the "non-essential" nature of identity. It is not inevitable that women are guided by a strong identification with women, nor is it the case that all women who are so identified act alike. People work out for themselves what it means to be certain types of people. Yet we can observe patterns because people do not do this in isolation. A large part of the fabric of culture is enacted through everyday social interaction.

Part of the development of social identity is the incremental process of deciding who constitutes the community with which one identifies and what it means to be a member of this community. For example, the Old Timers' responses to the survey question "What comes to mind when you think of an Ann Arborite?" illustrate that between the object of the social group and the psychological attachment there is an intermediate and socially situated process of definition. Conceptualized this way, social identity does not suffer from attributing a set of common characteristics to all members of a given identity, a theoretical move Young (1994) warns against.

Revising Traditional Views of Civic Life

The discussions observed in this study do not look like civic interaction as normally conceptualized by political theorists. Typically, civic life is conceptualized in one of two prevailing models, civic republicanism or liberal individualism.[3] "Briefly, the civic-republican model stresses a view of politics as people reasoning together to promote a common good that transcends the mere sum of individual preferences," Nancy Fraser explains. The liberal-individualist model assumes "that people's preferences, interests and identities are given exogenously in advance of public discourse and deliberation" (Fraser 1992, 129–30). The problem is that neither vision recognizes that through casual interaction people collectively create the perspectives with which they wade through public issues.

In the liberal-individualist picture of democratic life, citizens are first and foremost private individuals. Collectively defined concepts such as who constitutes "one of us" are not important because people are not presumed to act on the basis of attachments to social groups or communities. Instead, they listen to themselves. In this liberal-individualist view, political conflict is dealt with not by deliberation but by precommitment to procedural rules (Riker 1982). The role of the public sphere[4] in these models is not to facilitate the development of mutual understanding but to enable the exchange of information.

Civic republicanism, in contrast, views collective attachments such as a sense of community as central to civic behavior. Its shortcoming is that is does not acknowledge that these concepts are created through interaction. In this model, individuals either rely on socialized mutual understandings to guide policy preferences (Bell 1993) or pose their arguments for certain policies in an other-regarding fashion, thus legitimizing the final policy decision as representative of the community (Barber 1984; Bohman 1996). Either way, people are presumed to act in the name of a preexisting common good when in the realm of public affairs.

Both the civic-republican and the liberal-individualist perspectives are "visions" and "models" and are therefore more akin to outlines than detailed empirical descriptions of the nature of public discussion. However, these models are used as expectations in empirical work to judge political institutions and civic behavior. For example, Evans and Boyte argue that citizens can come together to form such visions of the broader good in free spaces, or arenas of association separate from the government (1986). In addition, Bellah and colleagues (1985) advise that American culture can be transformed through public discussion to recognize our "republican" traditions:

> It is evident that a thin political consensus, limited largely to procedural matters, cannot support a coherent and effective political system . . . [I]f we had the courage to face our deepening political and economic difficulties, we might find that there is more basic agreement than we had imagined. Certainly, the only way to find out is to raise the level of public political discourse so that the fundamental problems are addressed rather than obscured. (287)

Liberal-individualist appeals are also made as routes to improve actually existing democracy. Instead of invoking the belief that the morals of the community will guide citizens to an understanding, they advocate interaction as a means of discovering true opinion. Such arguments are based on J. S. Mills's idea that an exchange of information forces each participant to recognize their own inaccurate perceptions of the best policy. The National Issues Convention held in Austin, Texas, in February 1996, is an example of this. This deliberative opinion poll interviewed a random sample of citizens about various political attitudes, invited the respondents to attend a weekend retreat during which they learned policy information, asked questions of experts, and discussed the issues together to reach informed public opinions (Fishkin 1991, 1995; Luskin and Fishkin 1998). The presumption is that more information and more discussion will lead to better opinions. As with civic-republican arguments for public discussion, liberal-individualist pleas for talk are not just referring to the models as theoretical abstractions. These scholars are using them as models of what discussion *actually does achieve* under the right conditions.

Neither of these models is adequate for understanding the political consequences of informal talk. The people at the corner store are not intent on deciding a political issue or in engaging in reasoned debate. As is the case with many associations (Rosenblum 1998), the group whose members call themselves the Old Timers does not exist for the sake of democracy. The members gather because they like each other, or at least like taking part in the group. Their conversations are social, not civic. Any political talk that arises does so as a by-product of their social interaction.

If the civic-republican view were apt, we would have seen something akin to talk about the common good within the conversations in this study. The people would have set aside their specific social attachments to talk about the best policy for the community. On the other hand, if the liberal-individualist view were fit to capture the processes going on, we would hear people talking on behalf of themselves and gathering information, while bracketing their social attachments.

However, these behaviors were not apparent in the foregoing analyses. To probe even further, I operationalize discussion about the common good as conversation in which the participants are considering both majorities and minorities as members of their community, not dividing up the issue as if their interests were solely aligned with one specific subgroup. For example, during discussions of parking downtown, a discussion about the common good would have included statements such as "Think about the expense of maintaining roads in this town and maintaining the downtown," "It must be hard for commuters to have to pay such high rates," and "Disabled people have no choice—some parking should be free for them." In other words, talk about the common good would involve the active consideration of alternative perspectives on an issue. It would involve an attempt to think about the implications of a policy for people other than people like oneself.

But only rarely did the people I observe engage in this kind of discussion. Occasionally Dave, a former union member, generated discussion about economic divides between classes that was reminiscent of the civic-republican model. This kind of exchange was rare, as he himself noted. After a discussion about affirmative action, most of which had focused on the other Old Timers' beliefs that affirmative action discriminates against whites, Dave bluntly stated that the discussion neglected to consider the interests of the people whom affirmative action helps. He announced that discussion in general rarely entails consideration of the common good: "The problem with this country is that there's too much talk of *individual rights;* we don't think enough about what's good for the common, for the common good."[5]

The discussions among the Old Timers are a prime example of evidence that humans seem unable to completely set aside social attachments in their interactions with others. Theories of deliberation often expect that people bracket these differences prior to debate, as Fraser (1992) notes (see also Elster 1986), but even in formal settings this bracketing rarely if ever shows up empirically. When the public sphere is opened up to people from divergent backgrounds, particular interests distort the discourse (Calhoun 1992, 9; Fraser 1992; Sanders 1997). In an informal setting such as the corner store, theories of civic life that discount the influence of particularized attachments are especially inappropriate.

Just as attempts to speak from the perspective of an enlarged identity or to imagine alternative points of view were rare, the people I observed did not attempt to achieve a broader understanding of the common good through other means, such as increasing the diversity of people involved in their conversations. Although the women's craft guild consciously attempts to recruit new members, this is not done from a desire to consider more points of view. They simply wish to compensate for declining membership and prolong the history of their 130-year-old group. The men at the corner store also make no attempts to enlarge the group to consider more opinions but, instead, actively reinforce the boundaries around the two large tables.

If we only view discussion as talk about the common good, we neglect to recognize that talk does the work of clarifying interests and identities. Fraser writes that "the civic-republican view contains a very serious confusion, one that blunts its critical edge. This view conflates the ideas of deliberation and the common good by assuming that deliberation must be deliberation *about* the common good" (1992, 130). Although public discussion may make people aware of similarities, these may be less about *the* common good than about the clarification of particular points of view, such as among African Americans within subpublics (Dawson 2001) or women in consciousness-raising groups (Freeman 1975; Sapiro 1989).

If we ignore the way in which casual talk enables the clarification of social identities, we do not allow ourselves to understand how informal social interaction is one important source of the perspectives with which people view the political world. The public's part of public discussion may occur as a by-product of social interaction, but it involves the act of people relating themselves to the world around them in ways that are relevant to their understanding of political issues. Reinhardt, in a review of Bell's *Communitarianism and Its Critics,* makes this argument eloquently:

> The key limitation [to the liberal-communitarian debate] is the failure to
> provide theoretical tools that can make sense of struggles over the
> symbolic order and the ways political differences originate and are
> negotiated. . . . Either we speak in the name of transcendent right, or we
> show that the target of our complaint is at odds with our community's
> deepest principles. Each of these appeals has its philosophical strengths
> and important political uses, but this stark binary choice is not adequate
> to the diverse spaces and forms of contemporary ideological
> contestation. . . . Traditions are assumed to speak univocally, spheres of

> life are treated as if their boundaries were sharply delineated, and
> political argument is presented as if it took place entirely at the level of
> high philosophical principle. This model smells too much of the
> seminar and not enough like life. (1995, 699)

The political consequences of informal interaction lie outside the bounds of both liberal individualism and civic republicanism. Neither of these prevailing models of deliberation adequately captures how groups of people collectively define the boundaries of who "we" are. The social identities developed and defined during public discussion are central to "the pictures in our heads," or the perspectives with which people make sense of politics.

A Dark Side of Social Capital[6]

One might be tempted to read the results presented here as evidence that face-to-face interaction is a mechanism for strengthening social bonds. If social identities are our psychological attachments to social groups, then, the interpretation might go, this is evidence that more interaction is good for fostering bonds with others. However, a caution is in order. This study does not address whether or not extra opportunities for social interaction lead to a broadened sense of community or tolerance for contrasting points of view. What it does show, however, is that exposure to others' views enhances individuals' connections between their political opinions and their own social locations.

So, at a minimum, it would seem that this study provides encouraging evidence that casual interaction does enhance citizenship—it helps people see the relevance of their private lives to public concerns. The Old Timers' conversations reveal how informal interaction can help develop such conceptual links as well as higher levels of political knowledge and participation.[7] Taking part in a group that regularly talks about political events can have a "watercooler" effect; it can stimulate people to keep up with current events so that they can contribute to the conversation when the talk turns to politics.[8]

In addition, casual political conversation can even spur participation in activities such as voting, volunteering for an election campaign, attending a rally (Knoke 1990a), writing a letter to an official, or increase willingness to participate in a local deliberative forum (McLeod and Daily 1996; McLeod, Scheufele, and Moy 1999). Many of the Old Timers proudly wore their "I voted" stickers on election days, and one even sported a "Poll Official" button. Drinking coffee with a poll official as well as noticing that the rest of the group is proud to cast their votes likely has a mobilizing effect.

Despite these positive effects, this study suggests a troubling possibility. More interaction can strengthen social divisions and solidify identities that drive democracies apart. Rather than necessarily serving as opportunities to broaden and strengthen concern for others, participation in public settings— especially settings into which people self-select[9]—may fortify boundaries of *limited* communities of concern, perpetuating community divisions along the lines of "us" and "them."

For this reason, this study issues a caution to believers in "social capital." "Social capital," according to this argument's most prominent proponent, Robert Putnam, is "civicness" or a political culture that is conducive to democracy. It is "features of social organization, such as trust, norms, and networks, that can improve the efficiency of society by facilitating coordinated actions" (Putnam 1993, 167). Putnam has diagnosed a simultaneous decline in participation in voluntary associations and norms of reciprocity and trust within the United States (1995a, 1995b, 2000).[10] He and other scholars have argued that without social capital, democracy is threatened. For example, Francis Fukuyama argues that the continued stability of a democracy rests on the ability of citizens to "self-organize" and to cooperate together to "represent their passions and interests effectively in the political marketplace" (1997, 60). In other words, democracy rests on the ability of citizens to communicate with one another and with their government. If citizens are disconnected, democracy suffers.

It may be that a democracy functions best in a culture of civility and regard for the many different people that reside within it. However, such a culture does not automatically arise from high levels of participation in associations. Equating participation in voluntary associations with social capital obscures the dark side of social capital and confuses its sources and outcomes with the concept itself (Portes 1998). The field from which Putnam adopted the term,[11] structural sociology, defines social capital as "the ability to secure benefits through membership in networks and other social structures" (Portes 1998, 6). That is, social capital is the capacity, not the benefits, enabled by network membership. Participating in associations *enables* positive returns with respect to democracy, but it also enables negative effects.

To see how this works, we can follow Tarrow (1996) and define democracy as "popular sovereignty and the protection of individual rights." Participation in voluntary associations or other sites of social interaction is an important resource in such a system because this behavior enables people to collectively articulate their preferences, to recognize their shared interests, and to act on them. Thus a "positive" outcome of association participation for democracy is the opportunity to exercise popular sovereignty. However, taking part in associations threatens individual rights—not just by silencing people within the group but by excluding certain types of people and perpetuating the perception of these "types," or social divisions, in which patterns of inequality and unequal access to opportunities are embedded. Therefore, settings of informal interaction, especially the highly self-selected worlds of voluntary associations, are not necessarily the sources of a strengthened social fabric that nostalgia and recent research suggests.

The ways in which informal associations reinforce social divisions is even more alarming when we consider that these groups may be among the types of organizations whose members are most likely to talk about politics. Eliasoph (1998, 2000) found that people were more likely to talk about how their private lives are linked to a broader community of concern when they were participating in settings in which the role of public activist was not predominant. Thus, we might expect that it is in more informal, nonactivist groups that people will step outside their instrumental self-interest to consider their relationship to others and to political concerns.

A further problem is that the groups most likely to talk about politics in the American setting—groups of people who perceive that they agree with each other on public issues—are also the most likely to reinforce shared social identities. The shared acquaintances and experiences among the Old Timers facilitated their talk about politics yet simultaneously served as the basis for reinforcing their perception of themselves as true "Ann Arborites" and "middle Americans."

The relationship between informal interaction and particular social identities—a relationship that participation in associations enables—should not be ignored. Social identities are *fundamental* to processes of political understanding and evaluation. Who we perceive ourselves to be influences our sense of obligation and responsibility to others. It influences the kinds of issues we pay attention to and the considerations we use to interpret these issues and to form opinions.

Where Do We Go from Here?

One can imagine a world in which informal interaction both confers solidary benefits and fosters concern for the common good. Before proposing the means of achieving that end, it is necessary to ask whether a universal community of concern is what we want. Should discussion about the common good be the ultimate goal of civic life (Sanders 1997)? Perhaps interaction that clarifies specific interests and identities is more important. According to Ryan (1992), democracy needs the "articulation of opposing interests." If

Lippmann's "Public Opinion" is primarily the domain of the political elite, which is composed mainly of people from a particular stratum of society (Mills 1956) and "sings with an upper-class accent" (Schattschneider 1960), then politically marginalized groups can better recognize their collective political strength and legitimacy in groups that give them the space to develop their own identities (Evans and Boyte 1986).

Moreover, if we conceptualize associations as stepping-stones to political activism, homogeneity is indeed beneficial. If ideally associations foster empowerment and efficacy, why should we expect members of oppressed groups to welcome "opponents" into their discussions? Consciousness-raising groups in the women's movement demonstrated the effectiveness of having a women-only space in efforts to create an awareness among women of their common concerns. In this way, associations that are exclusive to the oppressed are potentially valuable sites for establishing the solidarity necessary for action. Notice also that even people who consider themselves members of the political mainstream, such as the men who comprise the Old Timers, feel oppressed and victimized. Their group serves as a safe haven from threatening groups. Whose place is it to demand that associations, the workplace, or any other forum for collective interaction should do otherwise?

In addition, interaction with "people like me" enables the clarification of concepts through which representation functions. If people interact with one another driven by attachment solely to entities larger than themselves, such as an entire city or nation, where do they learn how to articulate their particular interests in the political realm? Interaction with people of similar perspectives and concerns can help people recognize their membership in specific issue publics. It can also provide information about whether or not their particular interests are being represented. By talking together, the Old Timers form ideas of which kind of people represent them. They consider such things as, "Can we vote for someone like Elizabeth Dole or Colin Powell?" The "crazy liberals" on the city council were not representing their community of concern. Who was? Part of their above-average involvement in public affairs included the links they had developed between their private lives and the lives of particular public officials.

The benefit of an opportunity to clarify the linkages between identities and interests is undeniable, especially for members of politically disenfranchised groups. But the problem remains. Social identities are not only the label we give to a sense of common interests, fate, and membership, they also coincide with the distribution of power and resources across society. As long as inequalities in resources follow social divisions, members of a democracy that claims to uphold justice and equality must strive to foster a public in which individual members conceptualize their communities of concern as more than people of "my" race, "my" class, "my" gender, "my" generation, and so forth. The democratic value of discussion is diminished if the talk is carried out assuming that we already know what we have in common (Lichterman 1999; Schudson 1997). This does not mean that we should strive to do away with group interests or personalized concerns. It does mean, however, that we should strive for a society in which the concepts of "us" and "them" do not continually refer to the same groups of people. We should strive for ways to encourage all citizens to recognize interests that cut across major social divisions.

Notice, however, the tension that we must continually recognize: unity comes at the expense of exclusion and the endangerment of individual liberties. Consider again the national unity that erupted in the wake of the September 11, 2001, terrorist attacks. On the heels of a divisive presidential election, signs of a nation coming together, such as increased donations of blood and money to the Red Cross, near unanimous backing of an anti-terrorism bill in the Senate, and signs of support for the war effort from the Congressional Black Caucus (whose members were still furious with the Bush administration over the outcome of the 2000 election) were in some respects comforting. Yet at what expense? Is unanimous agreement on a bill that has the potential to endanger civil liberties what we want? Was the spike in flag sales[12] a sign of solidarity with those grieving over the attacks, patriotism, or a sentiment based in hatred of "the other"?

In order for us to build national unity that is rooted in a broad conception of the nation, an identification with the many different types of people who contribute to the body we call the American public, as opposed to a unity that is the product of excluding a portion of society that we refuse to imagine as one of us, we need the opportunity to interact with others unlike ourselves. The idea that interaction among diverse people can enhance civic life is not unlike Allport's contact hypothesis, the theory that bringing members of opposing groups into contact with one another reduces racial prejudice (1954). Allport suggested that intergroup hostility could be reduced if members of opposing groups had the ability to get to know one another on an intimate level, the ability to interact as equals in terms of status, the opportunity to engage in a cooperative effort, and institutional support in the effort to break down the barriers of prejudice (Brewer and Brown 1998). In a review of the subsequent social psychological research, Brewer and Brown note that theories that focus on group divisions as social identities have suggested that in order to overcome prejudice, contact should encourage the participants to view each other as individuals (Brewer and Miller 1984), make categories salient that encompass members of both groups (e.g., Gaertner et al. 1989), or make categories salient that cut across the preexisting divisions (Doise 1978). All of these theories suggest that a way to break down barriers is to foster an environment in which individuals have a chance to recognize the "other" as people who are more like oneself than previously imagined.

Both the civic-republican and liberal-individualist views value diversity within discussion. The civic-republican view expects that interaction with divergent others opens the participants' minds to different points of view. Politics begins with conflict (Barber 1984, 129), as controversy allows people to voice differences and therefore learn to empathize with one another (137). It is exposure to divergent views that enables the virtue of tolerance to exist (Sullivan, Piereson, and Marcus 1982).

Putnam (2000) recognizes the importance of exposure to diversity and advocates "bridging" social capital (chap. 22, pp. 22–23). This interaction with diverse others is distinct from "bonding" social capital, which is the act of interacting with like others. Achieving bridging social capital faces multiple obstacles. First, although bridging social capital, or interaction among people of diverse backgrounds, is more likely to foster generalized trust, it is people who are already more trusting who are more likely to self-select into diverse groups (Stolle 1998). Second, most interaction is not "bridging" social capital.

The cumulative effect of individuals acting in ways they think are appropriate for "people like me," self-selecting into groups on the basis of "the kind of people that I am" in opposition to "others," is a society in which social categories are institutionalized. And when institutionalized, these ideas of appropriateness affect the opportunity for policy making to consider divergent perspectives. The political processes underlying the formation of municipalities and special, or service, districts intentionally create racial and economic homogeneity (Burns 1994). Increasingly, racial segregation takes place by municipality, not just by neighborhood, meaning less white and black contact over time (Massey and Hajnal 1995). As Burns writes,

> The way in which Americans have constructed local autonomy means that we have created a space in American politics where race and class are embedded in boundaries. Because municipal boundaries can be boundaries between races and classes, boundaries that reinforce homogeneity, the possibilities for transformative public discussion are severely limited. (1994, 177)

Although social and economic processes have resulted in de facto segregation, the creation of special districts legislates such barriers. Thus, just as the federal government has institutionalized what it means to be an American through ascriptive citizenship laws (Smith 1997), municipalities have formalized what it means to be a member of a given geographic community.

The resulting pervasiveness of racial and socioeconomic segregation in American society means that the groups people participate in tend toward homogeneity with respect to major social divisions on the basis of both individual choice and institutional constraints. Among the nationally representative respondents in the 1990 Citizen Participation Study, there is a clear relationship between the racial composition of one's neighborhood and the racial composition of one's voluntary association.[13] This pattern is more than a matter of whites wanting to spend time with whites or of Latinos wanting to spend time only with Latinos, and so on. Members of the public sort out what kinds of people they are and which are their communities of concern, but they are aided by institutionalized chasms between people of different races, ethnicities, classes, and genders.

Evidence abounds that people choose to interact with perceived likes, and thus tend to talk with people who share similar views about politics (Huckfeldt and Sprague 1987, 1995; Berelson, Lazarsfeld, and McPhee 1954; Lazarsfeld, Berelson, and Gaudet 1944; Marsden 1987; Mutz and Martin 2001). This tendency operates even when the pool of discussion partners is constrained (Huckfeldt and Sprague 1995). For example, in a study of racial segregation and interaction in Detroit neighborhoods, Sigelman et al. (1996) found that the relationship between residential integration and interracial friendships is a tenuous one at best. Among whites, that relationship is curvilinear. Past a racial balance of 50–50 white/black neighborhoods, whites exhibit *less* interracial contact. Among blacks, the relationship between neighborhood diversity and interracial friendships is likely spurious: The racial composition of a neighborhood is a less significant predictor of interracial contact than whether the person came of age in an interracial environment.

Similar forces seem to operate even in the workplace, the most promising arena for exposure to cross-cutting viewpoints (Mutz 2002; Mutz and Mondak 1998). The positive affect for out-group members that work groups can create does not appear to transfer to other settings (Harding and Hogrefe 1952). Moreover, the American workplace continues to be heavily segregated along race and gender lines (Reskin et al. 1999). Hierarchical segregation reinforces social divisions; for example, even though it places women in direct contact with men it is typically as status subordinates (Bielby and Baron 1984). With respect to political attitudes specifically, when people are aware that they are political minorities in a workplace, such as Republicans working in an automobile factory where Democrats are predominant, they seek out others with the same minority points of view (Finifter 1974). Therefore, even in the workplace, institutional design would have to create a context conducive to bridging social capital and the development of a common identity.

Because informal political talk arises as a by-product of other topics, and perceived preexisting likenesses serve as the basis for beginning a conversation, the tendency to talk to like others about public matters is not easily overcome, even if unlike others are nearby.

This study illuminates a further obstacle to building bridging social capital: attachments to social groups are tools that people use to make sense of their world and thus are not easily set aside. People are not automatically tolerant, civil, or other-regarding in situations of diversity. What constitutes civility is, itself, constructed through interaction, and this has historically prevented the consideration of a wider array of viewpoints (Sapiro 1999). In addition, it is only when people perceive that crosscutting views are legitimate that exposure to them is accompanied by increased levels of tolerance (Mutz 2002). Discussion among diverse views has the tendency to suppress minority viewpoints rather than to incorporate them in the group's final decision (Moscovici and Zavalloni 1969; Doise 1969; Sanders 1997). Even when people engage in interaction with others unlike themselves in formal settings equipped with decision-making procedures, discussion on its own is likely to lead to disarray rather than consensus when perspectives about the desired ends diverge (Mansbridge 1983).

Any public is composed of many subpublics, or "subaltern counterpublics" (Fraser 1992), within which discussion likely takes place and across which discussion is most likely scarce (Granovetter 1973; Liu and Duff 1972; Dawson 2001). These subpublics of social attachments often trump attachment to the community as a whole. Therefore, diversity in public discussion does not necessarily function as independent opinions that when aggregated produce a more accurate perception of the "truth." Diversity is typically made up of discrete elements, and these elements, or particular reference groups, are tools of discussion, as this book has shown. As Sanders writes, traditional views of civic life miss this. "Indeed, democratic citizens as described in these theories seem to live on another planet (quite literally in the case of Ackerman 1980): they are devoid of race, class, and gender and all the benefits and liabilities associated by Americans with these features (1997, 353)."

It would seem that the key to improving civic life is not to ask people to set aside these attachments but to design institutions that cause us to recognize them. We cannot as a society arrive at solutions to common problems if we do not know how to communicate. This underlies the central paradox of citizen discussion, as normally described in models of civic life.

The problem is this: according to theories of deliberative democracy, a key criterion for good deliberation is that it be based on the idea of equality and joint membership in a given community. However, if this is a precondition, how can talk among citizens who do not share such understandings produce greater equality or identity as members of the same community? In a study of public participation in town meetings about school desegregation, Mendelberg and Oleske (2000) illustrate the obstacle. They found that when participating in an integrated meeting, whites were not motivated to speak on behalf of the broader community, but used language and arguments that were very similar to those used in a segregated meeting. They conclude that in order for deliberation to help dominant groups appreciate subordinate groups' concerns, citizens first need a common language based on common experience.

How do we go about achieving this? What institutions can break the "closed circle of deliberation" (Mendelberg and Oleske 2000, 186)? Putnam, in his prescription for greater social capital, proposes several potential remedies, among them new urbanist methods of urban planning (407–8) and the Internet (410–11).

Let us examine these in turn. New urbanism has been proposed by other scholars as a way to reduce segregation (e.g., Sandel 1996). However, solutions such as changes in urban planning and architecture hold very limited promise for fostering notions of community that are more inclusive with respect to race, and little if any promise for diminishing sex discrimination. New urbanism is a style of planning that promotes design oriented to pedestrians and public transportation, rather than design that caters to automobiles. Streets are designed as havens for pedestrians (Calthorpe 1993) and residential areas are designed to provide dense population within walking distance of amenities and services (Kunstler 1993, 1996). Although most proponents of this kind of design emphasize the ecological benefits of communities that encourage pedestrian traffic, some point to the social benefits. Reviving Jane Jacobs's (1961) claim, advocates of new urbanism believe that communities flourish when people have the opportunity to interact with each other. However, it glosses over the fact that neighboring is more likely in segregated contexts.

Moreover, while such a planning style does institutionalize opportunities for crosscutting discussions, it cannot ensure debate about a new public philosophy or talk about the common good. People that go about their daily lives may work to develop trusting friendships, but they are not necessarily intent on establishing respect for people who operate according to different models of appropriate behavior. Although social trust *can* arise from discussion among diverse perspectives (Mutz and Martin 2001; E. Smith 1998), informal talk among people of different status is not automatically civil or tolerant (Herzog 1998, chap. 4). Simply put, mere opportunity does not a diverse discussion make. Thinking back to the Old Timers, notice that people have shared the same small space of the corner store *for years* without interacting, let alone developing a common identity.

Another potential mechanism for bringing people of diverse backgrounds together is the Internet. As Putnam notes, however (410–11), there are some important cautions against making this claim. Because people do exhibit strong tendencies to talk only with people they perceive to be like themselves, new technologies are not guaranteed to foster bridging social capital. The ability to "point and click" to enter Internet Web sites and "chat rooms" (virtual discussion groups that address topics of specific interest) likely results in discussions among people who hold similar points of view.[14] This may serve as a source of exchange among mutually respecting people, nourishing perceptions that most people do *not* wish to take advantage of each other, *do* try to be fair, and in short, can be trusted. But what will it do for understanding and respecting other perspectives? Through hyper self-selection and narrowing of messages to particular groups of people, we may increasingly interact primarily with people who are trusting of others "like us" but who are wary of members of out-groups. Virtual communities may give rise to boundaries more impenetrable than those characterizing geographic communities.[15]

We might expect that mass media could foster individuals' psychological attachments to the communities in which they live (Friedland 2001). Left to market mechanisms, however, there is no guarantee that the news media will undertake the coverage such mobilization requires. Use of local media sources can foster positive affect toward one's community and attachment to the community as a whole as opposed to the larger society, specific neighborhoods, and voluntary associations, but an overemphasis on conflict can prevent a local news source such as a weekly newspaper from achieving this goal (McLeod and Daily 1996). Moreover, regardless of news media content, part of the work of forming perceptions of community is done at a level below the mass media environment—within the neighborhood or in face-to-face interaction (Friedland 2001, 383).

The power of face-to-face interaction cannot be overstated. Recall that the Old Timers often participated in discussions without words, only using their body language. This is a kind of involvement that only face-to-face interaction enables. The opportunity to look one another in the eye and relate as members of the same group without exchanging words forms the basis of social bonds that are unlike those formed through less personal means of communication.

With these potential remedies and their obstacles in mind, consider an alternative democratic project: intergroup dialogue programs. These are programs in which volunteers of diverse backgrounds agree to dialogue with one another over multiple sessions about pressing public issues, such as race relations, civil rights for gays and lesbians, violence, police-community relations, and education achievement gaps. The discussions are usually led by trained facilitators and often end in "action forums" in which the participants propose and plan ways to address the issues they have discussed.[16] Variations on this model include dinner dialogue programs, in which small groups of people representing a diversity of backgrounds meet regularly over dinner,[17] and communitywide book discussions organized by public libraries, local governments, local news media, and civic organizations.[18]

Such intergroup dialogue programs are taking place in communities across the United States, fostered by several national organizations. These include the Topsfield Foundation's Study Circles Resource Center, the National Conference on Communities and Justice, the YWCA, Hope in the Cities, the Anti-Defamation League, and the National League of Cities. The Study Circles Resource Center alone has provided instructional materials and program support to more than 230 dialogue programs in communities in forty-two states and the District of Columbia. In a 2000 best practices report, the Center reported that seventeen of its top programs had attracted more than twenty-eight thousand participants.[19] In 1997, the Center for Living Democracy published a list of eighty-five intergroup dialogue programs and estimated "conservatively that at least *hundreds of thousands of Americans are currently engaged in sustained, serious, community-based dialogues*" (DuBois and Hutson 1997, 12, emphasis in original). Yet another indicator of the ubiquity of these programs comes from a Western Justice Center Internet posting in 1999 that listed 440 intergroup dialogue programs around the nation.

Even though interpersonal dialogue programs date back to the 1870s and the Chautauqua adult education movement in New York, such programs have gained renewed energy at the turn of the twenty-first century (Schoem et al. 2001).[20] Arguably the leading force behind the communitywide intergroup dialogue programs is the Study Circles Resource Center, founded by the late Paul Aicher's Topsfield Foundation in 1989. The Center was designed to give people a chance to solve public problems through face-to-face discussion (McCoy 2001). After the Rodney King verdict in 1991,[21] many communities focused on race relations through the use of "Can't We All Just Get Along," an SCRC dialogue guide. And after September 11, 2001, many others formed discussions around another SCRC dialogue guide, "Facing the Future: How Should We Respond to the Attacks on Our Nation."[22]

Why are these programs promising? This is what we know: Institutions can place people of diverse backgrounds in close proximity to one another. In addition, this study has shown that through discussion, people can develop views of the world in which they define themselves as members of the same community. This study has also shown, however, that some type of mechanism is required for people to recognize their similarities and develop collective identities. Intergroup dialogue programs take into account each of these considerations.

Can such programs single-handedly eliminate intergroup tension? Of course not. Most obviously, the participants are a self-selected group. They have a desire to focus intently on public issues with people of diverse backgrounds. Second, improvement of intergroup divides requires institutional change and action beyond talking.

Intergroup dialogue programs can lead to concrete policy change. The City of Springfield, Illinois, diversified its fire and police forces after participants in Study Circles called for such a change.[23] Program organizers in Minneapolis and St. Paul, Minnesota, report changes in housing policy legislation and decision-making procedures (Reichler and Dredge 1997, 61); Oklahoma activists report changes in state criminal justice legislation (Houlé and Roberts 2000, 198). Officials in Portland, Maine; Decatur, Georgia; and Lima, Ohio, report changes in planning procedures partly as a result of the Study Circle programs (Houlé and Roberts 2000, 195; "Investing a Community of Stakeholders" 2000). News organizations that have opted to participate in the programs display changes in their coverage, such as is the case with the Aurora (Illinois) *Beacon News* and newspapers in Fort Myers, Florida, and North Little Rock, Arkansas (Houlé and Roberts 2000, 198). In addition, there is evidence that such dialogues give rise to new coalitions across organizations within communities[24] (Houlé and Roberts 2000, 184), spur new community festivals[25] (Houlé and Roberts 2000, 189), and encourage neighborhood initiatives to address racism in local schools (Flavin-McDonald 1998).

But notice what these programs achieve even if policy change is not an immediate output. Through the dialogues, participants lay open their different experiences, testify to their perceptions of other groups, and thereby gain an awareness of the perspectives through which other people view public problems. Does such dialogue result in a better understanding of different perspectives and the tools to communicate across lines of difference? Such outcomes are difficult to gauge, and are questions for future analyses, but some evidence exists. Most research on intergroup dialogue has been conducted in educational settings.[26] Work on intergroup dialogue in an undergraduate set-ting suggests that it can increase awareness of structural causes of inequality (Lopez, Gurin, and Nagda 1998) as well as personal growth and awareness of the role of identity in social relationships (Hurtado 2001).

Self-reports from participants in community dialogues suggest that these programs succeed in providing a safe haven for discussing openly di-vergent viewpoints as a route toward achieving a more pluralistic conception of community (Hurtado 2001; DuBois and Hutson 1997, 18–20). Participants in Study Circle programs report that the discussions gave them courage to talk about racial and ethnic differences and helped them to see people un-like themselves in new ways, to form friendships across lines of difference,[27] and to begin to conceptualize their communities in new ways (Houlé and Roberts 2000, 180–83). Studies of participants in communitywide intergroup dialogue programs suggest that participants felt positively about their expe-rience in the program,[28] believed it gave them a greater understanding of other groups and more awareness of issues related to intergroup relations in their community,[29] and left them with a greater perceived stake in the local community.[30]

Granted, the outcomes differ slightly for whites as opposed to people of color. People of color commonly call for the programs to lead to action and policy change, while white participants tend to be content with increased understanding (Flavin-McDonald 1998).[31] Whereas whites gain comfort in talking about race, people of color report that thinking about race is a con-stant fact of their lives and thus the main benefit from the intergroup dialogue programs is a recognition that talking can improve intergroup communica-tion and provide an opportunity to learn more about their own race.[32] In addition, a study of the Dayton [Ohio] Dialogue on Race Relations revealed that 51 percent of the white participants felt closer to blacks over the course of their participation, and 50 percent of the black participants felt closer to whites.[33] However, while only 11 percent of the whites felt less close to blacks over the course of the program, over a quarter, 27 percent, of the blacks who participated felt less close to whites (Keniston et al. 2002). Clearly this is not an entirely feel-good enterprise. In the dialogues people are confronted with many of the unspoken stereotypes members of groups hold about one another.[34]

Intergroup dialogue programs strive to address fears about confronting intergroup relations openly. Yet they do not assume that this work is com-fortable. They recognize that identity-based perspectives are central to the way people view problems and therefore must be acknowledged before peo-ple of varying standpoints can work together. Sandy Robinson, director of the Springfield Community-Wide Study Circles Program on Race Relations, phrases the rationale behind such programs this way:

> You have to come to know one another on a personal level, know one another's experiences, become a part of each other's story, and see where maybe your own personal biases, your own personal history, may cause you to see certain things in a certain way. Then and only then, after you've made that connection, can you begin to really deal with some of their innermost issues and see that the way you look at the world is not the only way. (Malick 1999, 8)

This philosophy builds on the dynamics uncovered in this book. On the one hand, a contrast with an out-group might seem necessary for the development of a group identity or for a sense of community to occur. But perhaps the opposing force against which the resource of identity can develop need not be other people but a societal ill such as racial achievement gaps in the public schools, escalating income gaps, or neighborhood crime. If provided the opportunity and the structure, interpersonal talk can forge bonds and develop ways of understanding that can improve the quality of our collective lives.

By enabling people to develop a shared identity, interpersonal talk arms people with a common language, a resource for collectively thinking through problems. This book has shown how groups of people develop collective identities. It has also shown that these definitions of one's group are not a given. People *create* them, through their actions and their words. Together, people create the lens through which they see the world. In the agency of this action, the potential for profound social change lies.

Dave, the Old Timer, said, "Government is us." If he was right, if democratic government is truly about popular sovereignty, then we, as citizens, govern each other. This is a substantial task. To make choices that will affect the lives of all people who share the world in which we live, we need, at a minimum, to be able to communicate. Therefore, part of our responsibility as citizens is to *collectively* develop our definitions of community while at the same time knowing enough about each other to respect our differences. Intergroup dialogue programs are just one of the projects we should pursue toward these ends.

Methodological Appendix

In this study, I investigated people doing public discussion in their own terms on their own turf. In other words, I made use of a data collection approach that is rather unorthodox in the study of public opinion, especially among political scientists. Participant observation (the act of simultaneously participating in and systematically observing human behavior) offered the best opportunity to watch informal political interaction in a natural setting. The balance was weighted on the "observer" rather than "participant" side of these two roles in each of my observation sites. This tradeoff was the most tipped toward "participant" in my observations of the Old Timers. Since such direct contact with my "subjects" influenced what I observed and how I observed it, the nature of my relationships with each of the groups requires some explanation.

As I explained in the introduction, I began observing the Old Timers after asking longtime Ann Arborites for suggestions of sites in which people met regularly to spend time with one another. One morning, during the period in which I was investigating potential places, I stopped at the corner store. In the middle of a cluster of retired folks sat the local member of Congress, holding a public question-and-answer session. She evidently thought this was a site for political interaction, and so did I.

Notably, even Representative Lynn Rivers did not sit at the large tables, but instead held court at the small tables across the way. I did not understand the significance of the spatial segregation in the store on that first day. However, over the next few weeks I noticed the many ways in which the Old Timers create themselves as a group, including the physical boundaries they enforce. I realized that gaining access to their portion of the room would take some time and caution. For the first month that I spent time there, I sat at the small tables. I did this even before I realized the boundaries around the large tables, because it was possible to sit alone there. If no small table was free when I arrived, I would sit outside the store and observe who was entering and exiting the place, the kind of cars they drove, and the way passersby regarded it.

During the first month, I observed the use of the place, the character of the people that spend time there, and made myself a familiar face. I talked frequently with the people sitting at the small tables, the African Americans and white blue-collar workers. While watching these behavioral patterns, I noticed one of the Old Timers' group norms. The Old Timers would take turns going behind the counter to get the "regular" and "decaf" coffee urns, and pour a round for each other. As they started inquiring about my purpose there and became used to my presence, I gradually included myself in this coffee etiquette by pouring coffee for Old Timers. Once they realized that I was not a new addition to the counter staff, I asked if I could join them at their tables.

My status as a relatively young woman might seem a barrier to gaining access to the group of Old Timers, an all-male group, or to the people who sit along the windows, of whom only one regular was female, but it may very well have enabled these observations. As a woman, my relative silence did not seem unnatural, especially among the Old Timers, a group of socially and economically conservative men. Although I joined in on the conversations enough to "earn my keep," my intent was primarily to listen and watch. When I visited, they often asked me questions. However, I bore less of a burden to bring up topics, crack jokes, and offer witty comments than did the rest of the Old Timers.

My status as a white person presented an obstacle in my attempts to observe both the Old Timers and the small table regulars. The morning crowd was clearly segregated by race, and according to this criteria, I "belonged" with the Old Timers. Since I spent time with members of both groups, this presented some tensions. I addressed this by being as open as possible about my desire to make acquaintances with members of both groups. Still, people sitting on opposite sides of the room for many years were obviously curious about what went on across the way. When anyone expressed discomfort with my attempts to traverse these boundaries, I paid close attention to it, answered their questions, and used their behavior to learn about their perceptions of each other.

At first, I explained my purpose in general terms. Since I wished to watch political conversations arise naturally, I said that I studied *social* science (not political science specifically), and was interested in group discussions. (After one year, I specified that my training is in political science.) I promised them confidentiality and asked them to please inform me if there was ever a time when they preferred that I not listen in on their conversations. (No one ever made this request.) As arranged through the University of Michigan's behavioral subjects committee, I established consent informally, without a signed consent form. Instead, I gave each member a letter explaining these details along with my name and telephone number, in the event that they wanted to ask additional questions. I also stated that when sitting with their group, I would remain in one spot. Therefore, they could avoid me by moving to another table. Although old Timers did occasionally switch tables, I have no reason to believe this was done to move out of my earshot.

To gain access to the guild, I attended one of their weekly meetings and asked if I could join the group. I explained that I was a graduate student at the nearby university studying social science and informal communication. I gave them a letter asking for their permission to be a part of their group and to use what I observed in my research. Over lunch, the leader of the group asked for a voice vote on whether or not to allow my observations, and the group kindly agreed.

While spending time with both groups, I tried to minimize my disruption of the usual flow of the conversations by acting as an engaged, yet neutral, participant. I spoke as little as possible, trying not to generate topics of discussion. However, during the first several weeks of participating, I found that I had to contribute to the conversations occasionally, in order to fit in. In participant observation, the participating enables the observing. The Old Timers, the mixed-gender group that met later in the morning, the small-table regulars, and the guild members each asked about my background and from time to time about my reasons for joining them. When asked direct questions about my research, I answered as completely as possible without revealing, until later, that my main interest was in the political content of their conversations.

Because of my age (and because of my gender in the context of the Old Timers), the members of the various groups regarded me as somewhat of a novelty. "What's a young thing like you doing in a place like this?" was a typical refrain from the Old Timers. My novelty status was especially apparent among them. They would joke about my marital status and about cheating on their wives with me. But this is just the surface of the relationship we developed. I thankfully had reason to not storm off in response to such comments and therefore had the time to realize that such joking was their way of including me.

My field notes convey that the transformation from observer to member did indeed take some time with the Old Timers. It took a full month before I had the courage to ask to sit with them, and several more months to overcome the worries about whether or not they resented my presence. The group in general was extremely warm and respectful toward me. However, several individuals never outgrew their skepticism of my motives. Also, several people worried me more than the others about my potential to have access to their conversations over an extended period of time. Early on in my observations, I sat down one morning with Dave and Baxter, who kept right on talking without taking a moment to greet me. I had not yet learned that this was typical, and not a form of shunning. The next morning, I sat at the small tables rather than the large tables, partly out of fear of being ignored again. But when Dave left for the day, he (uncharacteristically) stopped by the small tables to ask me how I was doing. I asked him how he was, and responded with a sarcastic "Aw, just great." "Are you pulling my leg?" I asked. He said, "No, but I would like to pull yours!"

I learned several things that morning. First, gaining access meant learning quickly about the many different personalities that comprised the Old Timers. Dave's grumpiness was part of his persona, not a sign that I was not welcome. Second, part of their way of including me was to flirt with me, deal with me as a woman in a way with which they were familiar. Finally, I realized that they liked having me around.

So at what point did I make the transition from being just an observer to also being a member? It seems common to remember transformations in our lives as focal events rather than the gradual processes that they typically are, but with respect to the Old Timers, one event stands out in my field notes as a key point in this transition. It was a common occurrence that a card would go around the Old Timers' tables for everyone to sign. This would be a card that would be sent to another Old Timer to celebrate a birthday, a major wedding anniversary, urge a "get well soon," or offer sympathy with respect to the death of a loved one. Several times, they signed cards addressed to the spouses and families of Old Timers who had died. During the first several months of my observations, these cards would pass by me. But then the key event occurred: one day, the Old Timers passed a card to me. I asked, "Do you want *me* to sign the card?" And the passer responded, "Yes, he [the recipient] would like that."

Other observable indicators help round out the nature of my "membership." I was given a membership card (printed in 1982) and a pin with the name of the place printed on it. When I became engaged and then married, many questions were asked and congratulations offered. And when I graduated from graduate school, and packed up to leave town, I was a recipient of one of the group cards. Moreover, the card included a generous gift certificate to a local department store. And it was signed by many of the Old Timers.

Another indicator of our relationship is at what point we introduced our family members to each other. As mentioned earlier in the book, many of them had known one another's families for years. This was not the case with me, obviously. Several people brought their wives to the corner store to meet me. Once when the store held a picnic, another member walked up to me and my then-fiancé and said, "Oh, I am so glad you are here. I was telling my wife I hoped you would come so that I could introduce you." And I did the same in return. When my family members visited, I took them to the corner store to meet the people there, who had by that time become a central feature of my life.

When I returned to the store in January 2001, I learned that one of the members, a man who had at first given me unwelcome looks but later regularly went out of his way to free up a chair for me, had died. It is indicative of the nature of my relationship with the group that this news was delivered to me gently, as it had been the several other times someone had to break bad news to me about a member of the group. Not only was I aware that I had developed personal relationships with the members of the group, and thus was myself a member, but the other Old Timers were aware of it, too.

In that sense I did become a member of the group, but I never did become a full-fledged participant. First, despite our friendships, the Old Timers and I were well aware that I was writing field notes about their conversations on a daily basis. Second, I did not continue on from the corner store to the golf course, with many of the others. And last, we did not share our lives as peers. Much of their interest in and curiosity about me was likely because I was *not* one of them. I did share my life with them, but perhaps it is the fate of all participant observers to be as much under the observation bell as the people one observes.

My relationship with the small-table regulars was slightly different. I spent a great deal of time with them early on in my observations, as I was attempting to gain access to the Old Timers. Although I continued to talk with them throughout my years of observation, they regarded me as a friendly acquaintance, but also as a member of the Old Timers. My relationship with the later morning regulars was somewhat similar. They knew me as the person who was writing a book about the Old Timers, and therefore treated me like a friend of a friend.

When I left Ann Arbor, I would occasionally send a letter saying hello to all the people in the corner store—the Old Timers as well as the small-table regulars. Once, my husband was in town on business and delivered a block of sharp cheddar cheese I had promised to a regular at the small tables. He offered greetings to a variety of people in the store on my behalf and gathered their latest news to report back to me.

I also corresponded with the guild after leaving town. They, like the Old Timers, treated me as a member. They enlisted me to help staff their occasional after-church sales. They inquired about my whereabouts when I disrupted my usual pattern of visits. I participated in the sewing projects, did the dishes after our lunches, and signed birthday or get well cards for other members.

Whether or not I was a full-fledged member is ultimately not as important as how my membership influenced what I observed. In conducting this study, I have paid close attention to these sources of bias, but one additional aspect deserves attention here. What I learned from this study about social identity more generally was mirrored in my own personal experience, especially with the Old Timers. In relationships with other people, we learn a great deal about ourselves. The Old Timers are much more conservative economically and socially than I am, and prior to spending time with them, I was rather self-righteous about my own political views. Fortunately, however, I had reason to listen intently to their thoughts and acknowledge as thoroughly as possible the perspectives through which they viewed the world. I not only enjoyed spending time with the Old Timers, I grew to respect them sincerely. This had one important effect on what I observed: I was slow to recognize aspects of their interaction that one might not want to publicize about friends. I was both surprised by and reluctant to address the extent to which race entered their conversations.

It is my ethical duty as a political scientist and a citizen who desires to improve race relations to acknowledge the centrality of race in their discussions. It was also my duty to admit to the Old Timers these processes as I observed them. Therefore, when I said good-bye to the group in July 2000 (unaware that I would return in January 2001 to listen to their conversations about the 2000 presidential election outcome), I wrote a four-page letter to them (on $5^{1/2} \times 8^{1/2}$-inch paper) explaining the crux of my dissertation and making plain the less palatable conclusions of my study (see appendix 7). I included with this letter a stamped, self-addressed envelope and asked them to please respond. I handed out the letter with peanut butter cookies expecting them to eat the cookies but stuff the letters into their pockets. Instead, they sat silently and took the time to read my letter. After awhile, one of them, John, said, "Thank you for this." And Arnie, who had earlier half-jokingly suggested that I was spending time with them just to study conservative people, said, "Thank you for your words." A few others said "very nice letter." This was the extent of their comments. No one used the self-addressed envelope to send me a response or rebuttal.

My presence did alter what I observed among the Old Timers in several other respects. They reported "cleaning up their language" when I was around, and claimed that they addressed issues dealing with "the university" more during my visits. (I was able to verify this by sitting at one table while close enough to another that I could eavesdrop on conversations that did not include me.) Neither of these effects were detrimental to the project at hand. Their attempts to swear less and tell fewer dirty jokes in my presence may mean that I was less often able to observe how these modes of conversation are used to make sense of politics and the world. But my eavesdropping suggests that these forms do not differ qualitatively from other means of making sense. The possibility that they more frequently talked about the university in my presence may have led to an overestimation of the salience of such issues to their lives, but it also may have enabled me to more accurately observe their interpretation of town-gown politics. How much of what they said was an attempt to show off for me? For example, when Dave remarked that he wanted to shoot all gays and lesbians when talking about the Big Three automakers' same-sex benefits policy, was that a reflection of his true beliefs or an exaggeration for my benefit? I have no doubt that this was an exaggeration. But it was also a relative indicator of the way Dave places himself in contrast to other people in the world. Thus I take the implied violence with a grain of salt, but the gist of the sentiment as a valid reflection of the tools Dave uses to understand public affairs.

As for the guild, my presence likely stimulated more conversations about the university in that context as well. Other potential sources of bias include an attempt to talk about topics that they perceived I would be interested in, out of politeness to me as a newcomer. It is also possible that they avoided controversial topics more in my presence, to avoid exposing me to arguments within the group. Ideally, to get a sense of how my presence altered the guild's conversations, I would have had a way to observe their interactions when I was not there. Because the group was small and sat in such a way that most conversations were conversations with the entire group,[1] I did not have the opportunity to eavesdrop on conversations behind me, as I did with the Old Timers. To get around this, I would occasionally arrive late to the meetings, to observe seating arrangements and conversation topics that emerged when I was not around. I observed no departures from the modes of interaction that took place when I was present.

Methods of Recording, Analysis, and Validity Checks

To record what I observed, I composed field notes immediately following the one- to two-hour visits with both groups.[2] I reconstructed as much of their conversations as I could recall, focusing on those portions that were explicitly political. I noted which portions I had forgotten, and which quotes were paraphrases. Throughout this study, portions of the conversations that I could not recall or that have been omitted for ease of exposition are denoted as follows: " ... [...] ... " I also recorded impressions about the speakers' tones, their body language, the manner in which topics changed, how conversations changed when others arrived, details about the physical setting, as well as anecdotes about the history of their groups.

To test the validity of this recording procedure, I tape-recorded several conversations and compared the transcripts to the field notes I composed from memory. In general, my field notes are abridged versions of the actual conversations, and capture the gist, tone, and basic language of their stories. I managed to record much of the original wording of their conversations, most of the factual information, and the order in which they spoke. What is missed are mostly side jokes to each other, elaborations of their stories or comments, and minor details such as the type of place in which an event occurred or the kind of food they reported eating. (Please see the end of this appendix for examples of such comparisons). To be sure, not tape recording all of the conversations limits the richness of the analysis I can conduct. I chose to not use a tape recorder initially for fear that it would complicate my ability to gain access to these groups. Duneier (2001) makes a strong statement that participant observers ought to use tape recorders if they are going to use conversations as an indicator of the meaning of a culture (339–40). Unlike Duneier in his (second) study of homeless street vendors (he had almost completed a study of one street vendor before deciding to expand the study and use a tape recorder), I did not have validation from an existing group member when I began my observations. I decided to err on the side of increasing my chances of gaining access, rather than increase the detail and accuracy with which I recorded the conversations.

As time went on, I could have recorded more of the conversations. I did not notice that the nature of their exchanges differed significantly when the machine was on, but my place in the exchanges changed. I felt overly intrusive, and the conversation became too much about me when I placed the machine in the center of the table. When people would arrive after the recorder had been placed there, we would have to go through a round of explanations for its presence. The validity checks I performed with the recordings led me to believe that the gain in accuracy I obtained from using the recorder was not worth the price of the arrogance I felt I conveyed when I introduced a recorder into their morning ritual.

To compensate for the lack of verbatim transcripts, I wrote the most detailed notes possible, and made concerted attempts to remember the gist of all relevant conversations by rehearsing them in my head as the talk turned to other topics. The data used in this study gains additional validity in chapter 7, in which most of the conversations forming the basis of analyses of interpretation of the 2000 election were taperecorded.

Methods of Analyzing the Conversations

This study has separated, for analytic purposes, the processes involved in informal talk into two parts: (1) the process of developing and clarifying social identities, and (2) the process of making sense of politics. To investigate social identity, I examined the way the groups talked about a variety of topics, not just politics, as well as their physical behavior toward in-group and out-group members in the sites in which they met. I used both counterfactuals of the variety of ways topics could be addressed as well as field notes from observation of the other groups as points of contrast to theorize the way they interpreted political issues and the resources they used to do so.[3]

To investigate the related process of making sense of politics, I focused specifically on all conversations dealing with political events, issues, or people, much like related focus-group research (Delli Carpini and Williams 1998; Gamson 1992). To reiterate, by "explicitly political," I mean topics that deal with the government directly, such as public policy issues, elections, or public officials.

In focusing on these types of conversations, I used a distinction between "political" and "social" that is more analytical than actual. Typically, political science has considered "politics" and "political behavior" as those actions that are connected to government institutions and elections (Bourque and Grossholtz 1974). But the political is not just the realm of people in power in the public (outside the home), nor is it removed from the private lives of individuals (Crow 1997). For example, the balance of power between husbands and wives and the level of respect women are given in the home affect male and female levels of political participation (Burns, Schlozman, and Verba 1997). The role of parenthood, a seemingly social one, also has political implications: for example, it appears to increase participation in local school politics while decreasing activity in national politics (Jennings 1979). The cultural norms that assume a division between public and private underscore their interconnection by hindering women's participation (Sapiro 1983). In order to acknowledge the overlaps between the public and private sphere and to further explain how this overlap works, I define "political" as behaviors and events that relate directly to the government, public officials, elections, or public policy, and define the "social" realm as the interconnection of lives of people outside government institutions.

With this focus on political topics, I read through the transcripts of conversations, looking for and coding general structures to the conversations (Delli Carpini and Williams 1998). For example, when a read-through led me to believe that conversations about Hillary Rodham Clinton often included references to women in their own lives, I was able to call up all conversations about her and assess this conclusion with focused scrutiny.

I attempted to bolster the validity of my conclusions in the observation portion of the study in a variety of ways. One was to simply ask the participants directly (in the later stages of the project) about their involvement in their groups, and their perceptions of the political conversations within them. Another was the use of the self-administered questionnaire to gauge their individually offered political attitudes and demographics and perceptions of the place. I also relied on other ethnographies to learn about the nature of identity processes within groups whose memberships drew from demographic categories other than those observed in this study. Finally, I attempted to validate stories and conceptions of the way "the community" used to be, using histories and historical documents about Ann Arbor in the twentieth century (such as maps and newspapers, and recent documentaries and biographies compiled by the neighborhood association). I checked such things as whether the neighborhoods were segregated by ethnicity and class when they were growing up (which they were.) Were many of the proprietors on Main Street German-speaking? (Yes). Has the city grown as much as they report? (Yes, it underwent a major population boom and geographic expansion after World War II [Marwil 1990; Eldersveld 1995].)

A Multimethod Approach

The multiple methods used in this study—content analysis of news, analysis of national sample survey data and self-administered questionnaires, along with participant observation—were employed because they informed each other. Each method has its weaknesses; in combination, they provide a robust view of a phenomenon of political communication (Neuman, Just, and Crigler 1992, chap. 2; Just et al. 1996). The observations helped uncover the processes of informal political talk, revealing that interaction in general, not just talk, and not just political talk, is relevant for understanding how people make sense of politics. The survey data enabled generalization of the processes observed to a broader population. Questionnaires administered to the Old Timers helped locate the limits of both the secondary data analysis and the analyses of observations. The self-administered questionnaires captured the political leanings of the Old Timers with greater specificity than was possible through conversations.[4] The respondents' marginalia also revealed confusion over survey questions that improved the analysis of national sample surveys by injecting a healthy dose of skepticism. For example, the Old Timers were confused over questions that asked whether they "felt close to" various social groups. As survey respondents, they were unclear whether the questions asked about affect, physical proximity, or psychological affinity. Observations of their conversations, conducted in their own language and understandings, clearly conveyed their social identification with whites, men, veterans, and the middle class, and in turn informed the data gathered through the questionnaire.

It is a happy circumstance to be a member of a field of inquiry that is home to scholars studying similar phenomena from a variety of angles and with a variety of methods. We should strive to develop methods appropriate to our questions, rather than design questions to fit the most revered methods. Participant observation may not provide the luxury of quantifiable confidence intervals around our parameter estimates. But giving up this luxury—as long as we are careful to specify how we know what we say we know (Manna 2000)—means a gain in detail and an insight into process that is unavailable by any other means.

Sample Field Note Validity Check

Following is an example of a comparison of my field notes (which I composed from memory immediately following the visits) to actual conversations. These examples include conversations on the first and last topic of conversations I observed during one visit in the summer of 1998 and a middle topic from one visit in November 1998.

Field Notes on the First Topic

As I started recording, Dave was telling a story about seeing a woman ride her bike around the Arc de Triomphe in Paris.

> Dave: As I was saying, this Champs-Elysées, cars go around the circle
> around the Arc de Triomphe, and I saw this woman on her bicycle in
> dark clothing riding around there, carrying loaves of French bread.
> One of the wildest things I've ever seen.
> Kathy: Didn't she get run over???
> Dave: No!

Actual Conversation on the First Topic

> Dave: Going back to that same line of stuff I was on—I walked down the
> Champs [Elysées], got into the Arc de Triomphe, and all this traffic is
> in circles around the Arc de Triomphe. And one of the most
> memorable things was a little old lady in dark clothing on her
> bicycle, right in the middle of all that circular traffic, peddling along
> with a couple of loaves of French bread in her basket.
>
> Jake: As if she didn't belong there but she did.
>
> Kathy: And she didn't get run over?
>
> Dave: Aw, she was right in the middle of it—the hell with 'em—she
> showed that French insolence.

Field Notes on the Last Topic

While we were talking about traveling they started talking about how
small the world is . . .

> Jake: Crazy thing is that my wife and I were in San Francisco, which is
> how far away?
>
> Kathy and Tim simultaneously: Three thousand miles, like three
> thousand miles . . .
>
> Jake: So three thousand miles away and who do we run into?! Tim!! You
> had a conference over there, right?
>
> Tim: Yeah.
>
> . . . [. . .] . . .
>
> Dave: The wife and I were at the Hong Kong Hilton checking in, met a
> man who said, "I'm from Dexter." In Hong Kong! Can you believe it?
>
> Jake: Yeah, my kids say to me, "Dad, can't you go anywhere without
> running into someone you know?" And I tell them, that's what
> happens when yuse impoooortent!
>
> Tim: I run into that same problem, too. . . . I was in Virginia the other
> day, about 50 miles north of Charleston at a gas station, and I ran
> into a guy who works out at the Y—swims over the lunch
> break. . . .

Actual Conversation on the Last Topic

> Jake: We leave town awhile ago, oh 25–30 years ago, all the way to San
> Francisco. And who do we run into standing in line? This guy!!

'member? My wife and I made a comment, "Man, if I was with a strange girl . . . whoo boy!!"

Tim: [laughs]

Jake: I mean you don't expect to go, how many miles is it to San Francisco?

Tim: Maybe three thousand.

Kathy: Three thousand.

Jake: Three thousand miles and run into Ann Arborites, okay?

Kathy: How funny.

Tim: Yeah.

Jake: They had a [business] meeting then, right?

Tim: Sure it was a [omitted] meeting.

Dave: They were surveying everything.

Jake: They were surveying, and I . . . he wasn't with his wife, all right. I don't know who that young chick was!! you know.

Tim: [laughs]

Jake: But *I* was with my bride, all right!

Dave: You'll have to get a different perspective on this.

Jake: Then we ran into [a different man from Ann Arbor], he was a . . . they had a meeting there also . . . the principals, teachers, whatever it was. . . . he was there . . . God!

Dave: What's this guy's name? Wilson [not his real name] in Dexter?

Alex: Who?

Dave: You know, Wilson?

Jake: Wilson, yeah, John Wilson.

Dave: Didn't he just lose his wife?

[several people nod]

Dave: A few years ago, [my wife] and I were in the Hong Kong Hilton, walked into an elevator, looked at him, he says, yeah, "I'm from Dexter." [laughs]

[Laughter]

Dave: We walk into the Hong Kong!! He and his wife . . . I thought I recognized him. He says, 'John Wilson, I'm from Dexter.' I says, 'Christ, I'm from Ann Arbor! How are you?'

Jake: You know, my . . . my kids always say, "Dad, can't you go anywhere where you don't know somebody?"

[Laughter]

Jake: I say, well, hey, I said, 'When yuse impooooooortant, you meet all kinds of people!'

[laughter]

Tim: I kind of have that problem, too.

Jake: You do? [laughs]

Tim: The other day I was going to Virginia, I was about fifty miles north of Charleston, West Virginia. I stopped at this little restaurant, I sat down, I looked at the guy next to me, you know at the next booth over, and it ... some guy, you know, who works out at the Ann Arbor, that works out at the Ann Arbor Y gym! He does swimming at noon. And I said, "Hi, you're from Ann Arbor, aren't you?" "Oh yeah!" "You know, I see you at the Y!"

Field Notes on a Topic from the Middle of a Conversation

Silas: They raised the price of coffee when the supply was low, but do you think they'll lower it when the supply goes back up? No way.

Dave: Same with orange juice. They say it's going up 10 percent across the board. That'll never come back down either.... but the conditions though that they raise those crops.... the wife and I once visited a banana plantation [here he launches into a long monologue, Kay is visibly trying to be polite yet is frustrated/bored/irritated. George stays silent as he has throughout the conversation.] The conditions. Jesus Christ. They harnessed people up like animals. Jesus Christ. I've never seen anything like it. Horrible.... and then one time we visited the Virgin Islands.... and one of the natives said to us, "Sometimes we go work up there," and pointed to a row of houses on a bluff. And do you know whose houses those were? Congressmen and Senators! "Sometimes they let us work up there"! Jesus Christ. Anyway, that's enough now but Jesus Christ, the conditions. The next day someone open fired on the Rockefeller Golf Course. I cheered for the rubbers when I read about it in the paper. Okay, that's enough now. Jesus Christ, it's just not right.

Actual Conversation on this Topic

Silas: ... Coffee went up, and the prices went up, and it'll never come back down.

Dave: Well that's true all of the time—it's like orange juice, going up 10 percent across the board, because of the severe frost, it'll never come down.

Ken: That's how they make their money ...

Dave: Well, it's like bananas—twenty-nine cents per pound or whatnot—but that's because of what we don't see. The wife and I were in Costa Rica a couple of times, visited a banana plantation. Boy, the way they exploit those workers. Jesus Christ, damned international banana consor-tee-ums. People living in hovels, Jesus Christ, harvesting bananas.

Silas: I wouldn't want to go up in a banana tree, Dave, there's spiders and I don't want to see the snakes.

Dave: You don't go up in a banana tree, you just look up at the tree. See the bananas point up, and then when they point down, ready, [inaudible] then the harvester takes a machete, hands it down with a wire . . . We were on a banana plantation in Jamaica, the workers were beautiful people, in good shape. They were plucking away, for the Chiquita banana consortium, [inaudible] . . . Then we were in the American Virgin islands, these big estates, [inaudible] big stores, these guys come in . . . [inaudible] "We work up there when they let us," they said [inaudible] There I go again . . . but the day before we left, out on the Rockefeller Golf Course, some of the natives open fired. They had had enough. BLEEEWwww it up. They had had enough. When I read about it in the paper I cheered for them. [long pause] Oh well. I can't change it.

Comparison of Old Timers to National Sample

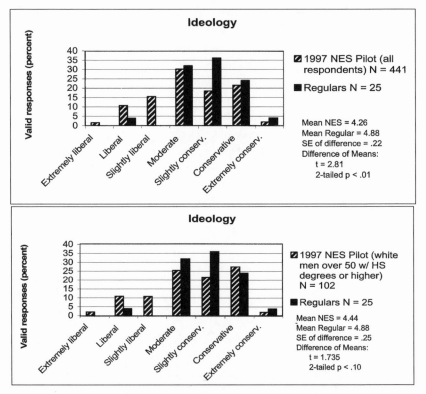

Figure A2.1 and A2.2 NES question wording: "We hear a lot of talk these days about liberals and conservatives. In your booklet is a seven-point scale on which the political views that people might hold are arranged from extremely liberal to extremely conservative. Where would you place yourself on this scale, or haven't you thought much about this?"

Wording in SAQ distributed to the Regulars (the Old Timers are referred to as the Regulars throughout appendix 2): "We hear a lot of talk these days about liberals and conservatives. Here is a seven-point scale on which the political views that people might hold are arranged from extremely liberal to extremely conservative. If you haven't thought much about this issue, check here —— and go to Question 62 [the next question]. If you have thought about it . . . where would you place yourself on this scale?"

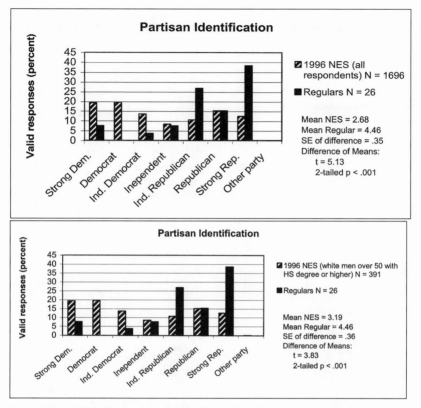

Figure A2.3 and A2.4 NES question wording: "Generally speaking, do you usually think of yourself as a Republican, a Democrat, an Independent, or what?" IF R CONSIDERS SELF REPUBLICAN / IF R CONSIDERS SELF DEMOCRAT:

>   a. "Would you call yourself a strong Republican or a not very strong Republican?"
>   b. "Would you call yourself a strong Democrat or a not very strong Democrat?"

IF R CONSIDERS SELF INDEPENDENT, NO PREFERENCE, OTHER: "Do you think of yourself as closer to the Republican Party or to the Democratic Party?"

Wording from SAQ given to the Regulars: "Generally speaking, do you usually think of yourself as Republican, a Democrat, an Independent, or what? *(Please circle one number)*" [Strong Republican, Weak Republican, Independent, Weak Democrat, Strong Democrat or Other]. IF YOU ANSWERED INDEPENDENT, "Do you think of yourself as closer to the Republican or Democratic party?"

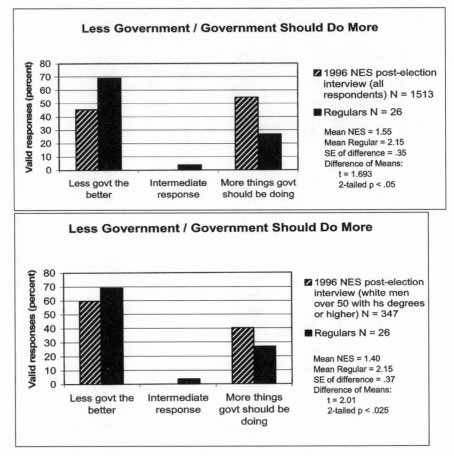

Figure A2.5 and A2.6 NES Question wording: "1, the less government the better, or 2, government should do more."

Question wording in SAQ given to Regulars: "Which is close to your opinion, The less government the better, or There are more things the government should be doing?"

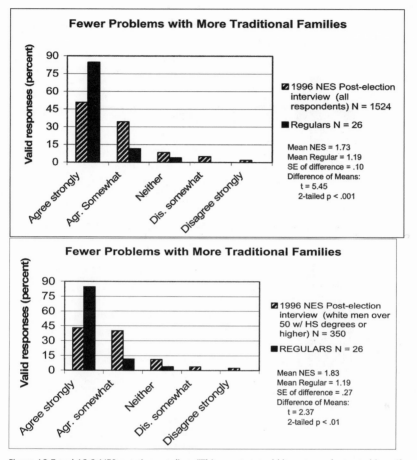

Figure A2.7 and A2.8 NES question wording: "This country would have many fewer problems if there were more emphasis on traditional family ties." [Agree strongly, agree somewhat, neither agree nor disagree, disagree somewhat, disagree strongly.]

Question wording in SAQ given to Regulars: "This country would have many fewer problems if there were more emphasis on traditional family ties." [Agree strongly, agree somewhat, neither agree nor disagree, disagree somewhat, disagree strongly.]

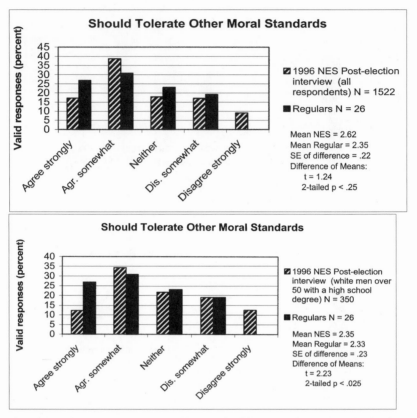

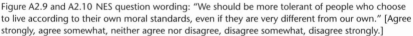

Figure A2.9 and A2.10 NES question wording: "We should be more tolerant of people who choose to live according to their own moral standards, even if they are very different from our own." [Agree strongly, agree somewhat, neither agree nor disagree, disagree somewhat, disagree strongly.]

Question wording in SAQ given to Regulars: "We should be more tolerant of people who choose to live according to their own moral standards, even if they are very different from our own." [Agree strongly, agree somewhat, neither agree nor disagree, disagree somewhat, disagree strongly.]

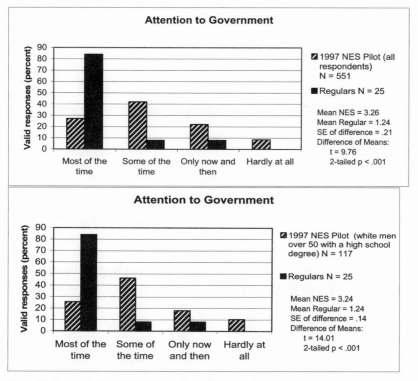

Figure A2.11 and A2.12 NES question wording: "Some people seem to follow what's going on in the government and public affairs most of the time, whether there is an election going on or not. Others aren't that interested. Would you say that you follow what's going on in government and public affairs most of the time, some of the time, only now and then, or hardly at all?"

Question wording of SAQ given to Regulars: "Some people seem to think about what's going on in government most of the time, whether there's an election going on or not. Others aren't that interested. How often do you follow what's going on in government?"

Survey Question Wordings

This appendix lists the question wordings and explains the indicator constructions for the variables used in analyses in chapters 4 and 5.

Self-Administered Questionnaire Given to Old Timers

Identities and Anti-Identities. "I am interested in finding out what kinds of people you think are most like you, in their ideas and interests and feelings about things. Please read over the following list and mark the groups you feel particularly close to." The list included: "Poor People," "Liberals," "The Elderly," "Ann Arborites," "Blacks," "Labor Unions," "Feminists," "Business People," "Young People," "Conservatives," "Residents of Michigan in general," "Hispanic-Americans," "Women," "Working-Class People," "Whites," "Environmentalists," "Middle-Class People," "Men," "Christian Fundamentalists," "Americans in general," "People at your place of worship," and "People in your neighborhood." I then asked, "Are there any other groups you feel close to that I have not listed? Please list them here."

The same list was provided after the anti-identities question: "Now, looking over the same list again, which of these groups do you think are different from you in their ideas and interests and feelings. That is, which of these groups do you feel particularly *not* close to?"

Media-Use Survey Questions

1. "Do you watch the nightly news more than 2 times per week?" (Yes or No) If "YES," "Which channel do you watch? Which program do you watch? (Local, National or Both)."
2. "Do you read a daily newspaper more than 2 days per week? (Yes or No)" If "YES," "Which newspaper(s) do you read? (Ann Arbor News, Detroit Free Press, USA Today, Other (Specify))."
3. "Do you listen to news on public radio more than 2 times per week? (Yes or No)" If "Yes," "Which station do you listen to? What time of day do you listen? (Morning, Noon, or Evening)"
4. "Do you subscribe to a national news magazine like Time or Newsweek? (Yes or No)" If "Yes," "To which one(s) do you subscribe?"

5. "Do you get local or national news on the internet? (Yes or No)" If "Yes," "Which web site(s) do you use most often?"

Trust in Government. "Over the years, how much attention do you feel the government pays to what the people think when it decides what to do? Would you say a good deal, some, or not much?" "Do you think that quite a few of the people running the government are dishonest, not very many are, or do you think hardly any of them are dishonest?" "Do you think that people in the government waste a lot of the money we pay in taxes, waste some of it, or don't waste very much of it?" "How much of the time do you think you can trust the government in Washington to do what is right—Would you say just about always, most of the time, or only some of the time?" "Would you say that the government is pretty much run by a few big interests looking out for themselves or that it is run for the benefit of all the people?" "Which one of the following levels of government do you have the most faith and confidence in? (national government, state government, local government)." "Which one do you have the least faith and confidence in? (national government, state government, local government)."

1990 Citizen Participation Study

Participation in Informal Interaction in Voluntary Associations. Two criteria were used to determine whether respondents took part in informal interaction in a voluntary association (using the 1990 Citizen Participation Data). First, was the respondent active in the association he or she considered most important in his or her life? This was determined in the following way. Respondents were asked, "In which of the organizations that you belong to or give time to are you the most active?" where possible responses were generated by a previous question, "Here is a list of organizations. Please read through this list and when you have finished, I'll have some questions. Are you a member of . . . " [each of the following groups were asked about, in this sequence]: service club/fraternal organization, veterans organization, group affiliated with respondent's religion, ethnic organization, senior citizen group, organization interested in women's issues, labor union, business/professional organization, political issue organization, nonpartisan or civic organization, liberal/conservative political group, organization active in elections, youth group, literary/art/discussion group, hobby or sports club, neighborhood association, health service organization, educational organization, cultural organization, other organization. Specifically, the wording ran as follows: "Are you a member of . . . any service clubs or fraternal organizations such as the Lions or Kiwanis or a local woman's club or a fraternal organization at school? A veterans organization such as the American Legion or the Veterans of Foreign Wars? Groups affiliated with your religion such as the Knights of Columbus or B'nai B'rith? A group representing your own particular nationality, or ethnic or racial group, such as the Polish-American Congress, the Mexican American Legal Defense and Education Fund, or the National Association for the Advancement of Colored People? An organization for the elderly or senior citizens? An organization mainly interested in issues promoting the rights or welfare of women—an organization such as the National Organization for Women, or the Eagle Forum, or the American Association of University Women? A labor union? Any other organization that is associated with your work such as a business or professional association, or a farm organization. Please include your own involvement in any such organization of which your employer is a member, even though you yourself are not a member. An organization active on one particular political issue such as the environment, or abortion (on either side), or gun control (again on either side), or consumer rights, or the rights of taxpayers, or any other issue? A nonpartisan or civic organization interested in the political life in your community or in the nation—such as the League of Women Voters or a better-government organization? An organization that supports general liberal or conservative causes such as the Americans for Democratic Action or the Conservative Caucus? An organization active in supporting candidates in elections such as a party organization? Youth groups such as the Girl Scouts or the 4-H? Literary, art, discussion or study groups? A hobby club, sports or country club, or some other group or club for leisure time activities? Any association related to where you live—like a neighborhood or community association or a homeowners' or condominium association, or a block club? An education institution—a local school or your own school or college or some organization associated with education such as the school alumni association or a school service organization like the PTA? Some cultural organization that is active in providing cultural services to the public—for example, a museum, the symphony, or public radio or television?

Then, respondents were asked, "In the past twelve months, to which of the organizations we have just discussed have you contributed the most money—beyond ordinary dues?" If this differed from most active group, the respondent was then asked, "Which of these two organizations is most important to you?" A respondent was considered to be active in this organization if they answered "yes" to either of the following questions: "Do you consider yourself an active member of this organization—that is, in the past twelve months have you served on a committee, given time for special projects, or helped organize meetings?" or "Have you attended a meeting of the organization in the past twelve months?"

To be categorized as a person who takes part in informal interaction in an association, respondents had to answer "very important" or "somewhat important" when asked, "Here is a list of reasons people give for being associated with organizations. Please tell me if each of these reasons is very important, somewhat important, or not very important in keeping you involved in the organization [that respondent indicated was his/her 'most important' organization]. . . . The chance to be with people I enjoy."

Homogeneity of Most Important Association. "Would you say that members of the organization are all (R's gender), mostly (R's gender), is it mixed, or are only a few (R's gender)?" "Would you say that members of the organization are all (R's race, for the analyses conducted in this study: white/black), mostly (white/black), is it mixed, or are only a few (white/black)?"

Informal Political Talk during Association Meetings. "Do people at these meetings sometimes chat informally about politics or government?"

Party Identification. A seven-point scale of party identification (Strong Democrat, Democrat, Independent-Democrat, Independent, Independent-Republican, Republican, Strong Republican) was constructed from responses to the following question and the appropriate follow-up question: "Generally speaking, do you usually think of yourself as a Republican, a Democrat, an Independent, or what?" If Republican or Democrat: "Would you call yourself a strong Republican/Democrat? Or not a very strong Republican/Democrat?" If answer other than Republican or Democrat in first question: "Do you think of yourself as closer to the Republican or Democratic party?"

Social Identification. If you think about the groups you feel particularly close to—people who are most like you in their ideas, interests and feelings about things—do you feel a lot closer to [women than to men/blacks than to other people], somewhat closer, or is there no difference in how close you feel to [women and men/blacks and other people]? A fourth code was a volunteered code used when the respondent reported feeling closer to "men" or "other people."

Union Membership. "Are you a member of a labor union?"

Education. Indicators of the highest level of education were computed by the principal investigators of the study, who used responses to the following questions: "What is the highest grade of regular school that you have completed and gotten credit for? [If necessary say: By regular school we mean a school which can be counted toward an elementary or high school diploma or a college or university degree.]" "Did you get a high school diploma or pass a high school equivalency test?" "What is the highest degree that you have earned?" The resulting eight-category indicator was coded as follows: 1 = Grammar school and less; 2 = Some high school; 3 = High school degree or equivalent; 4 = Some college; 5 = College graduate; 6 = Some graduate work; 7 = Master's degree; 8 = Ph.D. or professional degree.

Family Income. "Which of the income groups listed on this card includes the total 1989 income before taxes of all members of your family living in your home? Please include salaries, wages, pensions, dividends, interest, and all other income." Data analyzed in this study include responses corrected by the principal investigators of the study.

Political Ideology. "We hear a lot of talk these days about liberals and conservatives. Here is a scale on which the political views that people might hold are arranged from extremely liberal—point 1—to extremely conservative—point 7. Where would you place yourself on this scale?

Race. "What is your race?" Codes were "white," "black," "Asian," "Alaskan Native/Native American," "Hispanic/Latino," and "Other."

Gender. Respondent was assigned gender as "male" or "female" according to interviewer observations.

1996 American National Election Study

Participation in Informal Interaction in Voluntary Associations. "There are many kinds of organizations, groups, and charities that people might be involved with. We're interested in what kinds of groups you might be involved with. I'm going to read a list of different types of organizations. For each type, could you tell me the name or names of the organizations you are involved with." The list was nearly identical to the list of organizations asked about in the 1990 CPS study (described above), except for the following. Whereas the CPS asked about "an organization," the NES asked about "organizations." Other differences occurred in the question asking about youth groups ("Groups in which children might participate, such as Girl Scouts, 4-H, youth sports leagues such as soccer or Little League"); fraternal organizations ("Service or fraternal organizations such as the Lions or Kiwanis or a local woman's club or a college or fraternity or sorority"); religious organizations ("Other organizations affiliated with your religion besides that, such as the Knights of Columbus, or B'nai B'rith, or a Bible study group"); hobby clubs ("Hobby clubs, sports or country clubs, bowling leagues, or other groups for leisure time activities"); business or professional groups ("Other organizations associated with your work, such as a business or professional association or a farm organization"); racial/ethnic group ("Organizations representing your own particular nationality or ethnic group, such as the Polish-American Congress, the Mexican-American Legal Defense, or the National Association for the Advancement of Colored People"); election groups ("Organizations active in supporting candidates for elections such as a political party organization"). In addition, the NES asked about self-help groups ("Support or self-help groups such as AA or Gamblers' Anonymous"). Then respondents were asked, "In the last 12 months, have you taken part in any activities sponsored by this group or attended a meeting of this group?"

Political Talk during Association Meetings. "How often does this group discuss politics? Sometimes, rarely, or never?"

Social Identity. "Please read over the list and tell me the number of those groups you feel particularly close to—people who are most like you in their ideas and interests and feelings about things." "Poor people," "Asian-Americans," "Liberals," "The Elderly," "Blacks," "Labor Unions," "Feminists," "Southerners," "Business people," "Young people," "Conservatives," "Hispanic-Americans," "Women," "Working-Class People," "Whites," "Middle-Class People," "Men," "None (volunteered)."

Education. Indicators of the highest level of education were derived from responses to the following questions: "What is the highest grade of school or year of college you have completed?" "Did you get a high school diploma or pass a high school equivalency test?" "What is the highest degree that you have earned?" The resulting seven-category indicator was coded as follows: $1 = 8$ grades or less and no diploma or equivalency; $2 = 9$ to 11 grades, no further schooling; $3 =$ High school diploma or equivalent; $4 =$ More than 12 years of schooling, no higher degree; Some college; $5 =$ Junior or community college level degrees; $6 =$ B.A. level degrees; $7 =$ Advanced degree, including LLB (bachelor of laws degree).

Family Income. "Please look at page 21 of the booklet and tell me the letter of the income group that includes the income of all members of your family living here in 1995 [or if living alone: "that you yourself had in 1995"] before taxes. This figure should include salaries, wages, pensions, dividends, interest, and all other income." [IF UNCERTAIN: "What would be your best guess?"]

Political Ideology. Political ideology was assigned according to responses from two questions: "We hear a lot of talk these days about liberals and conservatives. Here is a scale on which the political views that people might hold are arranged from extremely liberal—point 1—to extremely conservative—point 7. Where would you place yourself on this scale or haven't you thought much about this?" Those who answered "moderate," "don't know," or "haven't thought much" were then asked, "If you had to choose, would you consider yourself a liberal or a conservative?" Summary responses were 1 = Liberal, 3 = Moderate, 5 = Conservative.

Union Membership. "Do you or anyone else in this household belong to a labor union?"

Race. Race was modeled with an indicator of whether or not the respondent was black (according to interviewer observations).

Gender. Respondent was assigned gender as "male" or "female" according to interviewer observations.

1965–1997 Political Socialization Study

Party Identification. A seven-point scale of party identification (Strong Democrat, Democrat, Independent-Democrat, Independent, Independent-Republican, Republican, Strong Republican) was constructed from responses to the following question and the appropriate follow-up question: "Generally speaking, do you usually think of yourself as a Republican, a Democrat, an Independent, or what?" If Republican or Democrat: "Would you call yourself a strong [Republican/Democrat]? Or not a very strong [Republican/ Democrat]?" If answer other than Republican or Democrat in first question: "Do you think of yourself as closer to the Republican or Democratic party?"

Persuade Others How to Vote (1997): "I have a list of some of the things that people do to help make an election come out the way they want it to. By that

I mean elections for public office or votes on issues, propositions, referenda, and so on. I wonder if you could tell me whether you have done any of these things during any kind of public election since you were interviewed in 1982? I know it might be hard to recall. First, did you talk to any people and try to show them why they should vote one way or the other?" [Note: Additional questions in this series were not used in the analyses reported in the text.]

Income. Household income was measured with the following questions.

In 1973: "Please look at this card [in face to face interviews, or sent to respondents prior to telephone interviews] and tell me the letter of the income group that includes the income of all members of your family in 1972 before taxes. This figure should include salaries, wages, dividends, interest, pensions, and all other income. What would be your best guess?" Response options were eighteen categories ranging from "none" to "$35,000 and over."

In 1997: "Now please look at page 16 of the booklet and tell me the income group that includes the income you had in 1996 before taxes. This figure should include salaries, wages, pensions, dividends, interest, and all other income." [IF UNCERTAIN: "What would be your best guess?"] Response options were twenty-three categories ranging from "none or less than $2,000" to "$150,000 and over." Responses were coded to the midpoint of the category and then rescaled within each wave and each generation from 0 (least) to 1 (highest).

Education. The indicator of education was constructed with use of the following questions.

In 1973: "Have you had any other schooling since leaving high school?" "What other schooling is that?" "Do you have a college degree?" "What degree(s) did you receive?"

In 1997: "Have you received a college degree since 1982?" "What degree(s) did you receive"? Responses in each wave and each generation were coded into seven categories: 0 = less than a high school degree; 1 = high school degree or equivalent; 2 = associate's degree or some college; 3 = bachelor's degree; 4 = master's degree; 5 = law, medical, or theological degree; 6 = Ph.D. This index was scaled from 0 (less than high school) to 1 (Ph.D.).

Union Member. "Does anyone in this household belong to a labor union?" 0 = no; 1 = yes.

Race. Race was modeled with an indicator of whether or not the respondent was black (according to cover sheets from previous waves, verified by interviewer observations).

Gender. Respondent was assigned gender as "male" or "female," according to cover sheets from previous waves, verified by interviewer observation.

Ideology. "We hear a lot of talk these days about liberals and conservatives. Here is a scale on which the political views that people might hold are arranged from extremely liberal to extremely conservative. Where would you place yourself on this scale or haven't you thought much about this?" $1 =$ extremely liberal, $2 =$ liberal, $3 =$ moderately liberal, $4 =$ moderate, $5 =$ moderately conservative, $6 =$ conservative, $7 =$ extremely conservative; responses were recoded to run 0 to 1.

Homogeneity Scores

Table A4.1 Number of Cases Used to Compute Homogeneity Scores Plotted in Figures 4.1 and 4.2

| Group Type | N Reporting Group Type Is Most Active and Most Important, and Were Active at Least 1 Hour Per Week | | | |
	Men	Women	Whites	Blacks
Youth group	26	39	51	10
Health/service group	29	26	41	7
Cultural organization	4	3	6	0
Hobby club, sports club, country club	57	42	73	14
Religious group	31	37	50	17
Education group	17	42	46	11
Service/fraternal organization	48	39	72	14
Senior citizens group	3	11	7	7
Literary group	13	16	23	3
Neighborhood group	8	8	11	3
Women's group	1	5	5	0
Racial/ethnic group	9	10	6	11
Business/professional group	39	30	58	5
Veterans group	9	2	6	2
Civic group	8	8	13	2
Labor union	30	9	28	5
Political issue group	22	12	30	3
Elections group	7	4	9	1
Liberal/Conservative group	1	2	1	2

Source: 1990 CPS

Supplementary Analyses, Chapter 5

Table A5.1 Party Identification as Function of Social Location and Informal Talk in Associations, Analyzed among the Half of Sample Most Involved in Associations

Constant	.07
	(1.76)
Female	−.07**
	(−2.78)
Black	−.23***
	(−4.43)
Family income	.32*
	(2.39)
Education	.20**
	(3.07)
Union membership	−.12***
	(−3.51)
Ideology	.61***
	(14.92)
Informal talk in voluntary associations	.57**
	(3.09)
Female × Informal talk	.22#
	(1.78)
Black × Informal talk	−.45*
	(−2.15)
Income × Informal talk	−.38
	(−.71)
Education × Informal talk	−.63*
	(−2.17)
Union membership × Informal talk	−.01
	(−.05)
N	1224
St. Error of the Estimate	.32
R square	.26
F test, set of interaction terms	3.40

Source: 1990 CPS.

Note: Dependent variable is 0 to 1 party identification, such that 0 represents strong Democrats and 1 represents strong Republicans. All variables are coded 0 to 1. Level of involvement in organizations was determined by count of associations in which R reported activity. Entries represent OLS coefficients. T-statistics are in parentheses.

*p < .05   **p < .01   ***p < .001   #p < .10.

Table A5.2 Party Identification as Function of Parent's Party Identification, Social Location, and Beginning to Persuade Others How to Vote, 1973–1997

Constant	$-.19^{**}$
	(-2.71)
Female	$-.02$
	$(-.64)$
Black	$-.20^{**}$
	(-2.70)
Family income	$.11$
	(1.42)
Education	$.12$
	(1.39)
Union membership	$-.02$
	$(-.42)$
Ideology	$.14^{***}$
	(12.81)
Began telling others how to vote by 1997	$-.00$
	$(-.05)$
Female × Began to persuade	$.06$
	(1.09)
Black × Began to persuade	$-.07$
	$(-.62)$
Income × Began to persuade	$.14$
	(1.23)
Education × Began to persuade	$-.24^{\#}$
	(-1.94)
Union membership × Began to persuade	$-.14^{*}$
	(-2.29)
Parent's Party ID	$.13^{***}$
	(3.49)
N	342
St. Error of the Estimate	.24
R square	.45
F test, set of interaction terms	2.28

Source: 1965–97 PSS.

Note: Dependent variable is 0 to 1 party identification, such that 0 represents strong Democrats and 1 represents strong Republicans. All variables are coded 0 to 1. Entries represent OLS coefficients. T-statistics are in parentheses. The small number of cases in this analysis (compared to $N = 501$ in the related table 5.3) is due to the smaller number of respondents for whom 1965 parental interviews were conducted. The total N for the cases for whom 1997 interviews as well as a 1965 parental interview are available is 636. The reduced N here is due to the fact that these analyses are only run on people who began persuading others how to vote by 1997.

$^{*}p < .05$ $^{**}p < .01$ $^{***}p < .001$ $^{\#}p < .10$.

Tables for Media Effects Analyses Reported in Chapter 6

Table A6.1 Public Affairs Topics Discussed during Media Effects Study among Old Timers

Topic	Who initiated topic?	Further discussion?	Date	Within 24 hours of breaking news?	
Breaking news					
Parking policy	Investigator	Yes	10/19/99	No	Story broke 10/16/99
Hillsdale College scandal	Old Timers	Yes	11/16/99	No	Story broke 11/10/99
Clinton fund-raiser	Old Timers	Yes, brief	12/14/99	No	Not ascertainable
New local shopping mall proposed	Investigator	Yes, brief	12/16/99	Yes	
Life sentence for 14-year-old murderer	Investigator	None	1/14/00	Yes	
Resignation of U of M athletic director	Old Timers	Yes	2/7/00	No	Story broke 2/5/00
Detroit Casino closing	Investigator	Yes, brief	6/8/00	Yes	
Same sex benefits	Investigator	Yes	6/9/00	Yes	
Drowning of local high school graduate	Old Timers	Yes	6/13/00	Yes	
Library official accused of embezzling money	Investigator	Yes	6/23/00	No	Story broke 6/20/00
Central Park beatings	Investigator	Yes, brief	6/23/00	No	Story broke 6/20/00
Supreme Court decisions of June 29, 2000	Investigator	None	6/29/00	Yes	
Nonbreaking news					
Native American sports team names	Old Timers	Yes	11/16/99	No	
Halo around Michigan Stadium	Investigator	Yes	12/13/99	No	
Homeless shelter	Old Timers	Yes	12/14/99	No	
Osama Bin Laden	Old Timers	Yes	12/15/99	No	
Panama Canal	Old Timers	Yes	12/16/99	No	
Y2K Potential for Terrorism	Investigator	Yes, brief	12/20/99	No	
Y2K Preparations	Investigator	Yes	12/20/99	No	
Y2K Potential for Terrorism	Investigator	Yes	12/21/99	No	
Y2K Preparations	Investigator	Yes	12/21/99	No	

Table A6.1 (continued)

Topic	Who initiated topic?	Further discussion?	Date	Within 24 hours of breaking news?
Police chief resignation	Investigator	Yes, brief	1/10/00	No
Elían Gonzales	Old Timers	Yes	1/10/00	No
Halo around Michigan Stadium	Investigator	Yes	1/14/00	No
Homeless shelter	Old Timers	Yes	1/14/00	No
Hillary Clinton announcing Senate candidacy	Investigator	Yes	2/7/00	No
Summer 2000 gas prices	Old Timers	Yes	6/13/00	No
G. W. Bush's stance on death penalty	Old Timers	Yes	6/23/00	No
Summer 2000 gas prices	Old Timers	Yes	6/30/00	No

Note: "Brief" further discussion refers to conversations that involved no more than an exchange of two comments between members of the group and/or the investigator.

Table A6.2 Correspondence between Perspectives Used by Old Timers and News Coverage: Firing of University of Michigan Athletic Director

	Media Coverage	Old Timers
Main Idea		
Criteria for judging performance	x	
Does current athletic director represent the University of Michigan tradition	x	
Performance and accountability of public administrators	x	
U of M tradition versus recent leadership	x	x
Affirmative action in hiring the current athletic director		x
Argument		
Not clear AD should be fired or is going to be fired; he has made mistakes but has not performed poorly	x	
AD should not be fired; has done a terrific job in a tough position	x	
AD hired in the spirit of U of M but unable to deal with big issues well	x	
Not clear AD should be fired; has made costly mistakes	x	
New AD should be someone from within the U of M family	x	x
AD made several good choices too	x	
U of M president has made controversial hiring decisions	x	x
Is this an example of local officials ignoring the public; or is rash of bad judgments by local officials just coincidence	x	
AD should not be fired because U of M athletics being overtaken by U of M president and regents	x	x
AD not the best person for the job because unqualified, not properly hired in the first place		x

(continued)

Table A6.2 (continued)

	Media Coverage	Old Timers
ACTORS		
Targets of blame		
President of U of M (Lee Bollinger)	x	x
Athletic Director (Tom Goss)	x	
Other actors mentioned		
African-Americans		x
Whites		x
Women		x
Homosexuals		x
Individual people	x	

Table A6.3 Correspondence between Perspectives Used by Old Timers and News Coverage: Hillsdale College Scandal

	Media Coverage	Old Timers
Main Idea		
Judging performance of leaders of private organizations	x	x
Reconciling institution's moral reputation with improper individual behavior	x	
Argument		
President of college (Roche) should step down; despite bringing in funds, evidence suggests he had been having long-term affair with his daughter-in-law	x	
Disbelief that he is guilty; seemed to be respectable and did a fine job	x	x
Reputation of the college intact; officials coming clean	x	
Scandal is harmful to members of the college community; disillusioning and hypocritical	x	
President not necessarilly guilty; his side of the story not yet heard		x
ACTORS		
Targets of blame		
President (Roche)	x	
Other actors mentioned		
College administrative board	x	
President (Roche Sr.)	x	x
President's son	x	x
President's daughter-in-law	x	x

Table A6.3 (continued)

	Media Coverage	Old Timers
Detective	x	
College vice president	x	
President's daughter	x	
News reporters	x	
William F. Buckley, Jr.	x	
William Bennett	x	
College professor	x	
College students	x	
Dean of the faculty	x	
The National Review	x	
The Weekly Standard	x	
President Clinton	x	x
Newt Gingrich	x	
College donors	x	x

Table A6.4 Correspondence between Perspectives Used by Old Timers and News Coverage: Auto Manufacturers' Same-Sex Benefits

	Media Coverage	Old Timers
Main Idea		
Corporate economic and personnel concerns	x	
Influence of corporate policies on norms of behavior	x	
Equality of opportunity	x	x
Feasibility of social policy		x
Argument		
Providing same-sex benefits is smart economically; attracts workers in a tight labor market	x	
Policy is good; symbolic in affirming equal rights of gays	x	
Policy is bad; some lifestyle should not be considered 'equal'		x
A just policy; same sex couples do not have the option to marry	x	
Policy is bad; implementation is impossible		x
ACTORS		
Targets of blame		
Auto companies	x	
Gay rights activists	x	

(continued)

Table A6.4 (continued)

	Media Coverage	Old Timers
Homosexuals		x
Greeks		x
United Auto Workers		x
Other actors mentioned		
Gay workers	x	
Auto companies	x	
Corporate America	x	
Workforce	x	
Heterosexuals	x	
Gay rights activists	x	
Southern Baptists	x	
Disney corporation	x	
Fortune 500 companies	x	
Homosexuals	x	x
United Auto Workers		x
Socialists		x
Academic liberals		x
Greeks		x
Lesbians		x
Blacks		x
Indians		x

Letter to Old Timers at End of Observation Period

July 2000

To everyone at the Corner Store,

At the end of July, I'll be moving to Madison, Wisconsin, to start a job as a professor of political science at the University of Wisconsin. Wisconsin is home to me, so in many ways it's a dream come true. I will miss all of you very much, probably much more than I could ever say in words.

It's because of all of you that I have been able to get this job and have the chance to live near my family doing the kind of work that I love to do. My dissertation is about you (although the place and individuals are anonymous). The time I have spent with you since the summer of 1997 has helped me understand a lot of things, some about political science and many about life.

I started coming to the corner store because I had heard that there was a group of retired men who hung out here every morning, and I was trying to find a group of people who met together often to just shoot the breeze. I wanted to study people talking informally about politics. Many political scientists believe that conversation is the soul of democracy. It's a hot topic these days, as many places (like Ann Arbor) are becoming more and more diverse with time. The idea is that that by talking to each other, Americans can create a "better" society and learn to get along with many different kinds of people.

By spending time with you (as well as a group of women who get together every week at a local church) I came to a different conclusion. When most people talk informally about politics, they aren't doing it to solve the world's problems. Their intent is not to improve democracy or foster brotherly love. Instead, their conversations are a way of sharing time, figuring out the world together, and feeling like a part of a community.

Some people who have read my work think that this is a pessimistic conclusion. I tend to agree. I think that there are some pretty rigid barriers in this society between different types of people, especially between whites and blacks. When we define "community," we often do so by excluding certain groups of people. And I don't think that casual conversation in places like the corner store has the potential to change that.

But in my dissertation, I also emphasize that the time you spend together is wonderful in its own right. I see it in your faces when you enter the door, look around the room and see two tables full of people you've known for many years. I feel it myself when I come in here. As I'm driving over, I smile to myself, just imagining the jokes I'll hear that day. You have provided a sense of community to me that I never would have experienced in Ann Arbor had I not met you. And I know you give that to each other as well.

In a few months, I'll start submitting my dissertation to publishers to try to turn it into a book. This means that I'll be revising it over the next year or so. I'm attaching a postage-paid envelope addressed to me. If you would like to comment on the things I have said here (or anything else), please do so. I will incorporate your comments (anonymously) in my book (unless you ask me not to). If you would like a copy of my dissertation, let me know that, too.

I will keep in touch. And I will miss you all very, very much. Thank you for everything.

Warmest regards,
Kathy Cramer Walsh

Chapter One

1. All of the names of people observed in this study have been changed to protect their confidentiality.

2. For one, such talk does not fit definitions of democratic deliberation because it is not performed for a public audience (Bohman 1996). Bohman builds on commonly asserted characteristics of democratic deliberation—" the inclusion of everyone affected by a decision, substantial political equality including equal opportunities to participate in deliberation, equality in methods of decision making and determining the agenda, [and] the free and open exchange of information and reasons sufficient to acquire an understanding of both the issue in question and the opinions of others" (16)—to emphasize that the key to deliberative democracy is the *public* exchange of reasons. See also Friedland (2001) for an argument on the importance of public talk for democracy.

3. In her investigation of the way people who are highly active in the political process read public opinion, Herbst (1998) opts for the terms "political professionals" or "political sophisticates" rather than "elites," saying the latter term is "both inexact and pejorative in this particular case" (32). Throughout this book, I use the terms "political professionals" and "political elites" interchangeably to refer to elected officials, policy makers, and journalists, in order to engage what Lee (2002) notes is the prevailing elite-driven model of public opinion.

4. A worldview is "a set of assumptions about the way the world is and ought to be organized" (Luker 1984, 193) or "basic assumptions about how the world works" (McLeod, Sotirovic, and Holbert 1998, 454). On culture, Johnson (2000) argues that it delimits the range of alternatives that people perceive to be possible and suggests the identities that are useful for thinking about a given issue.

5. Not all definitions of perspective contain social identity. McLeod, Sotirovic, and Holbert (1998) operationalize worldviews as "basic assumptions about how the world works" (454), such as the predictability and justness of events.

6. In an important exception to the view that deliberation worth noting is the domain of political professionals or is behavior that takes place in organized forums, Kim, Wyatt, and Katz (1999) use national sample survey data to investigate the existence, conditions, and consequences of everyday talk.

7. I follow Hochschild (1995) in calling this group by the name the members give themselves. For example, she uses the terms "blacks," "black Americans" and "African Americans" interchangeably, given survey evidence that there is no one preferred term among African Americans (6, n. 1). Incidentally, I use the terms "blacks" and "African Americans" interchangeably for the same reason.

8. For four months, I visited with the various groups at the corner store four to five mornings per week, and in subsequent months I visited with them one to three times per week. These visits generally lasted one to two hours.

9. I observed the first group during the winter and spring of 1998. I observed the guild from February 1998 to June 2000. The guild did not meet during July and August.

10. See Kuklinski and Hurley (1994, 747) on the importance of studying interpretations across multiple events. Their concern is discovering under which conditions people make sense of an issue aided by affect. I take away the broader point that styles of interpretation may differ across issues and therefore any theory of understanding will be more robust when tested on data about sense-making across a variety of topics.

11. I define voluntary associations as nonfamilial and nonwork groups into which people self-select themselves.

12. In the Citizen Participation Study, voluntary associations included the following types of groups: service clubs, veterans organizations, religious groups, ethnic organizations, senior citizens groups, organizations interested in women's issues, labor unions, business or professional organizations, political issue organizations, nonpartisan or civic organizations, liberal or conservative political groups, organizations active in elections, youth groups, hobby or sports clubs, neighborhood associations, health service organizations, educational organizations, cultural organizations, literary, art, or discussion groups, and "any other organization you belong to, give time to, or are associated with."

13. See Sigel (1996) for an investigation that suggests that gender identity is played out in everyday interactions, as opposed to political institutions. The conversations among women in her focus groups revealed that "For them, issues of equality, of dominance and subordination, and of rights and privileges are played out within the context of everyday life, in the workplace, the home, and the personnel office rather than in the polling booth, let alone the halls of Congress" (3).

14. Such studies include focus group approaches used by Gamson (1992) and Delli Carpini and Williams (1994, 1998), as well as multimethod approaches that combine qualitative and quantitative methods (Neuman, Just, and Crigler 1992; Just, Crigler, Alger, Cook, Kern, and West 1996).

15. *Voting* (Berelson, Lazarsfeld, and McPhee 1954) and *Personal Influence* (Katz and Lazarsfeld 1955) elaborated on the view that people make sense of politics partly through interacting with others to define opinion leadership in a web-like fashion.

16. Oliver and Mendelberg (2000) show a complex relationship between racial context and opinions in which socioeconomic status intervenes. In particular, they find that whites who live among low-status whites are more likely to exhibit out-group hostility (toward blacks). The authors assert that this response is better understood as a psychological orientation toward out-groups than as a group norm, because it is unlikely that enough interaction among the large number of people in the contexts they study takes place to communicate a given norm. The present study does not speak to this contention but to the act of small groups of individuals within

these larger contexts working out notions of who constitutes "us" and who constitutes "them."

17. Interpersonal interaction deserves attention especially when considering evidence that among whites, the opportunity to interact with African Americans is related to a smaller effect of prejudice on one's policy opinions (Kinder and Mendelberg 1995).

18. The work of Huckfeldt and Sprague (1992) has shown that the partisan composition of a neighborhood influences whether and which parties are active in a given neighborhood, which in turn is related to individuals' perceptions of neighborhood support for particular presidential candidates. They found that the distribution of preferences in a neighborhood is related to the extent to which people perceive whether they are in the minority or in the majority, and this consequently affects the effort they give to resisting dissonant messages (Huckfeldt and Sprague 1988). In addition, their work shows that the partisan context can influence whom people believe their acquaintances are likely to support in an election (Huckfeldt and Sprague 1987). Some observers contend that the study of South Bend, Indiana, on which this work is based, does not indicate that social interaction influences vote choice directly (Kinder 1998a, 816). However, other studies in the structural analysis tradition claim to show direct effects. In a study of the consistency of voting between 1956 and 1960, Zuckerman, Valentino, and Zuckerman (1994) showed that U.S. citizens who interact with people of similar partisan affiliations appear to be more influenced by their peers and exhibit more stability in vote choices than people who interact with people in dissimilar structural locations. Also, Knoke (1990a) shows a relationship between the partisan environment of a person's discussion network and votes for Reagan in 1984.

19. Salience is the prominence of a consideration in the information-processing tasks of political understanding and judgment (Schuman, Ludwig, and Krosnick 1986).

20. In association with Lane's study, James D. Barber "did arrange for some debate among [Lane's respondents] in a room where a recording apparatus had been set in motion (with the knowledge of the men) and where the men were then left alone to thrash out a problem by themselves. There were two groups of three; one group was selected because of the prickly personalities of the men, and another group for their rather more easygoing dispositions" (Lane 1962, 356). The purpose of this portion of the study was to gauge the rigidity of the men's political beliefs. Given the intent of this group investigation, as well as the lack of authenticity of these groups, it is difficult to determine from the small portion of one group's conversations printed in Lane (1962) whether or not the men relied on social identities more often in the group setting.

21. "The mass of absolutely illiterate, of feeble-minded, grossly neurotic, undernourished and frustrated individuals, is very considerable, much more considerable there is reason to think than we generally suppose. Thus a wide popular appeal is circulated among persons who are mentally children or barbarians, people whose lives are a morass of entanglements, people whose vitality is exhausted, shut-in people, and people whose experience has comprehended no factor in the problem under discussion. The stream of public opinion is stopped by them in little

eddies of misunderstanding, where it is discolored with prejudice and far- fetched analogy" (Lippmann 1947 [1922], 75).

Chapter Two

1. The frame concept appears across the social sciences. For approaches that differ from the studies cited here, see Goffman (1977, 1983) and Tarrow (1998).

2. A wide variety of framing effects have been demonstrated. A focus on the horse race as opposed to the issue substance of a campaign influences what people recall from a given news story (Cappella and Jamieson 1997; Valentino, Beckmann, and Buhr 2001). A focus on the potential recipients of policy influences whether affect toward those recipients influences evaluation of the policy (Nelson and Kinder 1996). Variations in the framing of a wide variety of policies, such as affirmative action (Kinder and Sanders 1990), gay rights (Brewer 2000), and partial birth abortion (Freedman 1997), have been shown to affect evaluation. Also, researchers have demonstrated that implicit appeals to race influence candidate and policy evaluation (Mendelberg 2001).

Does framing influence opinion because it alters the accessibility of certain categories or because it changes the importance of various categories? In earlier formulations of framing by political scientists, effects were considered to result from variations in the accessibility of certain schemata or schematic elements across different packages of a message (e.g., Lau et al. 1991). Recently, however, Nelson and colleagues (Nelson and Oxley 1999) have argued that framing works by making certain considerations seem more important; it is not necessarily the case that framing works by changing the accessibility of considerations (Nelson, Clawson, and Oxley 1997). These theories may be addressing two different problems. Both deal with the relevance of information. However, the accessibility argument appears to relate to the cognitive *fit* of a given piece of information, while the importance argument pertains to the socially driven *appropriateness* of an item of information to the problem. I am grateful to Dhavan Shah for help in clarifying this point.

3. Kuklinski and Hurley (1996), in a study of the effect of source cues on political interpretation, cite Lakoff (1987): "There is nothing more basic than categorization to our thought, perception, action, and speech" (127). Nelson (2000), in a recent framing study, writes, "We have at our disposal an impressive range of cognitive tools for culling, storing, and using social and political information; one of the choicest is *categorization:* the assignment of novel objects to familiar classes" (5, emphasis in original). Likewise, Kinder and Berinsky (1998), in a study of interpretation, write that "we think that understanding is typically achieved through categorization" (3). Each of these scholars are building from psychological research that shows that the categories people use to process information influence how that information is understood (e.g., Medin and Coley 1998; Chi, Feltovich, and Glaser 1981; Hinsley, Hayes, and Simon 1978).

4. For an overview of schema-based information processing, see Lau and Sears (1986), Graber (1988), and also the Lodge and McGraw (1991), Conover and Feldman (1991), and Miller (1991) replies to the Kuklinski, Luskin, and Bolland (1991) critique of schema conceptualizations within political science.

5. Tetlock's research program on the differences in styles of policy reasoning among elites supports the idea that motivation to think carefully about a policy domain results in complexity of thought. He finds that when elites are in a "low accountability" role, such as serving as a member of the opposition party (the party that does not make policy), they are more likely to exhibit reasoning that displays less complex connections among related considerations (Tetlock 1989).

6. This is why schema-based processing is called "theory-driven" rather than "data-driven" processing: storing and retrieving information is likely to be conducted consistent with the generic traits of the category rather than with respect to information specific to the particular instance.

7. For example, note the way Simon and Xenos (2000) begin a recent publication on framing effects and public deliberation: "Thanks to recent advances in public opinion research, we now know that the origins of public opinion—the sacred icon of democracy—lay in elite discourse. We also know that the public relies on the mass media for its political information" (363).

8. This is implied by his Reception Axiom (44).

9. As Lee (2002) argues, Zaller operationalizes awareness in a way that measures attention to elite discourse. Zaller conceptualizes awareness as attention to politics and understanding of political information (21), and measures it with knowledge of "neutral" factual information (333–45). Lee (2002) explains that "two of the three questions Zaller uses measure factual knowledge limited to the sphere of elite political actors and institutional politics. [These questions tap knowledge of the issue positions of elite actors, and the ability to recognize political actors on feeling thermometer items. The third indicator is the interviewers' global assessments of their respondents' political knowledge.] When Zaller controls for the transmission of political messages, he examines only mainstream media sources such as the *New York Times, Newsweek,* and *Time.* In this respect, although Zaller may be agnostic about where political information comes from, he is decidedly *not* agnostic about what constitutes political information" (28).

10. For the uninitiated, Converse's article displayed the following: He used survey interviews of a nationally representative sample of people to show that Americans are unfamiliar with the ideological labels "liberal" and "conservative." Also, he showed that Americans were not reasoning on the basis of liberal-conservative ideology (the most commonly mentioned set of ideological labels), even if not verbalizing them. Typically, a respondent's policy stances were neither generally liberal nor generally conservative. He also showed that citizens' opinions are unstable over time (from 1956 to 1960), again suggesting a lack of any coherent basis of reasoning. "On the average, less than two-thirds of the public came down on the same side of a policy controversy over a two-year period, where one-half would be expected to do so by chance alone" (Kinder 1983, 393). Therefore, Converse concluded that ordinary American citizens do not reason about politics on the basis of coherent belief systems. To top off his argument, he showed that people who *do* have reason to think about politics, candidates for the House of Representatives, showed a markedly higher degree of correlation among their attitudes (according to the left-right ideological scale), as well as more stability over time.

11. Relatedly, Sotirovic and McLeod (2001) estimate a structural equation model that suggests that values (postmaterialist vs. materialist [Inglehart 1990]) influence the use of information mediated by the mass media. They argue that postmaterialist values have a direct positive influence on newspaper use that in turn positively affects participation in diverse discussions. Conversely, materialist values have a positive effect on television entertainment use and a direct negative effect on exposure to diverse discussions.

12. Kuklinski, Luskin, and Bolland (1991) lodge this complaint against the concept of schema when they write, "A final limitation [in the use of schema theory] lies in the neglect of social context" (1346). The concept of schema does not prohibit recognition of the role of social context. However, researching political interpretation in a laboratory setting does inhibit our ability to investigate and theorize about socially rooted processes.

13. A further distinction in traditions underlying political science work on framing is the difference between two common points of departure, Gamson's sociological approach and Tversky and Kahneman's psychological approach. The latter's behavioral decision approach centers on prospect framing: an individual will pick a near-guaranteed option when a choice is framed in terms of gains, but will opt for a risky choice when the question is framed in terms of losses (Tversky and Kahneman 1988). Iyengar (1992, p. 163, n. 19) notes that the psychological and sociological conceptions are quite different. While Tversky and Kahneman approach framing as the act of altering choices by altering problem presentation, Gamson views framing as the act of affecting perceptions by stimulating the use of certain symbols and shared understandings to think about an issue. In addition, while Tversky and Kahneman focus on the mechanics of decision making, Gamson is attuned to the power associated with the ability to persuade populations of people to see an issue an a particular way. Lau et al. (1991) intentionally avoid the use of the term "frame" to "eliminate any confusion with the framing phenomenon documented in the behavioral decision theory literature [e.g., work by Tversky and Kahneman]" (645, n. 1). They distinguish framing effects in the behavioral literature by the process by which they cause preference reversals. They note, "In that literature, framing is the presentation of an identical set of consequences of a policy proposal in different ways. Typically, one frame presents the consequences in terms of gains and the other frame presents the consequences in terms of losses." The goal of the work of Tversky and Kahneman is to study changes in evaluations that result from alterations in problem presentation. The interest of Lau et al. (1991), instead, is on "framing" as it is commonly understood among political scientists: persuasion of preferences through the "strategic presentations of consequences" or emphasizing some consequences over others, rather than creating different portrayals of the same consequences (645, n. 1).

14. For example, whites tend to describe African Americans as lazy (Gilens 1999, chap. 7).

15. Graber (1988) makes a similar claim when drawing conclusions from her study of the way a panel of in-depth interview respondents processed the news. She notes that the slight variations in the way people processed public affairs information depended on "needs created by life-style. Insofar as life-style coincides with

demographic categories, such as age, sex, and ethnicity, life-style differences take on the appearance of demographic differences" (252).

16. For a careful reading of the reasons behind racially divergent interpretations of the O. J. Simpson trial, see Crenshaw (1997).

17. The average score among blacks who were not told the name of the speaker was 2.57.

18. Average agreement scores across the Jackson, Thomas, Kennedy, and Bush conditions were 3.37, 3.36, 3.29 and 3.15, respectively. The average score among whites who were not given the name of the speaker was 2.71.

19. In his definition, an ideology is "a world view readily found in the population, including sets of ideas and values that cohere, that are used publicly to justify political stances, and that shape and are shaped by society. . . . Cognitively, an ideology serves as a filter of what one sees and responds to in the social world" (4–5).

20. The relevance of race to the focus group discussions depended on the issue. For example, with respect to nuclear power, "more typically, the relevance of race was explicitly denied, and overall, there were very few differences between white and black groups in the framing of nuclear power" (Gamson 1992, 106).

21. See, especially, Lee (2002, chap. 6) for a display of the way racial identity is intertwined with the use of both group-based considerations and political principles.

22. Lau (1986) shows that there is considerable interpersonal variation by age in the schemata people employ to think about politics. People who were socialized in the New Deal era tend to evaluate presidential candidates on the basis of group-based schemata.

23. For example, in a study of political sophisticates' and professionals' interpretations of public opinion, Herbst (1998) argues that perceptions of interest are inextricably bound up with perceptions of collective identity. She argues that to understand someone's interpretation of a political event, it is essential to also understand their place in the world, including their roles and duties. Knowing how a given journalist or politician sees themselves in the world makes it easier to understand why they read political information as they do.

24. See, for example, definitions in *Webster's New Universal Unabridged Dictionary, 2d Edition* (1983): "1. the condition or fact of being the same in all qualities under consideration; sameness; oneness. 2. (a) the condition or fact of being some specific person or thing; individuality; (b) the condition of being the same as something or someone assumed, described, or claimed."

25. Tajfel (1969) argued that social identities were developed to provide a positive self-image. However, Huddy (2001, 134–36) explains that subsequent research has made various claims about the motivation behind social identification. She explains that identification with groups appears to fill affiliative needs for members of low-status and high-status group members alike. Also, the motivation might be better described as the need for positive distinctiveness, as her own research on national identity among various subgroups within "Latinos" illustrates (Huddy and Virtanen 1995). Similarly, Brewer's (1991) theory of "optimal distinctiveness"

views the motivation as a need to identify in a way that optimally provides differentiation and affiliation.

26. The process of identifying with a small group and the process of identifying with a large-scale social group are typically considered distinct traditions within the study of group identification. Lau (1989) explains that the "social interdependence model" draws from a definition of groups as entities within which the members interact with one another, while the "social identification" model does not require interaction, but rather a shared perception of membership in a social group (220–21). However, the two theories merge because the social-comparison function served by interaction (the first tradition) feeds identification with larger-scale social groupings (the second tradition).

27. A "minimal group effect" in which people show preference for in-group members has been demonstrated using categorizations that were made meaningful by the researcher in experimental settings, such as delimiting group memberships according to whether the subjects preferred a Klee or a Kandinsky painting (Tajfel et al. 1971) or whether the subjects were art or science students (Oakes, Turner, and Haslam 1991).

28. One might argue that this is not identity but merely affect. However, Brady and Sniderman argue that affect alone does not drive this "likability heuristic" in which individuals evaluate political issues on the basis of their feelings toward social and political groups and their perception of attitudes among members of these groups. Instead, they theorize that the heuristic operates on the basis of affect rooted in a cognitive framework in which social groups are arrayed as in-groups and out-groups.

29. See Sears et al. (1997) for work with respect to candidates and policies.

30. These analyses were conducted in the following manner. They estimated logit models in which, in addition to controls and the respondents' perceptions of the economic well-being of their families and the nation as a whole, they included perceptions of the economic well-being of social groups (women, blacks, Hispanics, poor people, the well-to-do, working men and women, and the middle class). To test whether membership in the groups caused perceptions of their economic well-being to matter, they investigated the significance of interactions between perceptions of each group and membership in it. To test identity, they investigated whether "statistical" interactions of perceptions and feelings of closeness to these groups (an indication of group identification) were statistically significant. To test whether respondents were engaging in social comparison, they included indicators derived from measures of the distance between the respondents' perceptions of their own economic well-being and that of each of the social groups.

Chapter Three

1. I passed out a self-administered questionnaire to thirty-nine people who usually sat down in the store between 8 A.M. and 9:30 A.M. I asked about their reasons for coming to the place, the histories of their lives in Ann Arbor, their perceptions of Ann Arborites and Americans in general, as well as many standard political attitude measures, standard participation measures, basic demographics, and closeness

measures. Thirty questionnaires were returned (for a response rate of 77 percent). Twenty-six questionnaires were completed by men who are Old Timers, one was completed by a woman who joins a mixed-gender group that meets after 9 A.M., and three were completed by regular patrons who sit at the smaller tables across from the Old Timers' section. Although the questionnaires were distributed to as many Old Timers as possible, as opposed to a random sample of them, the high response rate and the large proportion of the group's "regulars" given self-administered questionnaires allows me to use their responses to provide a suggestive profile of the group.

The reader might argue that the most politically attentive were more likely to complete the questionnaire. This is possible; thus, the results concerning the extent to which they follow government should be read with caution. Also, one might argue that the most extreme in their political views were also more likely to return the questionnaire. Although this might be the case, my perception is that the most conservative *and* the most liberal in the group were more likely to return the questionnaire, decreasing bias in one direction or the other.

I exclude the women and the small-table regulars from the results reported to focus on the Old Timers.

2. Note the difference between the argument that people avoid politics in a seemingly nonfriendly environment and the "spiral of silence" argument (Noelle-Neumann 1993), which states that people avoid talking about a political topic when they perceive that they do not hold the majority opinion. Evidence of the spiral of silence effect is inconclusive, as a recent meta-analysis of research on the phenomenon demonstrates (Glynn, Hayes, and Shanahan 1997). Rather than claim that people make judgments about the distribution of *political* preferences within an environment, I claim that people form perceptions about the general attitude environment, which includes, but is not restricted to, politics. Such assessments can take place without a single conversation about politics.

3. The complete wording of the question was, "One of the other things that I am interested in is finding out whether people ordinarily pay much attention to current events, public affairs, and politics. Do you ever discuss politics with your family or friends?"

4. It is possible that these self reports were biased upward by their knowledge that I was especially interested in their political conversations. At the time I administered this questionnaire I had been observing the Old Timers for over a year and had stated that my training was in political science. However, in the course of my observations, I mentioned this only rarely, and even two and a half years into my observations Dave, one of the most frequent regulars, asked what my degree would be in.

5. I am indebted to John Jackson for clarifying this point.

6. In other words, when asked to reach a collective opinion, people form ideas of the prototypical position. This is the position with the minimum distance from all group members—and the maximum distance from out-group members. When the discussants perceive that the group norm is near an extreme, polarization tends to occur (McGarty et al. 1992). This perception of the group norm has been likened to an identity, and it is a function of the discussion context: when subjects are encouraged to compare their group to an out-group, they tend to view their group identity in a

more extreme way (Doise 1969; Turner and Oakes 1986; Turner, Wetherell, and Hogg 1989; Abrams et al. 1990).

7. I use masculine pronouns in this section to remain consistent with the focus on the Old Timers.

8. I model these motivations after Wilson's (1973) trichotomy of incentives that political organizations use to obtain members.

9. The observations in chapters to come display that this updating process takes place even among elderly people, as people give meaning to their identities later in life. However, previous political socialization research suggests that priors on the content of identities tend to be stronger (more resistant to change) later in the life cycle. Major social changes, such as women's involvement in the workforce during World War II, appear to have a greater impact on people in younger generations, who are still in their precrystallization, formative years (Stewart and Healy 1989).

10. For example, Graber (1988), in her in-depth interviews of a panel of people over the course of a year that included the 1976 presidential election, found that her respondents rarely questioned the validity of a story, "except when a story ran directly counter to their personal experiences" (141).

11. This model of identity clarification can be construed as a model of identity persuasion. As such, it is similar to the persuasion model offered by Lupia and McCubbins (1998). They model persuasion over policy preferences (including jury decisions, vote choices, and policy stances), as opposed to perspectives or identities. They stipulate that in the absence of external enforcement mechanisms, persuasion can occur only when the receiver perceives that the speaker has common interests and is knowledgeable (49). In the present model, the judgment about whether or not to use the information the speakers in a group offer on appropriate perspectives for a person like oneself is based on perceptions of whether the speakers are knowledgeable about what it means to be someone like oneself (credibility) and have perspectives that resonate with one's prior (range of acceptability). These considerations are similar to the criteria of knowledge and interests, accordingly, in the Lupia and McCubbins model.

12. See Calvert (1985) for a formal model of this process with respect to preferences (as opposed to perspectives).

13. This is not to say that whatever a group such as the Old Timers talks about is consistent with their social identity. Rather, the group's expression of the kind of people they are before discussing a given topic structures how they make sense of it; that is, it predicts the resources that they use to communicate about politics.

14. I assume that the collective expression of social identity exists prior to the act of interpreting a given political event. In practice, the communication of social identity exists in a reciprocal relationship with the interpretation of political events. However, because informal public discussion occurs as a by-product of social interaction, it is more useful to conceptualize collective social identity as existing prior to comments made on a given political issue.

15. A vivid illustration of this on the individual level is Monroe's work on altruistic behavior (1996). In her theory, individuals' worldviews partly consist of their ideas about where they fit in the social world in relation to others. This

perspective drives perceptions of self-interest. Therefore, altruistic behavior is consistent with individuals' perceptions of material interests when they hold a perspective that all of humanity is part of a whole. Altruists conceptualize behavioral decisions as issues of how best to uphold humanity's best interests. This understanding constrains choice to such an extent that Monroe's altruistic respondents frequently described their altruistic behavior by saying "I had no other choice."

Chapter Four

1. "Corner store" is used in substitution of the actual name of the place.

2. Notice the implications for our standard methods of measuring participation in involuntary associations. In the previous chapter, I reported that only seven of twenty-six Old Timers admitted that they belong to an informal club or group. However, the frequency of participation and the behavior within the context of their morning meetings suggest that all of the Old Timers are members of an informal club or group.

3. Supportive evidence that a clear minority can foster in-group/out-group distinctions comes from Kanter's (1977) work on women in male-dominated organizations.

4. Lau (1989) also tested the effect of the (perceived) social density of respondents' friendship groups, neighborhoods, and nearest elementary schools, and found similar effects (229, n. 10).

5. Whether people refer to a subgroup identity rather than a larger-scale identity depends on whether doing so boosts their relative status. For example, while Latinos tend to identify with a more specific ethnic group than "Hispanics" (De la Garza et al. 1992), Cuban Americans appear to be especially likely to identify as "Cubans" because of the perceived higher status of that subgroup (Huddy and Virtanen 1995). This is another way in which the likelihood of a group of people communicating along the lines of collective as opposed to personal identity as well as the nature of that collective identity are both a function of the opportunity they have to recognize their similarities and to contrast themselves with out-groups.

6. Group consciousness, such as gender consciousness, differs from social identity because, in addition to identity with a social group, it entails an awareness that membership in that social category has implications for one's relative status and power in society (Miller et al. 1981; Gurin 1985; Tolleson-Rinehart 1992). I use consciousness-raising groups as an example here because group consciousness encompasses the concept of social identity.

7. This question was modeled after the question that was used by the ANES since 1972. The Old Timers expressed a good deal of exasperation with the vagueness of the question. For example, one man wrote in the margins of his questionnaire, "How can I be close to Black when I hardly know any or Christian fundamentalist or Resident of Michigan. I guess you could say I'm closest to people who work, are white and black who go to church and live [in] the neighborhood." Such marginalia suggested the question was interpreted in a variety of ways, from feelings of affect toward to experience with a given social group.

8. The relationship between identification with a group and social density ("the proportion of fellow group members in the immediate environment") is expected to be curvilinear (Lau 1989, 225). "At low levels of social density ... more group members should be associated with a higher probability of identifying with the group" (223), but past a certain point, more members should lead to a lower probability of identification (227).

9. These marginals were computed on data from the postelection interview using sampling weights. For men N = 689. For women N = 834. Whites N = 1,290. Blacks N = 183. See similar evidence in Wong (1998) and Lau (1989, 227) with respect to blacks.

10. Also, some closeness measures pose identity as an attachment to one group versus another and may have a difficult time capturing identity among people for whom such an attachment is not on the tip of their tongue. For example, the 1990 Citizen Participation Study (Verba et al. 1990) gathered data on gender identity by asking women, "If you think about the groups you feel particularly close to—people who are most like you in their ideas, interests and feelings about things—do you feel a lot closer to women than to men, somewhat closer, or is there no difference in how close you feel to women and men?" A fourth code was a volunteered code used when the respondent reported feeling closer to "men." Given the intimate linkages most women have with members of the out-group (men), when a heterosexual woman is asked this question, does a response that "there [is] no difference in how close [I] feel to women and men" indicate a lack of attachment to women? Or a reluctance to claim distance from men? The problem underscores that measures that ask people to label their social identities by claiming "closeness" to particular groups may miss the way people identify as social group members through their behavior and subtle us/them comments.

11. A similar argument can be made with respect to racial identity. For example, among African Americans, there are infinite definitions of what it means to be black (Cross 1991).

12. The population from which these ANES samples are taken is that of "all U.S. citizens of voting age [18] on or before election day 1996."

13. They do this even though, as of the 2000 Census, 27.2 percent of the population of Ann Arbor were not non-Hispanic white and 81 percent were younger than fifty years of age.

14. Throughout this study, portions of the conversations that I could not recall or that have been omitted for ease of exposition are denoted as follows: "... [...] ..."

15. For the CPS, identities were measured during the screener interview, which was conducted during the summer and fall of 1989. The follow-up main interview was conducted in the spring and summer of 1990. Although the screener measured closeness to "Asian-Americans" and "Hispanics" as well as to women and blacks, I do not investigate identification with Asian Americans here, in that only twenty of the main interview respondents were Asian Americans. I also do not investigate identification with Hispanics, given the ambiguity of the label "Hispanic." De la Garza et al. (1992) report that using the terms "Hispanic" and "Latino" to refer to the many diverse groups subsumed under those labels is "culturally demeaning and

conceptually indefensible" (7). Evidence from their Latino National Political Survey shows that Mexican Americans, Puerto Ricans, and Cubans prefer to identify with those subgroups, rather than with "Latinos" or "Hispanics" (13; see also Huddy and Virtanen 1995). Thus among people classified as "Latinos," we would not necessarily expect a relationship between closeness to "Hispanics" and participation. In addition, participation might actually foster identification with a more specific group such as Mexican Americans at the expense of identifying with "Hispanics." Please see appendix 3 for question wordings.

16. Although the women in the guild show signs of clarifying their identity with respect to women, most of their interaction is done through the lens of interpersonal difference. This suggests that not all association interaction fosters the clarification of identity. National sample survey data support this conclusion. I compared rates of social identification (with social groups in which respondents are objectively members) among people who reported participating in any kind of association in the past twelve months against rates among people who did not attend association meetings. Rates of identification among women, blacks, whites, senior citizens, and union members were analyzed with 1996 NES data, and identity with women and blacks was additionally analyzed with 1990 CPS data. The relationship between association participation and identification was only marginally statistically significant for women, blacks, and union members, although the direction of effects was as expected among all groups. To control for possible reverse causality, in the absence of longitudinal data, I compared differences in rates of identification between participants and nonparticipants versus the rates between members and nonmembers. The expectation was that if taking part in informal interaction within a group fosters social identity, then we should see a greater difference in rates of identification between nonparticipants and participants than we do among members and nonmembers. Mere membership, as opposed to exposure to group interaction, should not be associated with as strong an identification. A comparison of the gap in identification between members and nonmembers versus the gap in identification between participants and nonparticipants reveals that this expectation holds for women but not for African Americans.

17. The scale for figures 5.1 and 5.2 is as follows: 4 = Members of association are "all" respondent's race or gender; 3 = "Mostly" respondent's race or gender; 2 = "Mixed"; 1 = "Only a few" are respondent's race or gender.

18. The number of cases from which these homogeneity scores were computed varies widely across groups because the level of participation varies across group types. Please see table A4.1 for these numbers.

19. These figures were computed using weighted data. For racial homogeneity, $N = 188$, for gender $N = 189$. This difference is statistically significant: $t = 3.2092$, one-tailed $p < .000$. Unless otherwise noted, analyses of CPS data among women and respondents in general are conducted on weighted data (using variable "wt2517"), while analyses among blacks in that study are conducted on unweighted data. This is done to maximize the number of cases in each analysis while maximizing the representativeness of the sample. The CPS oversampled for African Americans. According to the study documentation, the unweighted sample of blacks is close enough to random that weights are not necessary. Also, unless otherwise indicated,

T-tests of differences in means in this chapter are one-tailed and do not assume equal variances across groups.

20. Both studies measured social identity through "closeness" questions, but the CPS used an item that obtained finer-grained responses. In that study, interviewers asked respondents whether they felt closer to a social group of which they were technically a member than to "others" (see note 9 in this chapter). Blacks were asked whether they felt closer to blacks "than to other people." I have rescaled and recoded these responses such that 1 corresponds to feeling "a lot" closer to one's social group than "others" or "men" and 0 corresponds to "feel closer to others/men."

21. When analyses within the 1990 CPS are conducted on women without using sample weights, the gap is slightly smaller, although still marginally significant at $p < .1$. When identification among blacks in the CPS is analyzed using weights the gap is larger and in the expected direction. When weights are not used in the NES analyses, the gap is larger for blacks, the elderly, and union members, and slightly smaller for women, though still marginally significant at $p < .1$. The negative relationship among whites disappears.

Chapter Five

1. Azziz was the Iraqi foreign minister at the time.

2. A difference of means test reveals $t = 3.944$, $p = .000$. When computed without weights, the gap is smaller, though significant at $p = .015$.

3. Of the 124 men reporting service or fraternal organizations as their most important group, 76 percent reported informal political talk, compared to just 51 percent among the 95 women who claimed such a group as their most important. (A weighted 2-tailed t-test, not assuming equal variances, gave $t = 3.909$, $p = .000$.) All of the five men who called a women's rights group their most important reported informal political talk, while 70 percent of the twenty-four women who said such a group was their most important did so. (A weighted 2-tailed t-test, not assuming equal variances, gave $t = 3.420$, $p = .002$.)

4. One caution is in order here. The wording of the questions asked in the ANES and my questionnaire are slightly different in several cases. Please see appendix 3 for exact question wordings. For this item in particular, the ANES asked, "Some people seem to follow what's going on in the government and public affairs most of the time, whether there is an election going on or not. Others aren't that interested. Would you say that you follow what's going on in government and public affairs most of the time, some of the time, only now and then, or hardly at all?" I asked only about government: "Some people seem to think about what's going on in government most of the time, whether there's an election going on or not. Others aren't that interested. How often do you follow what's going on in government?" (same response options offered). Despite the difference in wording, however, one would expect that asking about government and public affairs, as was done in the ANES, would elicit higher levels of attention than only asking about government. This was not the case—the Old Timers still showed higher levels of attention.

5. In reporting the marginals from the Old Timers as well as the ANES respondents, I am excluding "don't knows" and refusals.

6. One might argue that the attentiveness of the Old Timers may have something to do with the fact that they reside in a media market that is rich in local coverage. Although the television networks broadcast from Detroit, there are two local public radio stations, and the city sits within the broadcast area of three others. In addition, Ann Arbor has its own daily afternoon newspaper. Therefore, residents of the city may be more aware of local politics than in other places with less local coverage (Delli Carpini, Keeter, and Kennamer 1994) and also may be more likely to engage in political discussion (Mondak 1995). However, the guild members reside in the same location, so this does not adequately explain the differing levels of political talk.

7. In other words, the ability to exit means that repeated attendance is tacit agreement with the norms of the group.

8. One example occurred when the group was talking about the February 1999 trial of a white man who was convicted of killing an African-American man by dragging him behind a pickup truck in Jasper, Texas. Harold said, "Horrible. Yeah, they say he was alive when he hit the culvert, that's what tore his head off." Alex responded, "As a Caucasian, I am embarrassed."

9. See Eliasoph (1998) for a discussion of how jokes are a case of "the wider world enter[ing] the conversation in a backhanded way, in members' efforts to create a certain kind of interaction and present a certain kind of self" (103).

10. I use party identification rather than stances on specific policies to present a more global indicator of the use of identity to understand politics. I report results with respect to specific policies in a footnote below.

11. This approach is similar to methods used to investigate priming, or the alteration of the considerations individuals use when evaluating public figures. Iyengar and Kinder (1987, chaps. 7, 8) and Krosnick and Kinder (1990) use the magnitude of coefficients between presidential evaluations and evaluations on performance with respect to certain policy areas as indicators of the extent to which people "use" issue performance in evaluating the president.

12. When this analysis is run without using weights, the interactions on education become more significant, while the significance of the terms on the interactions with race and gender decreases. The F test remains significant at $p < .01$. When this same model is run on attitudes toward specific policy areas, more evidence emerges to support the claim that association interaction helps clarify the connection between social location and politics, although it is not as strong as the model of partisanship, arguably the most salient political attitude (Jennings and Niemi 1968). In particular, when modeling support without weights for government spending on programs for blacks, programs for women, a government-ensured standard of living, government spending, or abortion rights, a minimum of at least one interaction term on education, income, or union membership is significant. When the data are analyzed with weights, results still hold for attitudes toward programs for women and a government-ensured standard of living. The set of coefficients on the interactions is significant at $p < .05$ with respect to a government-ensured standard of living (with and without weights), but not for the other policies.

13. A rival explanation for the stronger linkages among people who are exposed to more casual political talk in associations is their higher levels of civic

engagement or characteristics that predispose people to be more civically engaged, rather than to exposure to informal political talk per se. However, when running this model just among the 50 percent of the sample that are most involved in associations, the significance of the interaction terms on African-American race and education persists. In addition, the interaction term on gender becomes marginally significant at $p = .075$. See table A5.1 (in appendix 5) for complete results.

14. To be sure, this measure only captures instrumental political talk, not the vast array of talk about politics that is uttered without a clear objective in mind. Unfortunately, there is no other survey data from a national sample of people studied over time that measures the level of informal political talk, instrumental or otherwise.

15. In 1965, 30 percent of the parent generation reported that one or more members of their household were union members, but just 25 percent of the offspring generation reported union membership in 1997, when they had reached the age of fifty (the approximate age of their parents in 1965). When we look only at people who identify as working class, a segment of the population in which we expect higher rates of union membership, 40 percent of the parent generation reported union membership, but just 30 percent of the younger generation did so in 1997 (Walsh, Jennings, and Stoker 2001).

16. In 1965, 39 percent of the parent generation had received some college education, and 13 percent had earned a bachelor's degree or higher ($N = 893$). But in 1997 (again, at an age comparable to that of their parents in 1965), 73 percent of the younger generation had received some college education, and 42 percent had earned a bachelor's degree or higher ($N = 935$).

17. In fact, when this same analysis is run while controlling for parent's party identification in 1965 (as reported by one parent in his or her 1965 interview), the effect of persuading others how to vote on clarifying the linkage between social location and partisan identification stands out more strongly. Results are displayed in table A5.2. With this control, not only is the interaction term on education significant at $p = .053$ but now the interaction term on union membership is also significant, at $p = .023$.

18. This correlation became larger between the 1950s and the 1990s. The exception is for votes in House and Senate races in the South, where support for the Democratic Party has dropped (Stonecash 2000, table 5.6, p. 110).

19. I am grateful to M. Kent Jennings for making this point.

20. Another example of this comes from the Press and Cole (1999) study of conversations about abortion shows on television. They found that the use of collective identities to talk about abortion is not restricted to working-class groups. Many of the middle-class as well as the working-class groups used their perceptions of their own social location to interpret the shows. As Press and Cole note, the television shows did not explicitly recognize group identity, but the viewers used cues about the identities of the characters as well as their own personal identities to talk about the content. Working-class women tended to view the messages oppositionally, disagreeing with the show's interpretations. The middle-class women tended to view women who had abortions as unlike, and of a lower class than, themselves. The

viewers used their interpretation of their own place in the social world as they engaged in a dialogue with each other and the television images.

21. Granted, they live on the rim of the Detroit metropolitan area, which Finifter (1974) described as overwhelmingly Democratic and pro-union. Even before "Reagan Democrats"—people who had been Democratic voters but strayed from the party to vote for Republican Ronald Reagan (Greenberg 1995)—emerged in the Detroit suburbs, Ann Arbor politics exhibited an unusually large degree of partisan competition (Eldersveld 1995).

22. I am grateful to Kimberly Gross for clarifying this point.

23. Women politicians are not a new phenomenon to this group. For example, throughout the course of this study, the mayor of Ann Arbor was a (Republican) woman. One might argue, however, that taking on a public role is one thing, but doing so while seeming to shirk a traditional duty such as that of wife is another, more threatening, thing for this group.

24. Earning money through the stock market is considered a legitimate route to wealth, as many of the Old Timers are themselves avid investors.

25. In the conversation, no one pointed out that Bradley is indeed from somewhere other than New Jersey: Missouri.

26. This was part of the analysis of correspondence between news and conversation frames, detailed in the next chapter.

27. For this reason, the "passing comments" label often given to informal political talk is partly apt. However, to say talk consists merely of "passing comments" misses the way in which these comments add up over time within a given group. For example, short comments, taken in isolation, may appear to have little impact, but, when taken as a whole, they create the boundaries of acceptable opinions.

28. Certainly, workplace settings might differ from less formal settings in which people have more control over with whom they talk. But even in workplaces, the everyday setting in which people are most likely exposed to cross-cutting opinions (Mutz and Mondak 1998), people seek out like-minded others with whom to chat about politics while on the job (Finifter 1974).

29. A persuasive bit of evidence on this point is provided by Lewin's (1952) research on campaigns to persuade housewives during World War II to serve "unpopular meats." The study, conducted in conjunction with the Food Habits Committee of the National Research Council, compared the relative effectiveness of persuasion attempts that involved lectures with those that used group discussions. In both conditions, the women were volunteers in a Red Cross home nursing program. They were brought together and given information about the health and economic benefits of serving sweetbreads, beef hearts, and kidneys. The facilitators and lecturers attempted to persuade the housewives to serve these meats with appeals to support the war effort. (An example argument was that serving these meats stretches a limited meat supply.) The subjects were given recipes for "delicious dishes," then asked whether they would try serving these dishes to their families. Women who participated in the group discussion were more likely to try serving one of these meats. According to follow-up contacts, of the women who attended lectures, only

3 percent tried serving the meats, while 32 percent of the participants in the group discussions served one of these unpopular foods. Subsequent experiments ruled out several alternative explanations for the differences between lecture and group treatments, including the potential that the conditions differed in the amount of time devoted to persuading each subject in the prompts provided about follow-up contacts, and the possibility that the results occurred as an artifact of the type of food product (similar results were achieved with respect to evaporated milk).

30. This is an admittedly minority opinion among contemporary public opinion researchers. In contrast to other historical periods, in the current era, "social scientists believe that our current American infrastructure of public opinion consists of (a) a shared meaning of public opinion as an aggregation of individuals, whose opinions are (b) measured through polls and surveys and then (c) diffused through print and broadcast media" (Herbst 2001, 452).

Chapter Six

1. In a study of agenda setting, Erbring and Goldenberg (1980) write, "Getting at the meaning of the news involves assessing its implications for the future, tracing developments from the past, comparing current events with previous experience, weighing the credibility of particular sources, and so forth. It calls, in short, for an *interpretation* of the news—not by individual intuition, but by 'social reality testing.' Informal communication with others is essential to help people make sense of news media content, and thus plays a critical role in shaping public perceptions of issue salience" (41).

2. For an important exception, see the recent study by Druckman and Nelson (2002).

3. Special thanks to Danna Basson for careful transcription of the television news broadcasts analyzed in this chapter.

4. Note that the present study is an investigation of processing news within a group context and thus is not a study of individual variations in media-use strategies.

5. I make this assumption in order to focus not on which news stories people discuss but on how they talk about news stories when they do so.

6. In October and November, I visited these groups once a week. In December, I went every day for a one-week period. In January and February, I visited once a week. In June, I went three to four days a week, and then once a week in July.

7. I did this by observing both groups on the day of the weekly guild meetings. On such days, I would visit the corner store in the morning, and then spend time with the guild over the lunch hour.

8. Table A6.1 displays the lag time between when the story broke and when the Old Timers discussed it.

9. The television coverage that was missed were stories aired on networks other than the ABC Detroit affiliate. Ten of the seventeen respondents to the media-use questionnaire (explained below) reported watching the ABC affiliate nightly news.

10. None of the Old Timers admitted to knowing a staff member of the *Ann Arbor News*.

11. I also used the content of the radio news program that was the most commonly used program, the morning news program of the University of Michigan's public radio station, but stopped doing so after several weeks. Only four people had reported using that program and after repeated attempts to generate a conversation based on that coverage, it appeared that their attention to this show was not frequent enough to merit inclusion in the study.

12. I defined "most prominent" by placement and headline size in newspapers and placement in the newscasts.

13. I had collected this content while conducting the fieldwork. To check that I had gathered all of the relevant articles, I looked at the local library's archives.

14. I randomly selected a subsample of 15 percent of the news stories and of the conversations included in the analyses and subjected my coding procedure to an interrator reliability test. The test coder was blind to the purposes of the study. Agreement across our coding was as follows: for the main idea of the stories: 85 percent; stance: 80 percent; groups mentioned: 98 percent.

15. Results with respect to the other issues are available upon request from the author.

16. The reader may wish to know which type of topics stimulated more or less divergence in interpretations. Because of the limited number of topics included in this analysis, I refrain from drawing such conclusions.

17. Several members of the Old Timers and the craft guild were connected to local leaders and therefore had access to firsthand information. What happens when we examine understanding among people who are clearly not among the people driving local policy? To further understand the process of interpreting news in small groups, I spent time with a group of homeless people who met over breakfast at a local church. Not only were the members of this group unlikely to have direct access to political professionals, they were also likely to have relatively less exposure to news. I had been volunteering at the free breakfast program at which they met for one year when, in the winter of 1999–2000, I began asking whether I could join the guests at their tables. (As with the Old Timers and the church guild, I gave the people in the setting a letter explaining that I was a social scientist and wanted to learn about small-group conversation from them. I explained that if anyone was uncomfortable with my presence I would leave.) The program served between one hundred and one hundred and fifty people each morning. The guests included a mix of men and women, the majority of whom were men. Ages ranged widely from infants to seemingly elderly people. The guests' racial backgrounds were also varied; on any given day, the majority was usually white, but a large proportion was African American, and occasionally several Latinos attended as well. The guests were exposed to very little news coverage. Most of the people I talked to did not watch the news on television or read a daily paper. Even though the *News* had printed a stream of articles, letters to the editor, editorials, and guest editorials about the homeless shelter plan in the preceding two months, most did not know what I was talking about when I asked them whether they had heard about it.

Although they did not have access to news from the mass media, they still went about the task of communicating about homelessness. They filled in the gaps in their knowledge about the specifics of the new shelter issue with reference to personal stories about the living conditions in shelters, such as their constant concerns about someone stealing their belongings and, in one case, concerns about physical violence.

This is not to say, however, that they were untouched by the mass media. Additional conversations suggest that they were influenced by news interpretations, but perhaps through a flow of information that included more steps than is the case for the average citizen. For example, one man was aware of the governor's policies with respect to homelessness. And when I attempted to validate their attention to the news by asking if they "knew what the weather was going to be like" that day, someone always had a reply that seemed consistent with the reports I had heard that morning on the radio. Given their lack of attention to news coverage, I was unable to use their conversations as part of this analysis of news interpretation. However, my observations of this group are a reminder that models of making sense of politics that place the media as the key linkage institution overlook processes among people who are politically interested but have relatively little access to news.

Chapter Seven

1. Many of the conversations in this chapter were recorded and transcribed. Footnotes designate which are reported verbatim.

2. Green Party candidate Ralph Nader also played a prominent role in the campaign, garnering 2.6 percent of the popular vote. Reform Party candidate Pat Buchanan was given attention by the mass media, but he won less than 1 percent of the vote.

3. See Just et al. (1996) for evidence that interpretations of the 1992 presidential election campaign were a function of the local media environment.

4. In his account of the dynamics of trust, Hardin focuses on social trust rather than trust in government. However, he suggests that the objects of trust in his model can be political officeholders (1993, 510). Like trust in other people, trust in government depends on a person's judgment about whether it is in the government's interest to do what the person trusts the government to do (506).

5. "As the old saying goes, the facts are not given, they are *taken*" (Sapiro and Soss 1999, 308, emphasis in original).

6. Studies by Lau and colleagues demonstrate that perceptions of trust depend upon the perspectives people use to think about politics. Using responses to open-ended questions in the National Election Studies panels of 1972–76 that capture what people like and dislike about the political parties, Lau (1986, 1989) determined whether respondents tended to think about politics using person-based or issue-based schemas. These schemas are related to the concept of perspective used here (see chapter 2). Erber and Lau (1990) found that changes in trust in government were most strongly related to evaluations of issue distance between the respondent and the candidates among people who typically use issue-based schemas when thinking about politics. Similarly, it was among people who tended to think about politics through person-based schemas that attitudes toward President Ford's pardon of Richard Nixon were significant predictors of their degree of political trust.

7. Tyler's (1990) survey and in-depth interview work on why people obey laws challenges the argument that identity-based perspectives are integral to the process

of updating attitudes toward government. In brief, he argues that compliant behavior can be explained by individuals' *direct experience with the law.* When people perceive that the procedures and the outcomes are just, they perceive the authority as legitimate and are therefore more likely to be compliant. Tyler found little variation across his respondents in their interpretation of what constitutes a fair procedure. However, perceptions of whether "people like me" are treated fairly do differ across groups, racial groups in particular. For example, decades of survey research have revealed that white and black Americans generally agree that success is a function of individual effort, but diverge widely when asked whether discrimination hinders African Americans' chances of getting ahead (Hochschild 1995; see table 3.1 [pp. 58–59], table 7.1 [p. 147], and pages 209–10 with respect to the political sphere and voting, specifically). In addition, Tyler finds it necessary to rely on the concept of identity with specific social groups on the last page of his book: "There appears to be a consensus among members of the group studied about what fair procedure means in the context of a particular dispute or problem. If people's concerns about fairness depend on their connections to social groups, then these concerns may have a limited range. People may feel less concerned about issues of fairness when they are dealing with others outside their own group" (178).

8. According to self-administered questionnaires and the observations, the Old Timers followed public affairs more closely on average than the people who sat near the windows.

9. This account of the election aftermath is based on the chronologies presented in Sunstein (2001) and Gillman (2001).

10. The official electoral college vote was held on January 6, 2001.

11. These observations were conducted on the mornings of January 9–12, 2001.

12. See chapter 3 for details of the survey, and appendix 3 for wording of the test measures.

13. These comparisons are made with 1996 ANES postelection data.

14. This conversation was recorded and then transcribed verbatim.

15. This conversation was recorded and then transcribed verbatim.

16. Referring to the Drudge Report, an on-line political news clearinghouse and gossip source.

17. Then somehow he segued into talking about liberal bias among university faculties and how "you know we have a course here [at the University of Michigan] now about how to be a homosexual."

18. This in itself is one indicator of their detachment from the government.

19. In addition, only one of the African Americans responded to the questionnaire. This person's responses displayed distrust in government, giving either the median response or the most nontrusting response to questions concerning the amount of attention the government pays to the people "when it decides what to do," whether people running the government are dishonest, whether the government wastes tax money, the level of trust in the government in Washington, and whether or not the government is "run by a few big interests." Like the majority of the Old Timers, this person indicated the least amount of faith in "national" government.

20. By referring to this, I do not mean to ignore the difference between trust in other people and trust in government but, instead, to use observations of the way they saw themselves within that setting as an indicator of their perceptions of their place within society as a whole.

21. My thanks to Dave Leheny for clarifying this means of observing identity.

22. I inserted this comment in reaction to comments Larry had made earlier in this exchange that referred to the Supreme Court's role.

23. This conversation was recorded and then transcribed verbatim.

24. See Mettler (2002) for a demonstration of the effect of obtaining an education through the G.I. Bill on political participation.

25. This conversation was recorded and then transcribed verbatim.

26. Additional support for this claim is provided by Valentino et al. (2001). They demonstrated with an experiment that when a campaign news story was framed such that a candidate's policy proposal was perceived as an attempt to win votes as opposed to an attempt to pursue important issue priorities, readers' trust in government was depressed, but only among people who identified as "Independents" as opposed to "Democrats" or "Republicans." It appears that people who view government actions from the standpoint of the disaffected are predisposed to perceive government action in a negative light.

Chapter Eight

1. Huddy and Sears (1995), in a study that examines whether racial prejudice or perception of threat to material interests explains white opposition to bilingual education programs, suggest in their conclusion that social identity theory may explain the reasons that both explanations appear to be at work (142).

2. As Young (1990b) states, groups are "real not as substances, but as forms of social relations" (44).

3. These labels roughly correspond to two main traditions among the variety of ways scholars have theorized democracy. Other labels are sometimes used. Smith (1997) describes the two perspectives as "liberal" and "republican" (1997). Bohman (1996) refers to a "precommitment" versus "proceduralist" model, which also maps to the civic-republican/liberal-individualist dimension. The "social choice" versus "democratic discourse" distinction (Van Mill 1996) is oriented in approximately the same direction. In addition, "communitarian" visions resonate with civic republicanism. I follow Fraser (1992) in the use of the terms "civic-republican" and "liberal-individualist" to describe in shorthand the ideas of public deliberation encapsulated within these two visions.

4. The public sphere, according to Habermas, is the realm of civic communication in society jointly occupied by citizens and mass media that exists independently of government and economic domination (Habermas 1995). Ideally, communication within the public sphere enables the exchange of ideas based in reason, among people who are treated as equals. Many debates have arisen over whether Habermas's conception of the public sphere is an ideal or a description of what actually existed. He bases his theory on communication that occurred within Western European, especially French, bourgeois societies in the late eighteenth and

early nineteenth centuries. In *The Structural Transformation of the Public Sphere,* Habermas details the decline of this public sphere, and in doing so he presents it as an ideal type against which modern forms of communication and opinion formation ought to be judged.

5. Because Dave is the most outspoken economic liberal of the group, and the only one to actively consider the effect of policy on other social groups, an argument might be made that the tendency of the other men to *not* consider the common good arises from a belief—given their conservative viewpoints—that individuals ought to rely on themselves, rather than the government, for assistance. This may indeed be the case. However, the use of the civic-republican model for understanding public discussion is all the more unsatisfactory if it can only be applied to people of certain ideological leanings. We should strive for a more widely applicable model for interpreting informal political talk.

6. I take this subhead from Robert Putnam (2000), "The Dark Side of Social Capital" (chap. 22). See also Fiorina (1999), "Extreme Voices: A Dark Side to Civic Engagement," in which Fiorina explains the dangers that can occur when only an unrepresentative portion of a community participates in civic action.

7. Robinson and Levy (1986) demonstrate higher levels of understanding of public-affairs news among people who report talking to others about politics.

8. Indeed, Lenart has found that talking to other people about politics enhances learning during election campaigns (1994). Using cross-section survey data, Kim et al. (1999) demonstrate a relationship between conversation about both political and personal topics and newspaper use, between political talk and participation within the political system, and between personal talk and participation outside formal channels of decision making, such as taking part in demonstrations, writing letters to the editor, and calling talk shows. One implication of this study is that participating in talk about political issues may spur attention to news and participation in public affairs.

9. McLeod, Scheufele, Moy, Horowitz et al. (1999) show that it is political discussion within homogenous social networks (in terms of age, gender, liberal-conservative ideology, and level of political knowledge) that is negatively related to willingness to participate in a citywide deliberative forum.

10. Not everyone agrees that these declines have occurred. First, the apparent decline in participation may be attributable to changing forms of participation in voluntary associations. For example, social and technological changes have brought about reduced participation in white, male, Protestant, "Main Street" organizations (Rich 1999). But participation in other kinds of organizations has surged, including soccer leagues (Ladd 1999) and centralized, expert-led organizations (Skocpol 1999). Second, using indicators of trust other than the one Putnam used suggests that levels of social trust among Americans have not necessarily declined (Jackman and Miller 1998).

11. In later work, Putnam (2000) uncovers the history of the term, tracing it back to a West Virginia Progressive-Era reformer in 1914 (19).

12. On September 11, 12, and 13, 2001, the Wal-Mart corporation sold four hundred and fifty thousand U.S. flags at their 2,746 stores nationwide. The tally for

U.S. flags sold at their stores one year earlier, on the same dates, was twenty-six thousand (personal communication with public relations office, October 10, 2001).

13. Among the people for whom group homogeneity data is available (people who said that their most active group is also their most important group) the correlation between perceived group racial homogeneity and perceived racial composition of one's neighborhood is $r = .341, n = 427, p < .000$.

14. Evidence that Internet use fosters exposure to like-minded others more than to crosscutting opinions is still forthcoming. Most claims to this effect in the scholarly literature, such as mine, above, are speculative (see Dahlgren 2001; Brown and Duguid 2000). For one study that supports this claim, which Dahlgren cites, see Fisher, Margolis, and Resnick (1996). One piece of attitudinal, albeit not behavioral, evidence to this effect comes from a Pew Research Center for the People and the Press Survey Report, "The Internet News Audience Goes Ordinary," released January 14, 1999. Among the questions asked was the following: "Some people say that the Internet is a good thing because it brings together people with similar interests. Others say that the Internet is a bad thing because it brings together small groups of people who share dangerous ideas. Which comes closer to your view?" Fifty-four percent responded "good thing," 28 percent responded "bad thing," and 18 percent did not know or refused to answer (N = 3,184).

15. However, among younger generations, use of the Internet for information seeking appears to foster social trust and civic participation more than does use of print and broadcast media (Shah, McLeod, and Yoon 2001).

16. This description most closely matches the Study Circles model.

17. Examples include St. Louis's FOCUS Bridges Across Racial Polarization and Baltimore BLEWS Dinner Dialogues.

18. Examples include the Madison Public Library-sponsored reading of *Caucasia*, by Danzy Senna, and the Cincinnati On the Same Page program reading of *A Lesson Before Dying*, by Ernest Gaines, in 2002.

19. "Toward Competent Communities" contained several caveats about this figure. Some of the figures from specific programs were estimates and not detailed counts. Also, some of the tallies may have counted the same individual more than once (81). A look at detailed counts of the enrollment in several of the more wide-reaching programs is instructive. The Aurora (Illinois) Community Study Circles has enrolled over 2,500 participants as of February 2003 (personal communication, Mary Jane Hollis, executive director). The first communitywide Study Circles program, in Lima, Ohio, had enrolled over four thousand individual community members as of the year 2000.

20. As Schoem et al. (2001) assert, the popularity partly results from the dialogues conducted and promoted as part of the Clinton administration's Initiative on Race. See the dialogue guide produced by the advisory board of the Initiative on Race (*One America* 1998).

21. Rodney King, an African American, was beaten with a baton and kicked in the head after being stopped for a traffic violation by Los Angeles police in March 1991. The violence fractured his skull and gave him kidney and brain damage. A

bystander captured the episode on videotape. A year later, the four officers involved were put on trial in Simi Valley, a suburb of Los Angeles. They were acquitted on April 29, 2002. As Lee (2002) describes it, "Almost instantly, the predominantly African American and Latino residents of South Central Los Angeles reacted to this verdict violently and the City of Angels burst into a raging hellfire" (186). Over the next five days, fifty-three people died, 2,400 were injured, more than $800 million worth of property was destroyed, and at least 11,500 people lost their jobs (Mydans 1993).

22. Hope in the Cities was founded in Richmond, Virginia, in 1990 as an attempt to foster racial reconciliation by bringing political, business, and community leaders together in dialogue (Robert Corcoran, national director, Hope in the Cities, personal interview; see also Greisdorf 2001). The National Conference for Community and Justice, formerly the National Conference for Christians and Jews, sponsors regional dialogue programs that range from the Greater Cincinnati Region NCCJ's CommUNITY program in which diverse groups of people gather in one another's homes for three sessions (Robert "Chip" Harrod, executive director, Greater Cincinnati Region NCCJ, personal interview) to the Des Moines NCCJ dialogues that invoke their "strategic screen" of empowering leaders by drawing together leaders from business, government, faith, and media to discuss specific community issues such as Native American mascots (Rudy Simms, executive director, Iowa NCCJ, personal interview; Jesse Villalobos, regional program director, Iowa NCCJ, personal interview).

23. Sandy Robinson, director, Springfield Department of Community Relations and Springfield Community-Wide Study Circles Program, personal interview.

24. Clifford Kessler of the Des Moines Neighborhood Circles reports such a result (interview).

25. One specific example is the annual Peace Bridge Event in Dayton, Ohio, spurred in part by the Dayton Dialogue on Race Relations, a program inspired by the Hope in the Cities project (interview, Dean Lovelace, Dayton City commissioner, and Audrey Norman-Turner, project leader of the Dayton Dialogue). They emphasize that this type of event, in which community members march across a bridge that spans what is generally regarded as the white and nonwhite sections of the city, is one of the many outcomes of intergroup dialogue programs that signal to the community at large a serious and sustained attempt to address intergroup relations.

26. See Schoem and Hurtado 2001.

27. These friendships have ranged from one-on-one ties to ongoing interracial book clubs, such as those formed in Kenosha and Racine, Wisconsin (interview, Roseann Mason, director, Kenosha-Racine Diversity Circles).

28. This is according to Keniston, Hubbard, and Honnold (2002) reporting on the Dayton Dialogue, with a 61-percent response rate for the pre- and post-participation questionnaires, and an evaluation conducted by this author of the Madison (Wisconsin) Study Circles on Race, response rate 49 percent (N = 33).

29. This is based on the Madison study.

30. This is according to the Goldstein and Sturm (1999) report on the MetroHartford (Connecticut) Community Conversations on Race. The response rate for these pre-post evaluations was 50 percent (N = 70).

31. Corroborating evidence comes from the Madison study.

32. See Keniston et al. (2002, 19) for evidence that African-American participants in the Dayton Dialogue learned to use the program to learn more about their own race.

33. The number of respondents providing answers to these questions was seventy-one whites and forty-two blacks.

34. As one multiracial participant in the Madison program observed, one outcome of the program was "the realization that the bigotry is every bit as bad as we dared to think, plus more."

Appendix 1

1. The exceptions were private conversations in the kitchen, such as the one in which Ruby divulged her past candidacy for office to me.

2. This approach is based on the recording procedure used by Kingdon (1989 [1973]) during his interviews with members of Congress, as well as by Fenno (1978) in his participant observation of members of Congress. I refrained from tape-recording all of the conversations because I wished to avoid, as much as possible, contaminating the naturalness of the settings.

3. To code the field notes, I used a qualitative software program called NU*DIST (Non-numerical Unstructured Data Indexing Searching and Theorizing).

4. The self-administered questionnaires could have revealed attitudes that the Old Timers were reluctant to state in the context of the group. However, analyses of their responses showed no such evidence.

Abrams, Dominic, Margaret Wetherell, Sandra Cochrane, Michael A. Hogg, and John C. Turner. 1990. "Knowing What to Think by Knowing Who You Are: Self-Categorization and the Nature of Norm Formation, Conformity, and Group Polarization." *British Journal of Social Psychology* 29: 97–119.

Abramson, Paul R., John H. Aldrich, and David W. Rohde. 1998. *Change and Continuity in the 1996 Elections.* Washington, D.C.: Congressional Quarterly.

Ackerman, Bruce. 1980. *Social Justice in the Liberal State.* New Haven: Yale University Press.

Allport, Gordon W. 1954. *The Nature of Prejudice.* Reading, Mass.: Addison-Wesley.

Baker, Keith Michael. 1975. *Condorcet: From Natural Philosophy to Social Mathematics.* Chicago: University of Chicago Press.

Barber, Benjamin R. 1984. *Strong Democracy: Participatory Politics for a New Age.* Berkeley: University of California Press.

Beck, Paul Allen. 1991. "Voters' Intermediation Environments in the 1988 Presidential Contest." *Public Opinion Quarterly* 55: 371–94.

Beckwith, Karen. 1998. "Collective Identities of Class and Gender: Working-Class Women in the Pittston Coal Strike." *Political Psychology* 19: 147–67.

Bell, Daniel. 1993. *Communitarianism and Its Critics.* Oxford: Oxford University Press.

Bellah, Robert N., Richard Madsen, William M. Sullivan, Ann Swidler, and Steven M. Tipton. 1985. *Habits of the Heart: Individualism and Commitment in American Life.* New York: Harper and Row.

Berelson, Bernard R., Paul F. Lazarsfeld, and William N. McPhee. 1954. *Voting: A Study of Opinion Formation in a Presidential Campaign.* Chicago: University of Chicago Press.

Bielby, William T., and James N. Baron. 1984. "A Woman's Place Is with Other Women." In *Sex Segregation in the Workplace: Trends, Explanations, Remedies,* edited by Barbara F. Reskin. Washington, D.C.: National Academy Press.

Billig, Michael. 1995. "Rhetorical Psychology, Ideological Thinking, and Imagining Nationhood." In *Social Movements and Culture,* edited by Hank Johnston and Bert Klandermans. Minneapolis: University of Minnesota Press.

Blumer, Herbert. 1948. "Public Opinion and Public Opinion Polling." *American Sociological Review* 13: 542–49.

Bohman, James. 1996. *Public Deliberation: Pluralism, Complexity, and Democracy.* Cambridge: MIT Press.

Bourque, Susan C., and Jean Grossholtz. 1974. "Politics an Unnatural Practice: Political Science Looks at Female Participation." *Politics and Society* 4: 225–66.

Boyte, Harry C., and Nancy N. Kari. 1996. *Building America: The Democratic Promise of Public Work*. Philadelphia: Temple University Press.

Burns, Nancy, Kay Lehman Schlozman, and Sidney Verba. 2001. *The Private Roots of Public Action: Gender, Equality, and Political Participation*. Cambridge: Harvard University Press.

Brady, Henry E., and Paul M. Sniderman. 1985. "Attitude Attribution: A Group Basis for Political Reasoning." *American Political Science Review* 79: 1061–78.

Brewer, Paul R. 2000. "Passive Receivers or Motivated Reasoners? An Experimental Study of How Citizens Process Value Frames." Paper presented at the 2000 annual meeting of the Midwest Political Science Association, Chicago.

Brewer, Marilynn B. 2001. "The Many Faces of Social Identity: Implications for Political Psychology." *Political Psychology* 22 (1): 115–23.

———. 1979. "In-group Bias in the Minimal Inter-Group Situation: A Cognitive Motivational Analysis." *Psychological Bulletin* 86: 307–24.

———. 1991. "The Social Self: On Being the Same and Different at the Same Time." *Personality and Social Psychology Bulletin* 17: 475–82.

Brewer, Marilynn B., and Rupert J. Brown. 1998. "Intergroup Relations." In *The Handbook of Social Psychology*, edited by Daniel T. Gilbert and Susan T. Fiske. 4th ed. Boston: McGraw-Hill.

Brewer, Marilynn B., and Donald T. Campbell. 1976. *Ethnocentrism and Intergroup Attitudes: East African Evidence*. New York: Halsted Press.

Brewer, Marilynn B., and Wendi Gardner. 1996. "Who IS This 'We'? Levels of Collective Identity and Self Representations." *Journal of Personality and Social Psychology* 71: 83–93.

Brewer, Marilynn B., and Norman Miller. 1984. "Beyond the Contact Hypothesis: Theoretical Perspectives on Desegregation." In *Groups in Contact: The Psychology of Desegregation*, edited by Miller and Brewer. Orlando, Fla.: Academic Press.

Brown, John S., and Paul Duguid. 2000. *The Social Life of Information*. Boston: Harvard Business School Press.

Burke, John P. 1994. "Democracy and Citizenship." In *Critical Perspectives on Democracy*, edited by Lyman H. Letgers, John P. Burke, and Arthur DiQuattro. Lanham, Md.: Rowman and Littlefield.

Burns, Nancy. 1997. "Gender and the Pathways to Participation." University of Michigan, typescript.

———. 1994. *The Formation of Local Governments: Private Values in Public Institutions*. New York: Oxford University Press.

Burns, Nancy, Kay Lehman Schlozman, and Sidney Verba. 1997. "The Public Consequences of Private Inequality: Family Life and Citizen Participation." *American Political Science Review* 91: 373–89.

Burt, Ronald S. 1992. *Structural Holes: The Social Structure of Competition*. Cambridge: Harvard University Press.

Calhoun, Craig. 1991. "The Problem of Identity in Collective Action." In *Macro-Micro Linkages in Sociology*, edited by Joan Huber. Newbury Park, Calif.: Sage.

———. 1992. "Introduction: Habermas and the Public Sphere." In *Habermas and the Public Sphere,* edited by Craig Calhoun. Cambridge: MIT Press.

Calthorpe, Peter. 1993. *The Next American Metropolis: Ecology, Community, and the American Dream.* New York: Princeton Architectural Press.

Calvert, Randall L. 1985. "The Value of Biased Information: A Rational Choice Model of Political Advice." *Journal of Politics* 47: 531–55.

Campbell, Angus, Philip E. Converse, Warren E. Miller, and Donald E. Stokes. 1960. *The American Voter.* Chicago: University of Chicago Press.

Cappella, James, and Kathleen Hall Jamieson. 1997. *Spiral of Cynicism: The Press and the Public Good.* New York: Oxford University Press.

Carmines, Edward G., and James A. Stimson. 1980. "The Two Faces of Issue Voting." *American Political Science Review* 74: 78–91.

———. 1989. *Issue Evolution: Race and the Transformation of American Politics.* Princeton: Princeton University Press.

Chi, Michelene T. H., Paul J. Feltovich, and Robert Glaser. 1981. "Categorization and Representation of Physics Problems by Experts and Novices." *Cognitive Science* 5: 121–52.

Chong, Dennis. 1996. "Creating Common Frames of Reference on Political Issues." In *Political Persuasion and Attitude Change,* edited by Diana C. Mutz, Paul M. Sniderman, and Richard A. Brody, 195–224. Ann Arbor: University of Michigan Press.

Citrin, Jack. 1974. "Comment: The Political Relevance of Trust in Government." *American Political Science Review* 68 (3): 973–88.

Conover, Pamela Johnston. 1984. "The Influence of Group Identifications on Political Perception and Education." *Journal of Politics* 46: 760–85.

———. 1988. "The Role of Social Groups in Political Thinking." *British Journal of Political Science* 18: 51–76.

Conover, Pamela Johnston, and Stanley Feldman. 1991. "Where Is the Schema? Critiques." *American Political Science Review* 85 (4): 1364–69.

Conover, Pamela Johnston, Ivor M. Crewe, and Donald D. Searing. 1991. "The Nature of Citizenship in the United States and Great Britain: Empirical Comments on Theoretical Themes." *Journal of Politics* 53: 800–832.

———. 1999. "Rights as Trumps or Nonsense upon Stilts?" Paper presented at the annual meeting of the Midwest Political Science Association, Chicago.

———. 2002. "The Deliberative Potential of Political Discussion." *British Journal of Political Science* 32: 21–62.

Converse, Phillip E. 1964. "The Nature of Belief Systems in Mass Publics." In *Ideology and Discontent,* edited by D. E. Apter. New York: Free Press.

Converse, Philip E., and Angus Campbell. 1968. "Political Standards in Secondary Groups." In *Group Dynamics: Research and Theory,* edited by Dorin Cartwright and Alvin Zander (3d ed.), 199–211. Evanston, Ill.: Row, Peterson.

Cowan, Jane K. 1991. "Going Out for Coffee? Contesting the Grounds of Gendered Pleasures in Everyday Sociability." In *Contested Identities: Gender and Kinship in*

Modern Greece, edited by Peter Loizos and Evthymios Papataxiarchis, 180–202. Princeton: Princeton University Press.

Crenshaw, Kimberlé. 1989. "Demarginalizing the Intersection of Race and Sex: A Black Feminist Critique of Antidiscrimination Doctrine, Feminist Theory, and Antiracist Politics." *University of Chicago Legal Forum* 139: 139–67.

Crenshaw, Kimberlé Williams. 1997. "Color-blind Dreams and Racial Nightmares: Reconfiguring Racism in the Post-Civil Rights Era." In *Birth of a Nation'hood: Gaze Script and Spectacle in the O. J. Simpson Case,* edited by Toni Morrison and Claudia Brodsky Lacour. New York: Pantheon.

Crigler, Ann N. 1998. "Making Sense of Politics; Constructing Political Messages and Meanings." In *The Psychology of Political Communication,* edited by Ann N. Crigler, 1–10. Ann Arbor: University of Michigan Press.

Cross, William E. 1991. *Shades of Black: Diversity in African-American Identity.* Philadelphia: Temple University Press.

Crow, Barbara A. 1997. "Relative Privilege? Reconsidering White Women's Participation in Municipal Politics." In *Women Transforming Politics: An Alternative Reader,* edited by Cathy J. Cohen, Kathleen B. Jones, and Joan C. Tronto. New York: New York University Press.

Dahlgren, Peter. 2001. "The Public Sphere and the Net: Structure, Space, and Communication." In *Mediated Politics: Communication in the Future of Democracy,* edited by W. Lance Bennett and Robert M. Entman, 35–55. Cambridge: Cambridge University Press.

Dawson, Michael. 1994. *Behind the Mule: Race and Class in African-American Politics.* Princeton: Princeton University Press.

———. 2001. *Black Visions: The Roots of Contemporary African-American Political Ideologies.* Chicago: University of Chicago.

De la Garza, Rodolfo O., Louis DeSipio, F. Chris Garcia, John Garcia, and Angelo Falcon. 1992. *Latino Voices: Mexican, Puerto Rican, and Cuban Perspectives on American Politics.* Boulder, Colo.: Westview Press.

Delli Carpini, Michael X., and Bruce A. Williams. 1994. "Methods, Metaphors, and Media Research: The Uses of Television in Political Conversation." *Communication Research* 21: 782–812.

———. 1998. "Constructing Public Opinion: The Uses of Fictional and Nonfictional Television in Conversations about the Environment." In *The Psychology of Political Communication,* edited by Ann N. Crigler, 149–76. Ann Arbor: University of Michigan Press.

Delli Carpini, Michael X., Scott Keeter, and J. David Kennamer. 1994. "Effects of the News Media Environment on Citizen Knowledge of State Politics and Government." *Journalism Quarterly* 71: 443–56.

Denton, Nancy A. 1994. "Are African Americans Still Hypersegregated?" In *Residential Apartheid: The American Legacy,* edited by Robert D. Bollard, J. Eugene Grigsby, and Charles Lee. Los Angeles: CAAS Publications.

Doise, Willem. 1969. "Inter-group Relations and Polarization of Individual and Collective Judgments." *Journal of Personality and Social Psychology* 12: 136–43.

———. 1978. *Groups and Individuals: Explanations in Social Psychology*. Cambridge: Cambridge University Press.

Domke, David, Dhavan V. Shah, and Daniel B. Wackman. 1998. "'Moral Referendums': Values, News Media, and the Process of Candidate Choice." *Political Communication* 15: 301–21.

Downs, Anthony. 1957. *An Economic Theory of Democracy*. New York: Harper and Row.

Druckman, James N. 2001a. "On the Limits of Framing Effects: Who Can Frame?" *Journal of Politics* 63: 1041–66.

———. 2001b. "Using Credible Advice to Overcome Framing Effects." *Journal of Law, Economics, and Organization* 17: 62–82.

Druckman, James N., and Kjersten R. Nelson. 2002. "Framing, Deliberation, and Opinions about Campaign Finance Reform." University of Minnesota, typescript.

Dubois, Paul Martin, and Jonathan J. Hutson. 1997. *Bridging the Racial Divide: A Report on Interracial Dialogue in America*. Brattleboro, Vt.: Center for Living Democracy.

Duncker, Karl. 1945. *On Problem Solving*. Washington, D.C.: American Psychological Association.

Duneier, Mitchell. 1992. *Slim's Table: Race, Respectability, and Masculinity*. Chicago: University of Chicago Press.

———. 2001. *Sidewalk*. New York: Farrar, Straus and Giroux.

Elster, Jon. 1986. "The Market and the Forum: Three Varieties of Political Theory." In *Foundations of Social Choice Theory*, edited by Jon Elster and Aanund Hylland. Cambridge: Cambridge University Press.

Eldersveld, Samuel J. 1995. *Party Conflict and Community Development: Postwar Politics in Ann Arbor*. Ann Arbor: University of Michigan Press.

Eliasoph, Nina. 1998. *Avoiding Politics: How Americans Produce Apathy in Everyday Life*. Cambridge: Cambridge University Press.

Entman, Robert M. 1989. "How the Media Affect What People Think: An Information Processing Approach." *Journal of Politics* 51 (2): 347–70.

Erber, Ralph, and Richard R. Lau. 1990. "Political Cynicism Revised: An Information-Processing Reconciliation of Policy-Based and Incumbency-Based Interpretations of Changes in Trust in Government." *American Journal of Political Science* 34: 236–53.

Erbring, Lutz, and Edie N. Goldenberg. 1980. "Front-Page News and Real-World Cues: A New Look at Agenda-Setting by the Media." *American Journal of Political Science* 24: 16–49.

Evans, Sara M., and Harry C. Boyte. 1986. *Free Spaces: The Source of Democratic Change in America*. New York: Harper and Row.

Farley, Reynolds, Charlotte Steeh, Maria Krysan, Tara Jackson, and Keith Reeves. 1994. "Stereotypes and Segregation: Neighborhoods in the Detroit Area." *American Journal of Sociology* 100: 750–80.

Feldman, Stanley. 1988. "Structure and Consistency in Public Opinion: The Role of Core Beliefs and Values." *American Journal of Political Science* 32 (2): 416–40.

Feldman, Stanley, and John Zaller. 1992. "The Political Culture of Ambivalence: Ideological Responses to the Welfare State." *American Journal of Political Science* 36 (1): 268–307.

Fenno, Richard F., Jr. 1978. *Home Style: House Members in their Districts.* Boston: Little, Brown.

Festinger, Leon. 1954. "A Theory of Social Comparison Processes." *Human Relations* 7: 117–40.

Festinger, Leon, Stanley Schachter, and Kurt Back. 1950. *Social Pressures in Informal Groups: A Study of Human Factors in Housing.* New York: Harper.

Finifter, Ada F. 1974. "The Friendship Group as a Protective Environment for Political Deviants." *American Political Science Review* 68: 607–25.

Fiorina, Morris P. 1999. "Extreme Voices: A Dark Side of Civic Engagement." In *Civic Engagement in American Democracy,* edited by Theda Skocpol and Morris P. Fiorina, 395–426. Washington, D.C.: Brookings.

Fisher, Bonnie, Michael Margolis, and David Resnick. 1996. "Breaking Ground on the Virtual Frontier: Surveying Civic Life on the Internet." *American Sociologist* 27: 11–25.

Fishkin, James S. 1991. *Democracy and Deliberation: New Directions for Democratic Reform.* New Haven: Yale University Press.

———. 1995. *The Voice of the People: Public Opinion and Democracy.* New Haven: Yale University Press.

Flavin-McDonald, Catherine, with Damon Higgins, Jennifer Necci Dineen, Martha McCoy, and Ruth Sokolowski. 1998. "New Castle County, Delaware: Study Circles on Racism and Race Relations, Year 1—1997, A Report on the Focus Groups." Pomfret, Conn.: Study Circles Resource Center and the YWCA of New Castle County.

Forgas, Joseph P. 1977. "Polarization and Moderation of Person Perception Judgments as a Function of Group Interaction Style." *European Journal of Social Psychology* 7: 175–87.

Fraser, Nancy. 1992. "Rethinking the Public Sphere: A Contribution to the Critique of Actually Existing Democracy." In *Habermas and the Public Sphere,* edited by Craig Calhoun, 109–42. Cambridge: MIT Press.

Freedman, Paul. 1997. "Framing the Partial Birth Abortion Debate: A Survey Experiment." Paper presented at the 1997 annual meeting of the Midwest Political Science Association.

Freeman, Jo. 1975. *The Politics of Women's Liberation: A Case Study of an Emerging Social Movement and Its Relation to the Policy Process.* New York: David McKay.

Friedland, Lewis A. 2001. "Communication, Community, and Democracy: Toward a Theory of the Communicatively Integrated Community." *Communication Research* 28 (4): 358–91.

Fukuyama, Francis. 1997. "Falling Tide: Global Trends and U.S. Civil Society." *Harvard International Review* (winter): 60–64.

Gaertner, S. L., J. Mann, A. Murrell, and J. P. Dovidio. 1989. "Reducing Intergroup Bias: The Benefits of Recategorization." *Journal of Personality and Social Psychology* 57: 239–49.

Gamson, William A. 1992. *Talking Politics.* New York: Cambridge University Press.

———. 1988. "The 1987 Distinguished Lecture: A Constructionist Approach to Mass Media and Public Opinion." *Symbolic Interaction* 11 (2): 161–74.

Gamson, William A., and Kathryn E. Lasch. 1983. "The Political Culture of Social Welfare Policy." In *Evaluating the Welfare State: Social and Political Perspectives,* edited by Shimon E. Spiro and Ephraim Yuchtman-Yaar. New York: Academic Press.

Gamson, William A., and Andre Modigliani. 1989. "Media Discourse and Public Opinion: A Constructionist Approach." *American Journal of Sociology* 95: 1–37.

Gastil, John. 1993. *Democracy in Small Groups: Participation, Decision Making, and Communication.* Philadelphia: New Society.

Gastil, John, and James P. Dillard. 1999. "Increasing Political Sophistication through Public Deliberation." *Political Communication* 16 (1): 3–23.

Gerteis, John, and M. Savage. 1998. "The Salience of Class in Britain and America: A Comparative Analysis." *British Journal of Sociology* 49 (2): 252–74.

Gilens, Martin. 1999. *Why Americans Hate Welfare: Race, Media, and the Politics of Anti-Poverty Policy.* Chicago: University of Chicago Press.

Gillman, Howard. 2001. *The Votes That Counted: How the Court Decided the 2000 Presidential Election.* Chicago: University of Chicago Press.

Glaser, Barney, and Anselm Strauss. 1967. *The Discovery of Grounded Theory: Strategies for Qualitative Research.* New York: Aldine de Gruyter.

Glynn, Carroll J., Andrew F. Hayes, and James Shanahan. 1997. "Perceived Support for One's Opinions and Willingness to Speak Out: Spiral of Silence: A Meta-Analysis." *Public Opinion Quarterly* 61: 452–63.

Goffman, Erving. 1977. "The Arrangement between the Sexes." *Theory and Society* 4: 301–32.

———. 1983. "The Interaction Order." *American Sociological Review* 48: 1–17.

Goldstein, Marc B., and Shimon Sturm. 1999. "MetroHartford Region Community Conversations on Race: Assessing the Impact, Report 2." Typescript, Central Connecticut State University.

Graber, Doris A. 1988. *Processing the News: How People Tame the Information Tide.* 2d ed. New York: Longman.

Granovetter, Mark. 1973. "The Strength of Weak Ties." *American Journal of Sociology* 78: 1360–80.

Greenberg, Stanley B. 1995. *Middle Class Dreams: The Politics and Power of the New American Majority.* New York: Times Books.

Grice, H. Paul. 1975. "Logic and Conversation." In *Syntax and Semantics,* Vol. 3: *Speech Acts,* edited by Peter Cole and Jerry L. Morgan, 41–58. New York: Academic Press.

Greisdorf, Karen Elliot. 2001. "An Honest Conversation on Race, Reconciliation, and Responsibility: Hope in the Cities." In *Intergroup Dialogue: Deliberative Democracy in School, College, Community, and Workplace,* edited by David Schoem and Sylvia Hurtado, 151–65. Ann Arbor: University of Michigan Press.

Gross, Kimberly. 2001. "Images of Others: The Effect of Media Coverage of Racial Unrest on Public Opinion." Ph.D. diss., University of Michigan.

Gurin, Patricia. 1985. "Women's Gender Consciousness." *Public Opinion Quarterly* 49: 143–63.

Gurin, Patricia, Shirley Hatchett, and James S. Jackson. 1989. *Hope and Independence: Blacks' Response to Electoral and Party Politics.* New York: Russell Sage Foundation.

Gurin, Particia, Timothy Peng, Gretchen Lopez, and Biren A. Nagda. 1999. "Context, Identity, and Intergroup Relations." In *Cultural Divides: Understanding and Overcoming Group Conflict,* edited by Deborah A. Prentice and Dale T. Miller, 133–70. New York: Russell Sage Foundation.

Habell-Pallán, Michelle. 1997. "No Cultural Icon: Marisela Norte." In *Women Transforming Politics: An Alternative Reader,* edited by Cathy J. Cohen, Kathleen B. Jones, and Joan C. Tronto, 256–58. New York: New York University Press.

Habermas, Jurgen. 1991 [1962]. *The Structural Transformation of the Public Sphere: An Inquiry into a Category of Bourgeois Society.* Cambridge: MIT Press.

Hanushek, Eric A., and John E. Jackson. 1977. *Statistical Methods for Social Scientists.* New York: Academic Press.

Hardin, Russell. 1993. "The Street-Level Epistemology of Trust." *Politics and Society* 21: 505–30.

Harding, J., and R. Hogrefe. 1952. "Attitudes of White Department Store Employees Toward Negro Co-Workers." *Journal of Social Issues* 8: 18–28.

Hart, Roderick P., and Sharon E. Jarvis. 1998. "Collective Language at the National Issues Convention." Paper presented to the annual meeting of the American Political Science Association, Boston, September.

Hartsock, Nancy C. M. 1998. "The Feminist Standpoint: Developing the Ground for a Specifically Feminist Historical Materialism." In *The Feminist Standpoint Revisited and Other Essays,* 105–32. Boulder, Colo.: Westview Press.

Herbst, Susan. 1998. *Reading Public Opinion: How Political Actors View the Democratic Process.* Chicago: University of Chicago Press.

———. 2001. "Public Opinion Infrastructures: Meanings, Measurement, Media." *Political Communication* 18 (4): 451–64.

Herzog, Don. 1998. *Poisoning the Minds of the Lower Orders.* Princeton, N.J.: Princeton University Press.

Hibbing, John R., and Elizabeth Theiss-Morse. 2002. *Stealth Democracy: Americans' Beliefs about How Government Should Work.* Cambridge: Cambridge University Press.

Higgins, E. Tory, W. S. Rholes, and C. R. Jones. 1977. "Category Accessibility and Impression Formation." *Journal of Experimental Social Psychology* 13: 141–54.

Hinsley, D. A., J. R. Hayes, and Herbert A. Simon. 1978. "From Words to Equations: Meaning and Representation in Algebra Word Problems." In *Cognitive Processes in Comprehension,* edited by P. A. Carpenter and Marion A. Just. Hillsdale, N.J.: Erlbaum.

Hirschman, Albert O. 1970. *Exit, Voice, and Loyalty: Responses to Decline in Firms, Organizations, and States.* Cambridge: Harvard University Press.

Hochschild, Jennifer L. 1995. *Facing Up to the American Dream: Race, Class, and the Soul of the Nation.* Princeton: Princeton University Press.

———. 2000. "Lumpers and Splitters, Individuals and Structures: Comments on *Racialized Politics.*" In *Racialized Politics: The Debate about Racism in America,* edited by David O. Sears, Jim Sidanius, and Lawrence Bobo, 324–43. Chicago: University of Chicago Press.

Hogg, Michael A., and John C. Turner. 1987. "Intergroup Behavior, Self-Stereotyping, and the Salience of Social Categories." *British Journal of Social Psychology* 26: 325–40.

Houlé, Kristin, and Rona Roberts. 2000. *Toward Competent Communities: Best Practices for Producing Community-Wide Study Circles.* Lexington, Ken.: Roberts and Kay.

Hovland, Carl I., Irving L. Janis, and Harold H. Kelley. 1953. *Communication and Persuasion.* New Haven: Yale University Press.

Huckfeldt, R. Robert. 1984. "Political Loyalties and Social Class Ties: The Mechanisms of Contextual Influence." *American Journal of Political Science* 28: 399–417.

Huckfeldt, Robert, and John Sprague. 1987. "Networks in Context: The Social Flow of Political Information." *American Political Science Review* 81: 1197–1216.

———. 1988. "Choice, Social Structure, and the Political Information: The Informational Coercion of Minorities." *American Journal of Political Science* 32: 467–82.

———. 1992. "Political Parties and Electoral Mobilization: Political Structure, Social Structure, and the Party Canvass." *American Political Science Review* 86: 70–86.

———. 1995. *Citizens, Politics, and Social Communication: Information and Influence in an Election Campaign.* Cambridge: Cambridge University Press.

Huckfeldt, Robert, Eric Plutzer, and John Sprague. 1993. "Alternative Contexts of Political Behavior: Churches, Neighborhoods, and Individuals." *Journal of Politics* 55: 365–81.

Huddy, Leonie. 1998. "The Social Nature of Political Identity: Feminist Image and Feminist Identity." Paper presented at the annual meeting of the American Political Science Association, Boston.

———. 2001. "From Social to Political Identity: A Critical Examination of Social Identity Theory." *Political Psychology* 22 (1): 127–56.

Huddy, Leonie, and David O. Sears. 1995. "Opposition to Bilingual Education: Prejudice or the Defense of Realistic Interests?" *Social Psychology Quarterly* 58: 133–43.

Huddy, Leonie, and Simo Virtanen. 1995. "Subgroup Differentiation and Subgroup Bias among Latinos as a Function of Familiarity and Positive Distinctiveness." *Journal of Personality and Social Psychology* 68: 97–108.

Hurtado, Sylvia. 2001. "Research and Evaluation on Intergroup Dialogue." In *Intergroup Dialogue: Deliberative Democracy in School, College, Community, and Workplace,* edited by David Schoem and Sylvia Hurtado, 22–36. Ann Arbor: University of Michigan Press.

Inglehart, Ronald. 1990. *Culture Shift in Advanced Industrial Society.* Princeton: Princeton University Press.

"Investing a Community of Stakeholders: Decatur, Georgia." 2002. ICMA University Best Practices Report, unpublished manuscript.

Iyengar, Shanto. 1991. *Is Anyone Responsible? How Television Frames Political Issues.* Chicago: University of Chicago Press.

Iyengar, Shanto, and Donald R. Kinder. 1987. *News That Matters: Television and American Public Opinion.* Chicago: University of Chicago Press.

Jackman, Mary R. 1994. *The Velvet Glove: Paternalism and Conflict in Gender, Class, and Race Relations.* Berkeley: University of California Press.

Jackman, Mary R., and Robert W. Jackman. 1983. *Class Awareness in the United States.* Berkeley: University of California Press.

Jackman, Robert W., and Ross A. Miller. 1998. "Social Capital and Politics." *Annual Review of Political Science* 1: 47–73.

Jacobs, Jane. 1961. *The Death and Life of Great American Cities.* New York: Modern Library.

Jennings, M. Kent. 1979. "Another Look at the Life Cycle and Political Participation." *American Journal of Political Science* 23: 755–71.

———. 1987. "Residues of a Movement: The Aging of the American Protest Generation." *American Political Science Review* 81: 368–82.

———. 1989. "The Crystallization of Orientations." In *Continuities in Political Action,* edited by M. Kent Jennings, Jan van Deth, et al. Berlin: De Gruyter.

———. 1990. "Women in Party Politics." In *Women, Politics, and Change,* edited by Louise A. Tilly and Patricia Gurin, 221–48. New York: Russell Sage.

Jennings, M. Kent, and Gregory B. Markus. 1984. "Partisan Orientations over the Long Haul: Results from the Three-Wave Political Socialization Panel Study." *American Political Science Review* 78: 1000–18.

Jennings, M. Kent, and Richard Niemi. 1968. "The Transmission of Political Values from Parent to Child." *American Political Science Review* 62: 169–84.

Jennings, M. Kent, and Laura Stoker. Forthcoming. "Political Socialization Study 1997." Ann Arbor, Mich.: Institute for Social Research Survey Research Center [producer]; Inter-University Consortium for Political and Social Research [distributor].

Johnson, James. 2000. "Why Respect Culture?" *American Journal of Political Science* 17: 405–18.

Johnston, David Cay. 1999. "Gap between Rich and Poor Found Substantially Wider." *New York Times,* September 5, A14.

Just, Marion R., Ann N. Crigler, Dean E. Alger, Timothy E. Cook, Montague Kern, and Darrell M. West. 1996. *Crosstalk: Citizens, Candidates, and the Media in a Presidential Campaign.* Chicago: University of Chicago Press.

Kahneman, Daniel, and Amos Tversky. 1984. "Choices, Values, and Frames." *American Psychologist* 39: 341–50.

Kanter, Rosabeth Moss. 1977. "Some Effects of Proportions on Group Life: Skewed Sex Ratios and Responses to Token Women." *American Journal of Sociology* 82: 965–90.

Katz, Elihu, and Paul F. Lazarsfeld. 1955. *Personal Influence: The Part Played by People in the Flow of Mass Communications.* New York: Free Press.

Kelley, Harold H. 1952. "Two Functions of Reference Groups." In *Readings in Social Psychology,* edited by Guy E. Swanson, Theodore M. Newcomb, and Eugene L. Hartley, 410–14. New York: Holt.

Keniston, Leonda Williams, Amy Seymour Hubbard, and Julie Honnold. 2002. "The Dayton Multiracial Dialogues: Expanding the Circle of Contact through Dialogue." Evaluation report for the City of Dayton Human Relations Council. Richmond, Va.: Social Sources, Inc.

Key, V. O. 1965 [1961]. *Public Opinion and American Democracy.* New York: Knopf.

Kim, Joohan, Robert O. Wyatt, and Elihu Katz. 1999. "News, Talk, Opinion, Participation: The Part Played by Conversation in Deliberative Democracy." *Political Communication* 16 (4): 361–85.

Kinder, Donald R. 1983. "Diversity and Complexity in American Public Opinion." In *Political Science: The State of the Discipline,* edited by Ada Finifter, 391–401. Washington, D.C.: American Political Science Association.

———. 1998a. "Opinion and Action in the Realm of Politics." In *The Handbook of Social Psychology,* edited by Daniel T. Gilbert, Susan T. Fiske, and Gardner Lindzey (4th ed.), 778–867. New York: McGraw-Hill.

———. 1998b. "Communication and Opinion." *Annual Review of Political Science* 1: 167–97.

Kinder, Donald, and Adam Berinsky. 1998. "Making Sense of Issues through Frames." Paper presented to the annual meeting of the American Political Science Association, August, Boston.

Kinder, Donald R., and Don Herzog. 1993. "Democratic Discussion." In *Reconsidering the Democratic Public,* edited by George E. Marcus and Russell L. Hanson. University Park: Pennsylvania State University Press.

Kinder, Donald R., and Tali Mendelberg. 1995. "Cracks in American Apartheid: The Political Impact of Prejudice among Desegregated Whites." *Journal of Politics* 57 (2): 402–24.

Kinder, Donald R., and Lynn M. Sanders. 1990. "Mimicking Political Debate with Survey Questions: The Case of White Opinion on Affirmative Action for Blacks." *Social Cognition* 8: 73–103.

———. 1996. *Divided by Color: Racial Politics and Democratic Ideals.* Chicago: University of Chicago Press.

Kinder, Donald R., and Nicholas Winter. 2001. "Exploring the Racial Divide: Blacks, Whites, and Opinion on National Policy." *American Journal of Political Science* 45 (2): 439–56.

Kingdon, John W. 1989 [1973]. *Congressmen's Voting Decisions.* 3d ed. Ann Arbor: University of Michigan Press.

Knoke, David. 1990a. "Networks of Political Action: Toward Theory Construction." *Social Forces* 68: 1041–63.

———. 1990b. *Political Networks: The Structural Perspective.* Cambridge: Cambridge University Press.

Krosnick, Jon A., and Donald R. Kinder. 1990. "Altering the Foundations of Support for the President through Priming." *American Political Science Review* 84: 497–513.

Kuklinski, James H., and Norman L. Hurley. 1994. "On Hearing and Interpreting Political Messages: A Cautionary Tale of Citizen Cue-Taking." *Journal of Politics* 56: 729–51.

———. 1996. "It's a Matter of Interpretation." In *Political Persuasion and Attitude Change,* edited by Diana C. Mutz, Paul M. Sniderman, and Richard A. Brody. Ann Arbor: University of Michigan Press.

Kuklinski, James H., Robert C. Luskin, and John Bolland. 1991. "Where Is the Schema? Going Beyond the 'S' Word in Political Psychology." *American Political Science Review* 85 (4): 1341–56.

Kunstler, James Howard. 1993. *The Geography of Nowhere: The Rise and Decline of America's Man-Made Landscape.* New York: Simon and Schuster.

———. 1996. *Home from Nowhere: Remaking Our Everyday World for the Twenty-First Century.* New York: Simon and Schuster.

Ladd, Everett Carll. 1999. *The Ladd Report: Voluntarism.* New York: Free Press.

Lakoff, George. 1987. *Women, Fire, and Dangerous Things: What Categories Reveal about the Mind.* Chicago: University of Chicago Press.

Lane, Robert E. 1962. *Political Ideology.* New York: Free Press.

Lasswell, Harold D., and Abram Kaplan. 1950. *Power and Society: A Framework for Political Inquiry.* New Haven: Yale University Press.

Lau, Richard R. 1986. "Political Schemata, Candidate Evaluations, and Voting Behavior." In *Political Cognition: The Nineteenth Annual Carnegie Symposium on Cognition,* edited by Richard R. Lau and David O Sears, 95–126. Hillsdale, N.J.: Erlbaum.

———. 1989. "Individual and Contextual Influences on Group Identification." *Social Psychological Quarterly* 52: 220–31.

Lau, Richard R., and David O. Sears. 1986. "Social Cognition and Political Cognition: The Past, the Present, and the Future." In *Political Cognition: The Nineteenth Annual Carnegie Symposium on Cognition,* edited by Richard R. Lau and David O Sears, 347–66. Hillsdale, N.J.: Erlbaum.

Lau, Richard R., Richard A. Smith, and Susan T. Fiske. 1991. "Political Beliefs, Policy Interpretations, and Political Persuasion." *Journal of Politics* 53 (3): 644–75.

Lazarsfeld, Paul F., Bernard Berelson, and Hazel Gaudet. 1944. *The People's Choice: How the Voter Makes Up His Mind in a Presidential Campaign.* 2d ed. New York: Columbia University Press.

Lee, Taeku. 2002. *Mobilizing Public Opinion: Black Insurgency and Racial Attitudes in the Civil Rights Era.* Chicago: University of Chicago Press.

LeMasters, E. E. 1975. *Blue-Collar Aristocrats: Life-Styles at a Working Class Tavern.* Madison: University of Wisconsin Press.

Lenart, Silvo. 1994. *Shaping Political Attitudes: The Impact of Interpersonal Communication and Mass Media.* Thousand Oaks, Calif.: Sage.

Levi, Margaret. 1997. *Consent, Dissent, and Patriotism.* Cambridge: Cambridge University Press.

Levi, Margaret, and Laura Stoker. 2000. "Political Trust and Trustworthiness." *Annual Review of Political Science* 3: 475–508.

Lewin, Kurt, and Paul Grabbe. 1945. "Conduct, Knowledge, and Acceptance of New Values." *Journal of Social Issues* 1 (3): 53–64.

Lichterman, Paul. 1999. "Talking Identity in the Public Sphere: Broad Visions and Small Spaces in Sexual Identity Politics." *Theory and Society* 28: 101–41.

Liebes, Tamar, and Elihu Katz. 1990. *The Export of Meaning: Cross-Cultural Readings of Dallas.* New York: Oxford University Press.

Liebow, Elliot. 1967. *Tally's Corner: A Study of Negro Streetcorner Men.* Boston: Little, Brown.

Lippitt, Ronald, and Ralph K. White. 1952. "An Experimental Study of Leadership and Group Life." In *Readings in Social Psychology,* edited by Guy E. Swanson, Theodore M. Newcomb, and Eugene L. Hartley. New York: Holt.

Lippmann, Walter. 1947 [1922]. *Public Opinion.* New York: Macmillan.

———. 1930 [1925]. *The Phantom Public: A Sequel to 'Public Opinion'.* New York: Macmillan.

Liu, William T., and Robert W. Duff. 1972. "The Strength in Weak Ties." *Public Opinion Quarterly* 36: 361–66.

Lodge, Milton, and Kathleen M. McGraw. 1991. "Where Is the Schema? Critiques." *American Political Science Review* 85 (4): 1357–64.

Lopez, Gretchen E., Patricia Gurin, and Biren A. Nagda. 1998. "Education and Understanding Structural Causes for Group Inequalities." *Political Psychology* 19 (2): 305–29.

Luker, Kristin. 1984. *Abortion and the Politics of Motherhood.* Berkeley: University of California Press.

Lupia, Arthur, and Mathew D. McCubbins. 1998. *The Democratic Dilemma: Can Citizens Learn What They Need to Know?* Cambridge: Cambridge University Press.

Luskin, Robert, and James Fishkin. 1998. "Deliberative Polling, Public Opinion, and Representative Democracy: The Case of the National Issues Convention." Paper presented to the annual meeting of the American Association for Public Opinion Research, St. Louis.

MacKuen, Michael. 1990. "Speaking of Politics: Individual Conversational Choice, Public Opinion, and the Prospects for Deliberative Democracy." In *Information and Democratic Processes,* edited by John A. Ferejohn and James H. Kuklinski. Urbana: University of Illinois Press.

Macy, Michael W. 1990. "Learning Theory and the Logic of Critical Mass." *American Sociological Review* 55: 809–26.

———. 1991. "Learning to Cooperate: Stochastic and Tacit Collusion in Social Exchange." *American Journal of Sociology* 97: 808–43.

———. 1993. "Backward-Looking Social Control." *American Sociological Review* 58: 819–36.

Malick, Amy. 1999. "An Interview with Sandy Robinson II." *Focus on Study Circles* 10 (4): 1, 7–9.

Manna, Paul F. 2000. "How Do I Know What I Say I Know? Thinking about *Slim's Table* and Qualitative Methods." *Endarch: Journal of Black Political Research* (spring): 19–29.

Mansbridge, Jane J. 1983 [1980]. *Beyond Adversary Democracy*. Reprint with new preface. Chicago: University of Chicago Press.

———. 1999. "Everyday Talk in the Deliberative System." In *Deliberative Politics: Essays on Democracy and Disagreement*, edited by Stephen Macedo, 211–39. Oxford: Oxford University Press.

Marsden, Peter V. 1987. "Core Discussion Networks of Americans." *American Sociological Review* 52: 22–131.

Marwil, Jonathan L. 1990. *A History of Ann Arbor*. Ann Arbor: University of Michigan.

Massey, Douglas S., and Nancy A. Denton. 1993. *American Apartheid: Segregation and the Making of the Underclass*. Cambridge: Harvard University Press.

Massey, Douglas S., and Zoltan L. Hajnal. 1995. "The Changing Geographic Structure of Black-White Segregation in the United States." *Social Science Quarterly* 76: 527–42.

McCoy, Martha. 2001. "Engaging the Whole Community in Dialogue and Action: Study Circles Resource Center." In *Intergroup Dialogue: Deliberative Democracy in School, College, Community, and Workplace,* edited by David Schoem and Sylvia Hurtado, 137–50. Ann Arbor: University of Michigan Press.

McGarty, Craig, John C. Turner, Michael A. Hogg, Barbara David, and Margaret S. Wetherell. 1992. "Group Polarization as Conformity to the Prototypical Group Member." *British Journal of Social Psychology* 31: 1–20.

McLeod, Jack M., and Katie Daily. 1996. "Community Integration, Local Media Use, and Democratic Processes." *Communication Research* 23 (2): 179–209.

McLeod, Jack M., Dietram A. Scheufele, and Particia Moy. 1999. "Community, Communication, and Participation: The Role of Mass Media and Interpersonal Discussion in Local Political Participation." *Political Communication* 16: 315–36.

McLeod, Jack M., Dietram A. Scheufele, Particia Moy, Edward M. Horowitz, R. Lance Holbert, Weiwu Zhang, Stephen Zubric, and Jessica Zubric. 1999. "Understanding Deliberation: The Effects of Discussion Networks on Participation in a Public Forum." *Communication Research* 26 (6): 743–74.

McLeod, Jack M., Mira Sotirovic, and R. Lance Holbert. 1998. "Values as Sociotropic Judgments Influencing Communication Patterns." *Communication Research* 25: 453–80.

McPherson, J. Miller, and Lynn Smith-Lovin. 1986. "Sex Segregation in Voluntary Associations." *American Sociological Review* 51: 61–79.

Medin, Douglas L., and John D. Coley. 1998. "Concepts and Categorization." In *Perception and Cognition at Century's End,* edited by Julian Hochberg, 403–39. San Diego: Academic Press.

Melucci, Alberto. 1989. *Nomads of the Present: Social Movements and Identity Needs in Contemporary Society.* London: Hutchinson Radius.

———. 1995. "The Process of Collective Identity." In *Social Movements and Culture,* edited by Hank Johnston and Bert Klandermans. Minneapolis: University of Minnesota Press.

Mendelberg, Tali. 2001. *The Race Card: Campaign Strategy, Implicit Messages, and the Norm of Equality*. Princeton: Princeton University Press.

Mendelberg, Tali, and John Oleske. 2000. "Race and Public Deliberation." *Political Communication* 17: 169–91.

Merei, Ferenc. 1952. "Group Leadership and Institutionalization." In *Readings in Social Psychology*, edited by Guy E. Swanson, Theodore M. Newcomb, and Eugene L. Hartley. New York: Holt.

Merelman, Richard M., Greg Streich, and Paul Martin. 1998. "Unity and Diversity in American Political Culture: An Exploratory Study of the National Conversation on American Pluralism and Identity." *Political Psychology* 19: 781–807.

Merton, Robert K. 1957 [1949]. *Social Theory and Social Structure*. Revised and enlarged edition. Glencoe, Ill.: Free Press.

Mettler, Suzanne. 2002. "Bringing the State Back in to Civic Engagement: Policy Feedback Effects of the G.I. Bill for World War II Veterans." *American Political Science Review* 96 (2): 351–65.

Mill, John Stuart. 1956 [1859]. *On Liberty*. Edited by Currin V. Shields. New York: Liberal Arts Press.

Miller, Arthur H. 1991. "Where Is the Schema? Critiques." *American Political Science Review* 85 (4): 1369–80.

Miller, Arthur, Patricia Gurin, Gerald Gurin, and Oksana Malanchuk. 1981. "Group Consciousness and Political Participation." *American Journal of Political Science* 25: 494–511.

Mills, C. Wright. 1956. *The Power Elite*. London: Oxford University Press.

Mizruchi, Mark S. 1992. *The Structure of Corporate Political Action: Interfirm Relations and Their Consequences*. Cambridge: Harvard University Press.

Mondak, Jeffery J. 1995. *Nothing to Read: Newspapers and Elections in a Social Experiment*. Ann Arbor: University of Michigan Press.

Monroe, Kristin. 1996. *The Heart of Altruism*. Princeton: Princeton University Press.

Morley, David. 1992. *Television, Audiences, and Cultural Studies*. London: Routledge.

Moscovici, Serge, Willem Doise, and Renauld Dulong. 1972. "Studies in Group Decision II: Differences of Positions, Differences of Opinion, and Group Polarization." *European Journal of Social Psychology* 2: 385–97.

Moscovici, Serge, and Marisa Zavalloni. 1969. "The Group as a Polarizer of Attitudes." *Journal of Personality and Social Psychology* 12: 125–35.

Mutz, Diana C. 1997. "Mechanisms of Momentum: Does Thinking Make It So?" *Journal of Politics* 59: 104–25.

———. 1998. *Impersonal Influence*. Cambridge: Cambridge University Press.

———. 2002. "Cross-Cutting Social Networks: Testing Democratic Theory in Practice." *American Political Science Review* 96: 111–26.

Mutz, Diana C., and Paul S. Martin. 2001. "Facilitating Communication across Lines of Difference: The Role of Mass Media." *American Political Science Review* 95: 97–114.

Mutz, Diana C., and Jeffery J. Mondak. 1997. "Dimensions of Sociotropic Behavior: Group-Based Judgements of Fairness and Well-Being." *American Journal of Political Science* 41 (1): 284–308.

———. 1998. "Democracy at Work: Contributions of the Workplace Toward a Public Sphere." Paper presented to the annual convention of the Midwest Political Science Association, April, Chicago.

Mydans, Seth. 1993. "Los Angeles Lays Plans to Avoid Repeat of '92 Riots." *New York Times,* March 28, A16.

Myers, David G., and George D. Bishop. 1971. "Enhancement of Dominant Attitudes in Group Discussion." *Journal of Personality and Social Psychology* 20: 386–91.

Myers, David G., and Helmut Lamm. 1976. "The Group Polarization Phenomenon." *Psychological Bulletin* 83: 602–27.

Nelson, Thomas E. 1999. "Public Rhetoric, Policy Goals, and Political Attitudes." Paper presented to the annual meeting of the American Political Science Association, September 2–5, Atlanta.

———. 2000. "Goals and Values in the Language of Issue Framing." Paper presented to the annual meeting of the American Political Science Association, Washington, D.C., August 31–September 3.

Nelson, Thomas E., and Donald R. Kinder. 1996. "Issue Frames and Group-Centrism in American Public Opinion." *Journal of Politics* 58 (4): 1055–78.

Nelson, Thomas E., and Zoe M. Oxley. 1999. "Issue Framing Effects on Belief Importance and Opinion." *Journal of Politics* 61 (4): 1040–67.

Nelson, Thomas E., Rosalee A. Clawson, and Zoe M. Oxley. 1997. "Media Framing of a Civil Liberties Conflict and Its Effect on Tolerance." *American Political Science Review* 91 (3): 567–83.

Neuman, W. Russell, Marion R. Just, and Ann N. Crigler. 1992. *Common Knowledge: News and the Construction of Political Meaning.* Chicago: University of Chicago Press.

Newcomb, Theodore M. 1951. "Social Psychological Theory." In *Social Psychology at the Crossroads,* edited by John H. Rohrer and Muzafer Sherif. New York: Harper.

Niemi, Richard G., and Larry M. Bartels. 1985. "New Measures of Issue Salience: An Evaluation." *Journal of Politics* 47: 1212–20.

Noelle-Neumann, Elisabeth. 1993. *The Spiral of Silence: Public Opinion—Our Social Skin.* 2d ed. Chicago: University of Chicago Press.

Norton, Anne. 1988. *Reflections on Political Identity.* Baltimore: Johns Hopkins University Press.

Oakes, Penelope J., John C. Turner, and S. Alexander Haslam. 1991. "Perceiving People as Group Members: The Role of Fit in the Salience of Social Categorizations." *British Journal of Social Psychology* 30: 125–44.

Oliver, J. Eric, and Tali Mendelberg. 2000. "Reconsidering the Environmental Determinants of White Racial Attitudes." *American Journal of Political Science* 44 (3): 574–89.

One America in the Twenty-First Century: The President's Initiative on Race, One America Dialogue Guide. 1998. Washington, D.C.: The White House.

Page, Benjamin I. 1996. *Who Deliberates? Mass Media in Modern Democracy*. Chicago: University of Chicago Press.

Page, Benjamin I., and Robert Y. Shapiro. 1992. *The Rational Public: Fifty Years of Trends in Americans' Policy Preferences*. Chicago: University of Chicago Press.

Pettigrew, Thomas F. 1967. "Social Evaluation Theory: Convergences and Applications." In *Nebraska Symposium on Motivation*, 241–311. Lincoln: University of Nebraska Press.

Pitkin, Hanna Fenichel. 1981. "Justice: On Relating Public and Private." *Political Theory* 9: 327–52.

Polanyi, Livia. 1989. *Telling the American Story: A Structural and Cultural Analysis of Conversational Storytelling*. Cambridge: MIT Press.

Portes, Alejandro. 1998. "Social Capital: Its Origins and Applications in Modern Sociology." *Annual Review of Sociology* 24: 1–24.

Press, Andrea L., and Elizabeth R. Cole. 1999. *Speaking of Abortion: Television and Authority in the Lives of Women*. Chicago: University of Chicago Press.

Putnam, Robert D. 1993. *Making Democracy Work: Civic Traditions in Modern Italy*. Princeton, N.J.: Princeton.

———. 1995a. "Bowling Alone: America's Declining Social Capital." *Journal of Democracy* 6: 65–78.

———. 1995b. "Tuning In, Tuning Out: The Strange Disappearance of Social Capital in America." *PS: Political Science and Politics* 28: 664–83.

———. 2000. *Bowling Alone: The Collapse and Revival of American Community*. New York: Simon and Schuster.

Rahn, Wendy. 1993. "The Role of Partisan Stereotypes in Information Processing about Political Candidates." *American Journal of Political Science* 37: 472–96.

Reichler, Patricia, and Polly B. Dredge. 1997. *Governing Diverse Communities: A Focus on Race and Ethnic Relations*. Washington, D.C.: National League of Cities.

Reinhardt, Mark. 1995. "Look Who's Talking: Political Subjects, Political Objects, and Political Discourse in Contemporary Theory." *Political Theory* 23: 689–719.

Reskin, Barbara. 1993. "Sex Segregation in the Workplace." *Annual Review of Sociology* 19: 241–70.

Reskin, Barbara F., Debra B. McBrier, and Julie A. Kmec. 1999. "The Determinants and Consequences of Workplace Sex and Race Composition." *Annual Review of Sociology* 25: 335–61.

Rich, Paul. 1999. "American Voluntarism, Social Capital, and Political Culture." *Annals of the American Academy of Political and Social Science* 565: 15–34.

Ridgeway, Cecilia L., and Lynn Smith-Lovin. 1999. "The Gender System and Interaction." *Annual Review of Sociology* 25: 191–216.

Riker, William H. 1982. *Liberalism against Populism: A Confrontation between the Theory of Democracy and the Theory of Social Choice*. San Francisco: W. H. Freeman.

Robinson, John P., and Mark R. Levy with Dennis K. Davis in association with W. Gill Woodall, Michael Gurevitch, and Haluk Sahin. 1986. *The Main Source: Learning from Television News*. Beverly Hills, Calif.: Sage.

Rosenblum, Nancy L. 1998. *Membership and Morals: The Personal Uses of Pluralism in America*. Princeton: Princeton University Press.

Rosenstone, Steven J., Donald R. Kinder, Warren Miller, and the National Election Studies. 1998. "Pre-and Post-Election Survey" [computer file]. Ann Arbor: University of Michigan, Center for Political Studies, 1996 [producer]; Inter-University Consortium for Political and Social Research [distributor].

Ryan, Mary P. 1992. "Gender and Public Access: Women's Politics in Nineteenth-Century America." In *Habermas and the Public Sphere*, edited by Craig Calhoun, 259–88. Cambridge: MIT Press.

Sandel, Michael J. 1996. *Democracy's Discontent: America in Search of a Public Philosophy*. Cambridge: Harvard University Press.

Sanders, Lynn M. 1997. "Against Deliberation." *Political Theory* 25: 347–76.

Sapiro, Virginia. 1981–82. "If U.S. Senator Baker Were a Woman: An Experimental Study of Candidate Images." *Political Psychology* (spring/summer): 61–83.

———. 1983. *The Political Integration of Women: Roles, Socialization, and Politics*. Urbana: University of Illinois Press.

———. 1989. "The Women's Movement and the Creation of Gender Consciousness: Social Movements as Socialization Agents." In *Political Socialization, Citizenship Education, and Democracy*, edited by Orit Ichilov. New York: Teachers College, Columbia University.

———. 1999. "Considering Political Civility Historically: A Case Study of the United States." Paper presented at the annual meeting of the International Society of Political Psychology, Amsterdam.

Sapiro, Virginia, and Joe Soss. 1999. "Spectacular Politics, Dramatic Interpretations: Multiple Meanings in the Thomas/Hill Hearings." *Political Communication* 16 (3): 285–314.

Schattschneider, Elmer Eric. 1960. *The Semi-Sovereign People: A Realist's View of Democracy in America*. New York: Holt, Rinehart and Winston.

Schoem, David, and Sylvia Hurtado. 2001. *Intergroup Dialogue: Deliberative Democracy in School, College, Community, and Workplace*. Ann Arbor: University of Michigan Press.

Schoem, David, Sylvia Hurtado, Todd Sevig, Mark Chesler, and Stephen H. Sumida. 2001. "Intergroup Dialogue: Democracy at Work in Theory and Practice." In *Intergroup Dialogue: Deliberative Democracy in School, College, Community, and Workplace*, edited by David Schoem and Sylvia Hurtado, 1–21. Ann Arbor: University of Michigan Press.

Schudson, Michael. 1997. "Why Conversation Is Not the Soul of Democracy." *Critical Studies in Mass Communication* 14: 297–309.

Schuman, Howard, Jacob Ludwig, and Jon A. Krosnick. 1986. "The Perceived Threat of Nuclear War, Salience, and Open Questions." *Public Opinion Quarterly* 50: 519–36.

Schumpeter, Joseph. 1942. *Capitalism, Socialism, and Democracy*. New York: Harper.

Sears, David O., and Carolyn L. Funk. 1991. "The Role of Self-Interest in Social and Political Attitudes." *Advances in Experimental Social Psychology* 24: 1–91.

Sears, David O., and Donald R. Kinder. 1971. "Racial Tensions and Voting in Los

Angeles." In *Los Angeles: Viability and Prospects for Metropolitan Leadership,* edited by Werner Z. Hirsch, 51–88. New York: Praeger.

Sears, David O., Collette Van Laar, Mary Carrillo, and Rick Kosterman. 1997. "Is It Really Racism? The Origin of White Americans' Opposition to Race-Targeted Policies." *Public Opinion Quarterly* 1: 16–53.

Sears, David, and Richard E. Whitney. 1973. "Political Persuasion." In *Handbook of Communication,* edited by Ithiel de Sola Pool and Wilbur Schramm, 253–63. Chicago: Rand McNally.

Shah, Dhavan, David Domke, and Daniel B. Wackman. 1996. "'To Thine Own Self Be True': Values, Framing, and Voter Decision-Making Strategies." *Communication Research* 23 (5): 509–60.

———. 1997. "Values and the Vote: Linking Issue Interpretations to the Process of Candidate Choice." *Journalism and Mass Communication Quarterly* 74: 357–87.

Shah, Dhavan, Jack M. McLeod, and So-Hyang Yoon. 2001. "Communication, Context, and Community." *Communication Research* 28 (4): 464–506.

Sigel, Roberta S., ed. 1989. *Political Learning in Adulthood.* Chicago: University of Chicago Press.

———. 1996. *Ambition and Accommodation: How Women View Gender Relations.* Chicago: University of Chicago Press.

Sigelman, Lee, Timothy Bledsoe, Susan Welch, and Michael W. Combs. 1996. "Making Contact? Black-White Social Interaction in an Urban Setting." *American Journal of Sociology* 101: 1306–32.

Simon, Adam, and Michael Xenos. 2000. "Media Framing and Effective Public Deliberation." *Political Communication* 17 (4): 363–76.

Skocpol, Theda. 1999. "Associations without Members." *American Prospect* 45: 66–73.

Skocpol, Theda, and Morris P. Fiorina, eds. 1999. *Civic Engagement in American Democracy.* Washington, D.C.: Brookings Institute.

Smith, Elizabeth. 1998. "Political Socialization Research, Social Capital, and the Making of Citizens." *Political Psychologist* 3: 19–23.

Smith, Rogers M. 1997. *Civic Ideals: Conflicting Visions of Citizenship in U.S. History.* New Haven: Yale University Press.

Smith-Lovin, Lynn, and J. Miller McPherson. 1993. "You Are Who You Know: A Network Approach to Gender." *Theory on Gender/Feminism on Theory,* edited by Paula England. New York: Aldine de Gruyter.

Sniderman, Paul M., and Edward G. Carmines. 1997. *Reaching Beyond Race.* Cambridge: Harvard University Press.

Sniderman, Paul M., and Thomas Piazza. 1993. *The Scar of Race.* Cambridge: Belknap/Harvard University Press.

Sniderman, Paul M., and Sean M. Theriault. 1999. "The Dynamics of Political Argument and the Logic of Issue Framing." Paper presented at the annual meeting of the Midwest Political Science Association, Chicago.

Sotirovic, Mira, and Jack M. McLeod. 2001. "Values, Communication Behavior, and Political Participation." *Political Communication* 18: 273–300.

Stewart, Abigail J., and Joseph M. Healy Jr. 1989. "Linking Individual Development and Social Change." *American Psychologist* 44: 30–42.

Stoker, Laura. 1992. "Interests and Ethics in Politics." *American Political Science Review* 86: 369–80.

Stolle, Dietlind. 1998. "Bowling Together, Bowling Alone: The Development of Generalized Trust in Voluntary Associations." *Political Psychology* 19: 497–524.

Stonecash, Jeffrey M. 2000. *Class and Party in American Politics.* Boulder, Colo.: Westview Press.

Stoner, J. A. F. 1968. "Risky and Cautious Shifts in Group Decisions: The Influence of Widely Held Values." *Journal of Experimental Social Psychology* 4: 442–59.

Sulkin, Tracy, and Adam F. Simon. 2001. "Habermas in the Lab: A Study of Deliberation in an Experimental Setting." *Political Psychology* 22 (4): 809–26.

Sullivan, John L., James Piereson, and George E. Marcus. 1989 [1982]. *Political Tolerance and American Democracy.* Midway reprint. Chicago: University of Chicago Press.

Sunstein, Cass R. "Of Law and Politics." 2001. In *The Vote: Bush, Gore, and the Supreme Court,* edited by Cass R. Sunstein and Richard A. Epstein. Chicago: University of Chicago Press.

Tajfel, Henri. 1969. "Cognitive Aspects of Prejudice." *Journal of Social Issues* 15: 79–97.

Tajfel, Henri, M. G. Billig, R. P. Bundy, and Claude Flament. 1971. "Social Categorization and Intergroup Behavior." *European Journal of Social Psychology* 1: 149–78.

Tajfel, Henri, and John Turner. 1979. "An Integrative Theory of Inter-group Conflict." In *The Social Psychology of Inter-group Relations,* edited by William G. Austin and Stephen Worchel, 33–47. Belmont, Calif.: Wadsworth.

———. 1986. "The Social Identity Theory of Intergroup Behavior." In *Psychology of Intergroup Relations,* edited by Stephen Worchel and William G. Austin, 7–24. Chicago: Nelson.

Tarrow, Sidney. 1996. "Making Social Science Work across Space and Time: A Critical Reflection on Robert Putnam's *Making Democracy Work." American Political Science Review* 90: 389–97.

———. 1998. *Power in Movement: Social Movements and Contentious Politics.* 2d ed. Cambridge: Cambridge University Press.

Taylor, Marylee C. 2000. "The Significance of Racial Context." In *Racialized Politics: The Debate about Racism in America,* edited by David O. Sears, Jim Sidanius, and Lawrence Bobo, 118–36. Chicago: University of Chicago Press.

Teixeira, Ruy, and Joel Rogers. 2000. *America's Forgotten Majority: Why the White Working Class Still Matters.* New York: Basic Books.

Tetlock, Philip E. 1989. "Structure and Function in Political Belief Systems." In *Attitude Structure and Function,* edited by Anthony R. Pratkanis, Steven J. Breckler, and Anthony G. Greenwald, 129–51. Hillsdale, N.J.: Erlbaum.

Tocqueville, Alexis de. 1981 [1835]. *Democracy in America.* New York: Modern Library.

Tolleson-Rinehart, Sue. 1992. *Gender Consciousness and Politics.* New York: Routledge.

Turner, John C., and Penelope J. Oakes. 1986. "The Significance of the Social Identity

Concept for Social Psychology with Reference to Individualism, Interactionism, and Social Influence." *British Journal of Social Psychology* 25: 237–52.

Turner, John C., Michael A. Hogg, Penelope J. Oakes, S. D. Reicher, and Margaret S. Wetherell. 1987. *Rediscovering the Social Group: A Self-Categorization Theory.* Oxford: Blackwell.

Turner, John C., Penelope J. Oakes, S. Alexander Haslam, and Craig McGarty. 1994. "Self and Collective: Cognition and Social Context." *Personality and Social Psychology Bulletin* 20: 454–63.

Turner, John C., Margaret S. Wetherell, and Michael A. Hogg. 1989. "Referent Informational Influence and Group Polarization." *British Journal of Social Psychology* 28: 135–47.

Tversky, Amos, and Daniel Kahneman. 1988. "Rational Choice and the Framing of Decisions." In *Decision Making: Descriptive, Normative, and Prescriptive Interactions,* edited by David E. Bell, Howard Raiffa, and Amos Tversky. Cambridge: Cambridge University Press.

Tyler, Tom R. 1990. *Why People Obey the Law.* New Haven: Yale University Press.

U.S. Bureau of the Census. 1999. "Household Income at Record High; Poverty Declines in 1998, Census Bureau Reports." Prepared by Economics and Statistics Administration, Bureau of the Census, Washington, D.C.

Valentino, Nicholas A. 1998. "Who Are We on Election Day? Mass Media and the Salience of Group Identifications during Political Campaigns." Ph.D. diss., University of California, Los Angeles.

——. 1999. "Crime News and the Priming of Racial Attitudes during Evaluations of the President." *Public Opinion Quarterly* 63: 293–320.

Valentino, Nicholas A., Matthew N. Beckmann, and Thomas A. Buhr. 2001. "A Spiral of Cynicism for Some: The Contingent Effects of Campaign News Frames on Participation and Confidence in Government." *Political Communication* 18: 347–67.

Van Mill, David. 1996. "The Possibility of Rational Outcomes from Democratic Discourse and Procedures." *Journal of Politics* 58: 734–52.

Verba, Sidney, Kay Lehman Schlozman, and Henry Brady. 1995. *Voice and Equality; Civic Voluntarism in American Politics.* Cambridge: Harvard University Press.

Verba, Sidney, Kay Lehman Schlozman, Henry Brady, and Norman H. Nie. 1990. "American Citizen Participation Study, 1990." [Computer file]. ICPSR Version. Chicago: University of Chicago, National Opinion Research Center (NORC) [producer], 1995. Ann Arbor, Mich.: Inter-university Consortium for Political and Social Research [distributor], 1995.

Walsh, Katherine Cramer, M. Kent Jennings, and Laura Stoker. 2001. "The Dynamic Effects of Social Class Identification on Orientations toward Government." Paper presented to the annual meeting of the American Political Science Association, San Francisco.

Walsh, Katherine Cramer, M. Kent Jennings, and Laura Stoker, forthcoming. "The Effects of Social Class Identification on Participatory Orientations toward Government." *British Journal of Political Science.*

Warren, Mark E. 2001. *Democracy and Association.* Princeton: Princeton University Press.

Webster's New Universal Unabridged Dictionary, 2d Edition. 1983. New York: Simon and Schuster.

West, Candace, and Don H. Zimmerman. 1987. "Doing Gender." *Gender and Society* 1: 125–51.

Wilson, James Q. 1973. *Political Organizations.* New York: Basic Books.

Wong, Cara. 1998. "'Who Is This "We" We keep Talking About?': Conceptualization and Measurement of Community." Paper presented at the annual meeting of the American Political Science Association, Boston, September 3–6.

——. 2002. "Membership and Morality in American Politics: Obligation to Racial, National, and Geographic Communities." Ph.D. diss., University of California, Berkeley.

Young, Iris Marion. 1990a. "The Ideal of Community and the Politics of Difference." In *Feminism/Postmodernism*, edited by Linda J. Nicholson, 300–23. New York: Routledge.

——. 1990b. *Justice and the Politics of Difference.* Princeton: Princeton University Press.

——. 1994. "Gender as Seriality: Thinking about Women as a Social Collective." *Signs* 19: 713–38.

Zaller, John R. 1992. *The Nature and Origins of Mass Opinion.* Cambridge: Cambridge University Press.

Zaller, John R., and Stanley Feldman. 1992. "A Simple Theory of the Survey Response: Answering Questions Means Revealing Preferences." *American Journal of Political Science* 36: 579–618.

Zuckerman, Alan S., Nicholas A. Valentino, and Ezra W. Zuckerman. 1994. "A Structural Theory of Vote Choice: Social and Political Networks and Electoral Flows in Britain and the United States." *Journal of Politics* 56 (4): 1008–33.

Kinder and
Mendelberg 2000
ed David   Racialized Politics:
The Debate about

Racasm in America